Lance E Davis i   f econc
         Incti   2c

D0915298

INSTITUTIONAL CHANGE AND
AMERICAN ECONOMIC GROWTH

INSTITUTIONAL CHANGE
AND AMERICAN
ECONOMIC GROWTH

---

by LANCE E. DAVIS
California Institute of Technology

and DOUGLASS C. NORTH
University of Washington

with the assistance of
CALLA SMORODIN

CAMBRIDGE *at the University Press 1971*

Published by the Syndics of the Cambridge University Press
Bentley House, 200 Euston Road, London NW1 2DB
American Branch: 32 East 57th Street, New York, N.Y.10022

© Cambridge University Press 1971

Library of Congress Catalogue Card Number: 70-155584

I S B N: 0 521 08111 4

Composed in Great Britain by
William Clowes and Sons Ltd., London, Beccles, and Colchester
Printed in the United States of America

CONTENTS

v

PREFACE

It is difficult to believe that the exploration of long-run economic change can be achieved without development of a body of theory that can incorporate the innovation, mutation, and demise of institutions. If the theory employed in economic history (and economic growth) continues to be restricted to the tools of traditional micro–macro economics, further advances in knowledge are, by the very nature of the theory, severely restricted. The objective of this book is to break out of these strictures and develop a theory of institutional change. The model is consistent with, and built upon, the basic assumptions of neo-classical theory. Therefore, it allows us to integrate standard economic analysis with an explanation of the emergence and decline of institutional arrangements as we attempt to explore the past. The limits of the model will be readily apparent to the reader since we have attempted to specify its shortcomings as well as its accomplishments. Certainly it is only a first step – but we hope a major stride – in developing a theory of institutional change. In Part One, the theory is developed; Part Two applies the theory to American economic history; Part Three explores some further implications and limitations of the analytical framework.

We ask the reader to keep in mind three limitations of the study: (1) the model is a simple one which explains a given, and specified, range of institutional innovations, but explicitly does not explain all institutional change; (2) the historical chapters make no pretense of being a complete history of the particular product or factor market under examination. They were written to illustrate the promise, the achievements, and the limitations, of the theory. The coverage, therefore, is selective and arbitrary. Some sections apply the model to familiar issues; others examine neglected issues. The variation in the extent of historical coverage has reflected in good part the the authors' interests and the limitations of their knowledge. (3) Even as the book is going to press, further developments in the theory are occurring which might modify or improve upon our model. We have chosen to call a halt to further refinements and get the study in print in the expectation that this will encourage other colleagues to build upon and modify or destroy and replace our theory. Moreover, it is also our hope that it will encourage

Preface

economic historians to broaden their canvas to encompass institutional change in their research.

We think that the book will be of value to others besides economists interested in long-run economic change. It is our conviction that the future of historical research, if it is to improve its explanatory power, must come from the application of advances in social science theory. The model developed in this study treads the borderlines between political, social, and economic history. With this in mind, we have attempted to keep the language non-technical (or at least to provide explanation for technical terms and concepts) in the hope that it may be of interest to historians and social scientists of other disciplines as well as to economists.

We are greatly indebted to many of our colleagues for advice and comments. Without in any way implying that they share in the book's shortcomings, the following colleagues have contributed to improving the quality of the study by reading part or all of the earlier drafts of the manuscript: Steven Cheung, Stan Engerman, Burton Klein, Roger Noll, Jim Quirk, George Stigler, and Alan Sweezy. In addition, Edith Taylor and Sharyl Weber have typed and retyped the manuscript until, we are sure, they are sick to death, and Roberta Berry has become something of a guru on questions of economic history while doing much of the research on which the historical chapters are based.

L.E.D.

April, 1971   D.C.N.

PART ONE

THE THEORY DEVELOPED

CHAPTER I

A THEORY OF INSTITUTIONAL CHANGE: CONCEPTS AND CAUSES[1]

(I) Introduction

Historians have traditionally displayed an interest in the institutions within which human action occurs, and much of their work has involved an examination of the interaction between people and these institutions. Economic historians, especially the 'new' group, have, on the other hand, focused their efforts on economically rational behavior as an explanation of past events; institutions have been taken as given, and the 'antiquarian' interests of the more traditional historians have sometimes been scorned.[2] Perhaps because of their concern with long-run change, traditional historians have recognized that institutions do have something to do with the speed and pattern of economic growth (a relationship that was obvious to them but one that economists have only gradually perceived). Much of written history is devoted to the study of the evolution and development of political, military, and social institutions; and just as these sophisticated institutions have evolved through history, so have complex economic institutions emerged to provide a part of the framework within which a highly technical society can survive and flourish. While there are few pieces of history that do not lean heavily upon some form of theory, unfortunately, there has been little theory to help understand the phenomena of institutional change. In the absence of such theory, history is limited to narration, classification, and description. There are relatively few historians who would willingly accept such a limitation.

---

[1] This chapter draws heavily on the work of J. Buchanan and G. Tullock, *The Calculus of Consent* (Ann Arbor, Mich., 1962); K. Arrow, 'Political and Economic Evaluations of Social Effect and Externalities', paper given at the NBER Conference on the Economics of Public Output, April 1968; and A. Downs, *An Economic Theory of Democracy* (New York, 1957).

[2] For a discussion of the 'new' economic history, its method, proponents, and critics, see either L. Davis, 'And It Will Never Be Literature', *Explorations in Economic History*, 2nd ser., vol. 6, Fall 1968, or R. Fogel, 'The New Economic History: Its Findings and Methods', *Economic History Review*, December 1968.

The theory developed

If the historian's explanation of the process of economic development has been less insightful than one might wish, a substantial part of the blame must rest on the set of blueprints of the causal structure that the economists have provided. The best of the historian's work has all too often been rooted not in sound logical deductions from explicit premises but in brilliant historical intuition. This triumph of intuition over mathematics rests not on the blind refusal of the historian to kneel at the altar of science, but on the fact that the theories that he might have used have been poorly specified, totally irrelevant, and, at times, marked by errors in logic. Until 'better' theories are created, no one can blame him for depending on the intuition that has served him so well in the past.

It is unlikely, however, that these theories will spring full-grown from the forehead of some ivory-towered theorist. It is more probable that theories capable of predicting the future and explaining the past will emerge in bits and pieces from some interaction between the theorist who worries about logic and the historian concerned with explaining the past. In his search for a theory that explains the process of economic evolution, the scholar must continually move from theory to fact and back again to theory.

This book is a 'day-by-day' account of an intellectual journey through American economic history. The journey was planned to provide a description of the processes that have produced the present structure of economic institutions. That description, in turn, is the basis for a first (and very primitive) attempt at the formulation of a specified, relevant, and logical theory of the birth, growth, mutation, and, perhaps, death of these institutions. The book is a study of the sources of institutional change in American history. It is specifically concerned with the relationship between economic organization and economic growth, but it is no more than a preliminary study. The theory is at some points woefully weak and the explanations at times incredibly simplistic. The book does, however, represent a first step towards a useful theory of economic growth, and it does provide some new interpretations of the American economic experience.

Since the book is written for historians (as well as economists), it may be well to digress briefly on the role of models and theories in the writing of history. Although it is technically inaccurate to do so, for simplicity's sake we will use the words 'model' and 'theory' interchangeably. They will both refer to a logical structure that relates a set of assumptions to a certain set of conclusions. In economics, it is initially assumed that a firm attempts to maximize its profits and that it is constrained in its production possibilities by a combination of its technological capabilities and existing resources, and in its sales opportunities by certain market conditions. From these assumptions it follows that if it pays a firm to produce at all, it will choose to

4

operate at a level that will return the greatest possible profit – i.e. where the difference between total revenue and total cost is the greatest. This assertion is only a logical deduction, and like any such conclusion it has predictive or explanatory power in the real world only if, in addition to being logically valid, its initial conditions are met. It is under these circumstances that the theory is said to be 'operational'. If, for example, we were attempting to explain the production decision of a Soviet firm whose goals were the maximization of output, rather than profit, the theory would not be very useful.

Even if the theory is conjoined with a relevant set of initial conditions and is in principle operational, the historian must realize that the 'laws' (i.e. predictive or explanatory statements) that can be derived from the theory are probabilistic, not mechanical. In the same way that a physicist cannot predict the behavior of an individual sub-atomic particle but is quite able to predict the average behavior of large groups of such particles, the economic theorist can predict the behavior of typical firms and consumers but cannot make meaningful predictions about the behavior of single decision-making units.

If the model is to be completely useful, ideally it ought to be able to predict two kinds of things:

(1) Given any established set of institutions and some disequilibrating force, the model ought to predict whether the newly emerging institutions will be purely individual (i.e. involve only a single decision maker), depend upon some form of voluntary cooperation, or rely on the coercive power of government.

(2) It should provide some estimate of the period of time that is likely to elapse between the initiating disequilibrium and the establishment of the new (or mutated) institutions.

In the remainder of Part One (Chapters 1–4), we attempt to spell out the model and the initial condition in their simplest form. In Part Two (Chapters 5–10), the model is applied to a number of facets of the American economy, and its ability to explain institutional developments in those sectors is evaluated. In the final part (Chapters 11–12), we summarize the impact that institutional innovation has had on the public–private mix and attempt to reformulate the model along the lines suggested by the experience of Part Two. This particular form of exposition was chosen to make it easier for the reader to follow the argument, as well as to show him why the modifications were important.

This book, then, attempts to specify a theory of institutional change and to apply that theory to certain facets of American development. It is hoped that the theory will contribute to our understanding of that process and that

5

such an experiment might make it possible to modify the model so that in the future it can be used to explain change in certain non-economic institutions and in certain non-American environments. The model has been formulated in a manner that makes it in principle operational, although, like many models in the social sciences, it predicts much less than we would like. As our narrative unfolds it will become increasingly clear that the model yields particularly poor results: when the potential gains and losses are large and relatively equal, but received and/or incurred by different groups; when the predictions involve a mixed result – an institution that is not purely public or purely private; when the fundamental legal and social rules that govern economic and political behavior are altered by the 'predicted' changes in the institutional structure. Despite these qualifications and limitations, we argue that the exercise is worthwhile. It focuses attention on the need for some theory of institutional change if we are ever to have a useful theory of economic growth; and, even in its present crude form, the model has, we feel, allowed us to take a new and productive look at certain aspects of the American historical experience.

(II) Some definitions

While Humpty Dumpty was obviously correct when he said, 'When I use a word it means just what I choose it to mean', Alice also had a point when she complained that words should not mean so many different things. In deference to Alice, it seems appropriate to define some terms as we intend to use them in the remainder of this study and to draw some distinctions between concepts that are sometimes lumped together.

(1) The *institutional environment* is the set of fundamental political, social, and legal ground rules that establishes the basis for production, exchange, and distribution. Rules governing elections, property rights, and the right of contract are examples of the type of ground rules that make up the economic environment. In the American economy, the environment is established by: a written document, the Constitution, and the interpretations that the judiciary have placed on it in decisions dating back to the earliest years of the Republic; and the views of the nation's citizens about the type of institutions that they prefer.[1]

The environment can, of course, be altered. In the context of the American

---

[1] In other countries the environment is set in other ways and different rules for amendment apply. In the United Kingdom, for example, there is no written constitution, and court decisions alone establish the rules of the game. In a totalitarian country, the rules are established by political fiat and altered by decree. We distinguish between fundamental legal ground rules and other types of legislation. The former we treat as exogenous; the latter as endogenous. However, we admit that the line between the two is not always clear cut, and to that extent the analysis contains an element of ambiguity.

legal structure such changes can come from an amendment to the Constitution either by political action or a change in judicial interpretation, or from a shift in citizens' preferences. Thus, for example, property rights were fundamentally altered both by the Thirteenth Amendment and by the court decision in the case of *Ogden* v. *Saunders*. Similarly, election rules have been changed both by constitutional amendment (the Fifteenth, for example) and by judicial reinterpretation. (The twin decisions in *Baker* v. *Carr* and *Reynolds* v. *Sims* are cases in point.) In this study we make no attempt to explain changes in the economic environment. Such changes have certainly occurred and any study of their causes would be interesting. They are, however, exogenous to this model of institutional innovation.[1]

(2) An *institutional arrangement* is an arrangement between economic units that govern the ways in which these units can cooperate and/or compete. The institutional arrangement is probably the closest counterpart of the most popular use of the term 'institution'. The arrangement may be either a formal or an informal one, and it may be temporary or long-lived. It must, however, be designed to accomplish *at least one* of the following goals: to provide a structure within which its members can cooperate to obtain some added income that is not available outside that structure; or to provide a mechanism that can effect a change in laws or property rights designed to alter the permissible ways that individuals (or groups) can legally compete.

The laws legalizing the corporation provide an example of an institutional arrangement that is designed to accomplish both of these ends. The corporate form provides an organizational structure that makes it possible for management to control a much larger and more diverse set of economic activities than could be effectively directed within a more primitive organizational form; and it gives the organization itself legal life. A business so constituted can, therefore, compete in areas that are closed to other types of organizations.

The arrangement may involve a single individual, a group of individuals voluntarily cooperating together, or the government (alone or in cooperation with one or more individuals). The last mentioned innovation frequently implies some legal change, but the first two, while resting on the legal structure that constitutes the environment, involve only the private sector directly; and it is possible that innovation could occur without a change in the law.[2] It is the process of innovation of these institutional arrangements

[1] A survey of changes in the environment is presented in Chapter 4.
[2] The government can act, for example, through executive fiat (as the President did in ordering black employment in the defense industries) and in these cases one might say no legal change has occurred.

that the model of 'institutional change' is designed to predict – specifically it is designed to predict their level (individual, voluntary cooperative, or governmental) and the timing of their emergence.

(3) A *primary action group* is a decision-making unit whose decisions govern the process of arrangemental innovation. The unit may be a single individual or a group of individuals, but it is the action group that recognizes there exists some income – income that their members are not presently receiving – that *they* could accrue, if only they could alter the arrangemental structure. At least one member of any primary action group is an innovating entrepreneur in the Schumpeterian sense, and within the context of this model the group initiates the process of arrangemental innovation. The action group always increases its income if its innovation survives the test of competition. The group pays a portion of the innovation costs, but it may or may not have to bear all or part of the operating costs of the new arrangement (if, in fact, there are operating costs).

The New York manufacturers who informally banded together in 1811 to lobby for the passage of a general incorporation law provide an example of a successful primary action group. They saw that income could be earned if easy incorporation were possible, they paid the costs involved in pushing the revised law through the legislature, and they reaped the profits from their innovation.[1]

(4) A *secondary action group* is a decision-making unit that has been established by some change in the institutional arrangement to help effect the capture of income for the primary action group. The secondary action group makes some of the tactical decisions that bring about the capture, but it does not accrue all of the additional income (it may, in fact, quite likely accrue none).

If the New York law had established the office of Commissioner of Corporations charged with the task of receiving, reviewing, and approving applications for corporate charters, the commissioner (together with his staff) would have constituted a secondary action group. In the normal course of events the secondary action group might accrue none of the income arising from the innovation, but if the law granted them some discretionary powers, they might be able to effect a transfer of a portion of that extra income from the primary action group to themselves. If one wishes, it is possible to view the American tradition of bribing public officials as an arrangement

---

[1] Although the history is not clear, it is possible that the lobbyists might have effected an even more profitable innovation had they been able to convince the legislature to pass a *temporary* general incorporation law. However, the costs of such an arrangement may have been prohibitive either because of the legislative response or because of the rules laid out in the institutional environment.

designed to redistribute income between primary and secondary action groups.

(5) *Institutional instruments* are documents or devices employed by action groups to effect the capture of income external to the existing arrangemental structures when those instruments are applied within the new arrangemental structure. The corporate charter granted to a manufacturing company under the New York general incorporation act is an example of an institutional instrument.

The arrangement, if it is a governmental one, will directly involve the coercive power of government; if it is a voluntary one, it may have underlying it the coercive power of an existing structure of property rights. The effectiveness of the instruments may depend on some fundamental legal concept that is part of the economic environment. An officer of a corporation may sign a contract and in so doing effect a decision to buy a machine. While the contract once signed can be enforced in the courts, the enforcement power does not rest with the institutional arrangement, but depends upon some fundamental constitutional rule.

In an attempt to make the reader more familiar with these definitions, consider for a moment the case of a factory that produces smog as well as products. The smoke is part of the production process; it would be costly to eradicate it, but the people living near the factory find it very disagreeable. Assume that the real cost to them of the smoke (as measured by the amount they would be willing to pay to eliminate it) is greater than the cost the factory owner would have to incur if he were to install a smog control device. Clearly total income could be increased if the smog were eliminated; however, it may well be that there is no way the bargain can be effected within the existing institutional arrangement (where the costs of the smoke accrue to one group, the costs of elimination to another). This problem is typical of those faced by residents of most every city in the United States, and often it appears that some type of government institution should be innovated to effect the smoke abatement.[1] At least two alternatives are open to those who seek the additional income. They could band together to form a political coalition (a *primary action group*), and, if successful at the polls, they (or their representatives) could enact a law (an *institutional arrangement*) that prohibited the factory from emitting smoke. Alternatively the successful political coalition could underwrite legislation establishing a zoning board (a *secondary action group*), and that board could, in turn, issue a cease and

---

[1] The explanation for the choice of government as opposed to some other form of institution is the thrust of the argument in the next three chapters. Here for simplicity we merely assume that that choice is 'best' in some sense.

9

The theory developed

desist order against excessive air pollution.[1] The cease and desist order is an *institutional instrument* backed by the coercive power of the government. Either plan, however, depends on an *economic environment* within which it is possible by political action to abrogate certain of the 'rights of private property'. If the fundamental rules of society prohibited such interference (as in fact they did in the United States until the late nineteenth century), either arrangement (and its complement of instruments and secondary action groups) would be ruled out unless (or until) the rules were changed.

(III) A theory of institutional innovation: a first approximation

Economic institutions and property rights are assigned distinct and constant values in most economic models, but in the study of long-term economic growth, these values are always subject to fundamental change. We postulate that economic institutions are innovated or property rights are revised because it appears desirable for individuals or groups to undertake the costs of such changes; they hope to capture some profit which is unattainable under the old arrangement.

An institutional arrangement will be innovated if the expected net gains exceed the expected costs.[2] Only when this condition is met would we expect to find attempts being made to alter the existing structure of institutions and property rights within a society. For example, if production can be carried on more cheaply by large firms than small, it may be cheaper for a corporation to operate than for a sole proprietorship; if prices differ widely between two markets, it may be profitable to organize a third market to move goods from the low-priced to the high-priced market; if theft and brigandage are widespread, the creation of an efficient police force will raise the value of private property. If an entrepreneur contemplates the construction of a dam designed to produce hydroelectric power that also reduces flood damage downstream, the builder might appropriate a share of these benefits by the prior purchase of some of the downstream property. On the other hand, he might appeal to government to impose a tax on the downstream beneficiaries to help subsidize his construction costs.

As to form, arrangements can range from purely voluntary to totally government controlled and operated. Between these extremes exists a wide

---

[1] Alternatively they could band together to pay off the factory owner. As we shall see, the alternative of choice depends, like the choice between government and private arrangement, on the costs incurred and the revenues accruing to each.

[2] To avoid confusion we will use the term 'innovation' to refer to any change in the institutional technology embodied in an institutional arrangement and the term '*new* innovation' to the first such application.

variety of semi-voluntary, semi-government structures. Voluntary arrangements are simply cooperative arrangements between consenting individuals, and any individual can legally withdraw.[1] This ability implies, of course, that decisions must be unanimous, as the costs of acceding to the decisions are less than those incurred by withdrawal. Government arrangements, on the other hand, do not provide the withdrawal option. Action, therefore, does not require unanimous consent but only conformity with some decision rule.[2] In a democracy, for example, a simple majority frequently determines the course of action.

Both voluntary and government arrangements have been innovated to realize economies of scale, gains from transaction costs, internalization of externalities, the reduction of risk, and the redistribution of income.[3] For example, the corporation has aided the realization of the benefits of the economies of scale sometimes inherent in large-scale operations, and the TVA has yielded similar benefits from power generation and distribution. The stock exchange is an example of a voluntary arrangement whose innovation has reduced transaction costs, and an insurance company is an example of a voluntary arrangement designed to reduce risk. At the same time government employment exchanges and the Federal Deposit Insurance Corporation are examples of parallel government innovations. The Union Pacific's development of Sun Valley, Idaho – a development that turned a primitive area into a major resort – is an example of a voluntary cooperative group effectively capturing the externalities associated with the development of a complex of diverse economic activities. The enactment of a zoning ordinance, a government solution, might be aimed at the same goals in an already established community.[4] Trade unions and the American Medical

[1] We recognize that the costs of withdrawal from both voluntary and government arrangements can vary from zero to infinity (i.e. death of the withdrawing individual). Typically, however, the costs of withdrawal from voluntary organizations have been substantially lower than from government ones. Therefore, for purposes of simplicity in exposition, we have followed Buchanan and Tullock in assuming that voluntary organizations abide by unanimity rule and the cost of withdrawal is zero, whereas government arrangements abide by some political decision rule and do not permit withdrawal.
[2] In line with the argument in footnote 1 above, since emigration is always an alternative, withdrawal from governmental decisions are possible, but the larger is the area of sovereignty, the higher are the costs.
[3] These sources of reorganizational profits are spelled out in detail in Section IV of this chapter.
[4] In William Baumol's *Welfare Economics and the Theory of the State*, 2nd ed. (Cambridge Mass., 1968), he explores the rise of government as the method by which externalities may be internalized in a society. But in his second edition he acknowledges the point developed by Buchanan and Tullock in *Calculus of Consent*; it may be equally possible to internalize externalities, in many cases, through the use of voluntary organization as well as via government.

The theory developed

Association are examples of voluntary arrangements designed to redistribute income. Tariff laws and the progressive income tax are governmental illustrations. What factors underlie the choice between individual, voluntary cooperative, and government arrangements?

The choice rests upon the benefits and costs of each, and on the relative market and non-market power of the affected groups. There are neither organization nor coercive costs associated with individual arrangements, but the revenues are limited to only those that can accrue to an individual. There are organizational costs in the innovation of both the other types of arrangement. In voluntary and in democratic governmental arrangements, the total costs of organization tend to rise with the number of participants.[1] However, in the former case, the need for unanimity may further increase the organizational costs. Given the same number of participants, the organizational costs may be lower for government arrangements than for voluntary arrangements; however, there is an additional element of cost inherent in government arrangements. Each participant is subject to the coercive power of government, and no matter how much he may dislike the government-imposed solution, he may not withdraw.[2] It is possible, however, that a government-imposed solution may yield higher revenues, as a government can utilize its coercive power and impose a solution that might not be achieved by any voluntary bargain.

(IV) The sources of external gains

Let us now be more specific about the sources of gains which could induce people to strive toward changes in their institutional arrangements. In theory there are many outside events that can lead to the generation of profits which, given the existing state of economic arrangements, remain unharvested. We refer to such gains as 'external profits'. In this book we shall limit our analysis to only four: (A) economies of scale, (B) externalities, (C) risk, and (D) transaction costs, since they appear to have played the most important role in American development. If an arrangemental innovation can successfully internalize these profits, then total income is increased, and it is possible that the innovator can gain without anyone having lost.

(A) *Economies of scale*

Economies of scale in production are a technological phenomenon and reflect the fact that the most efficient (lowest cost per unit) output may entail a size

---

[1] In the case of totalitarian institutions, the organization's costs may not rise proportionately, but political and policing costs may be quite high.

[2] The costs and benefits of voluntary organization versus the use of government are discussed in detail in Buchanan and Tullock, *Calculus of Consent*, Chapter 6.

of firm so large that it requires more complex organization than the single proprietor or partnership type of firm can underwrite.

In the jargon of the economist, a firm is faced at any moment in time by a technological constraint. To the layman, this statement need mean no more than given any state of the arts, limits are set by the existing technology on the ways inputs can be combined to form output. The economist's shorthand for the technical relationship between physical inputs and outputs is the term 'production function', an expression often written:

$$O = P(L, K, T)$$

where O refers to output and L, K and T to Labor, Capital and Land. P refers to the technical function that governs the transformation of those inputs into output. There are no *a priori* constraints on the form of this relation; thus it is possible that a doubling of all inputs might lead to less than a doubling of output, exactly a doubling of output, or more than a doubling of output. If the former holds, the production function is said to be subject to *decreasing returns* to scale (it takes more and more inputs to produce equal changes in output); if the second condition holds, it is said to be subject to *constant returns* to scale; and in the last condition, to *increasing returns* to scale (you need fewer inputs to produce an extra unit of output at high levels of production than at low levels). Moreover, since the relationship is unconstrained, it may be subject to increasing returns with regard to some part or range of the output, constant returns over another, and decreasing returns over yet a third. In particular, if the process requires investment in a large and complex plant that must be erected on an all or nothing basis, one might expect increasing returns until the capacity of that plant is reached, at which time decreasing returns set in.

For example, the petroleum refining industry in the 1850s was characterized by something close to constant returns to scale. All that was required to operate was a still (basically a copper boiler and several hundred feet of tubing). Small firms had one still and larger firms more than one, but costs per unit of output were not a function of the size of the operation. Over the next two decades, however, a new technology was innovated, and this technology was subject to increasing returns over a wide range of outputs. The new techniques required very heavy investment in a sophisticated refining plant. That plant, in turn, could produce a large volume of refined petroleum much more cheaply than under the old technology, but the entire plant was needed (i.e. it was 'indivisible') even if the output were very small. As a result, large firms could produce much more cheaply than small, and there was great pressure for small firms to adopt the new technology, increase their size, and capture the profits inherent in the lower costs of

13

production. Most efficient firm size and the number of firms in the industry were, of course, a function of the technology and the relevant market size.

If all firms had equal access to capital and knowledge, there would be no way of predicting which firms would grow and which would die. In the real world, however, capital is not equally available to all firms. The firm's own organizational form may well be the determining factor in the supply of capital available to it. Since both sole proprietorships and partnerships are characterized by limited life and unlimited liability, the supply of long-term external finance available to such firms is frequently quite restricted. Equity finance tends to be scarce because of the unlimited liability attached to such investments; and debt finance, because the enterprise may die (with its owner) while the capital still has a portion of its life remaining. The latter constraint becomes more binding the more specific is the capital[1]. The innovation of the corporation with its unlimited life and limited liability lifts the restrictions on obtaining capital and therefore allows its innovators to reap the profits inherent in the economies of scale.

In terms of the American experience, the last third of the nineteenth century was marked by the development of a number of manufacturing technologies which required large-scale production in order to obtain the lowest per unit cost. At the same time, the limited supply of capital available to the traditional single owner or partnership firm prevented the expansion of these types of organizations into the large-scale firm which was a prerequisite to the utilization of the new technologies. Thus technology made it more economical to produce on a very large scale, but the unavailability of capital to enterprises organized in traditional fashion prevented them from attaining those 'efficient' levels of production. The corporation had access to capital and was able to take full advantage of scale economies; its innovation permitted the capture of the external profits existing in the new technology.

(B) *Externalities – changes in external costs and revenues*[2]

Traditional micro economic theory can be used to explore the relationship between some exogenous event (i.e. an event external to the theory), the reaction to some manifestation of that event by a decision-making unit, and

[1] If the finance is invested in capital for which there is a ready market, the problems exist but their effect is minimized. If, however, the capital has no market, the demise of the owner may signal the default of the loan.

[2] In a recent article that appeared after most of this manuscript had been completed, Stephen Cheung suggests that there be substituted for the term externalities, the degree to which a contract is inclusive of all potential gains and costs to the transacting parties.

the ultimate reestablishment of an equilibrium position as the system adjusts to the new decision. Within the structure of a free enterprise system, for example, a change in consumer tastes (an exogenous change) may result in an increase in demand for some commodity. A businessman (a decision-making unit) notes the higher prices that result and in an attempt to increase his profits responds by increasing his output. The result of the rise in demand, therefore, has been an increase in the quantity of the commodity supplied – that increase followed from the recognition by the businessman that the increase in demand gave him a chance to make more profits if he responded in the correct manner. The search for profits, then, provides the drive that pushes the economy towards a new equilibrium.

The system works less well if the potential profits (or the costs of the expansion in output) are not received (or borne) by the unit that makes the output decision. The term 'externality' refers to the fact that some costs or revenues are external to the decision-making unit. Whenever these external costs and revenues exist it is possible that unaided the market may not yield the most efficient result. If such is the case, some new institutional arrangement that does permit a counting of all costs and revenues (both private and external; i.e. social) would increase the total net revenue accruing to society.

Every homeowner realizes that the value of his property reflects not only his own building, upkeep, and improvement decisions, but those of his neighbors as well. In fact, these 'neighborhood' effects are the basis for community improvement drives, for anti-litter laws, and for the profit potential in 'block busting' in areas undergoing racial integration. What every homeowner may not realize is that these neighborhood effects are only one example of a large class of 'externalities' and that institutional reorganization can increase total income when other types of externalities are present in the same way that a community improvement drive (an institutional innovation) can increase the value of everyone's home.

Leaving economics for a moment, consider the following situation: A college professor finds that his research output is closely linked with his ability to interact with his secretary. Although she is hired only to type manuscripts, it becomes clear that her contribution is far in excess of the number of pages pushed through the typewriter. In this case, since a part of the research process lies outside of the control of the decision maker, an externality exists. Since the secretary bears no additional costs because of

---

This may be a useful alternative, but it appeared too late to permit us to change our terminology. Moreover, our terminology is in line with the economists' traditional vocabulary. See Stephen Cheung, 'The Structure of a Contract and the Theory of a Non-Exclusive Resource', *The Journal of Law and Economics*, 13, no. 1, 49–70.

The theory developed

her extra contribution (her costs may be negative if she views interacting as more fun than typing), no problems are raised and the system operates as it should.[1] A problem does arise if the secretary's husband becomes jealous and tells her to quit her job. The costs (a jealous husband to face each evening) are borne by the secretary while the revenues (fame in the profession, promotion, and salary increases) accrue to the professor. Faced by her dis-equilibrating resignation, the proper response should be an offer of an increased salary (a bribe), and if she accepts, the external costs have been internalized (i.e. assumed by the decision-making unit), and production – albeit higher cost production – continues. The new equilibrium is Pareto efficient. If the highest bribe that the professor can afford is less than the costs she incurs by remaining on the job, the production will cease, but the result will still be Pareto efficient. If, however, something in the existing institutional arrangement makes it impossible to pay the bribe – a bribe that the professor can afford and that if paid would be sufficient to keep her on the job – then the result will not be efficient. Such a situation might occur if, for example, university regulations forbad personal payments between employees or if the scandal engendered by such side payments would cause the professor to lose his job. In these circumstances some institutional arrangement would be necessary if the external profits are again to be realized, and it is the analysis of the processes through which these rearrangements are invented and innovated that constitute an important part of the subject matter of this book.[2]

Externalities in production exist whenever the firm making the production decision does not bear all the costs inherent in the decision or whenever it is unable to accrue all the revenues from selling the output that results from that decision. Similarly, consumption externalities exist whenever the utility of the consuming unit depends not only on that unit's consumption but on the consumption of some other unit as well.[3] In each case the production or consumption decision will have been made without a full assessment of the relevant costs and revenues. As a result the decision may not be Pareto efficient (that is, it might be possible to make a different decision that would make at least one person better off without making anyone worse off). To better describe the potential source of profits from reorganization, let us examine a few examples of externalities.

[1] An economist would call it Pareto efficient, which is nothing but a fancy word for a situation that cannot be altered to make someone better off without making anyone worse off.
[2] The rearrangement could take the form of out-of-office interacting or, perhaps, a suitable bribe might make the husband 'less jealous'.
[3] Utility is a word that economists use to refer to a measure of consumer satisfaction or well being. The greater the utility derived from any commodity the greater the satisfaction.

16

A theory of institutional change

Returning to the manufacturing plant that produced not only its saleable output, but a large volume of black noxious smoke as well, assume that the volume of the smoke increases as output rises. Moreover, assume that while the smoke is not poisonous, people would prefer to breathe clean rather than polluted air.[1] Since, by assumption, the utility of everyone who breathes the smoke is adversely affected, this reduction in utility is certainly a part of the *total* cost of the firm's production. In addition, since people prefer less smoke to more smoke, that element of cost rises as the firm's output increases. The utility reduction, however, is a cost item that, while real, is not borne by the firm, and it is, therefore, not included in the calculations undertaken to determine the firm's most profitable level of output. Since the firm will choose an output level that maximizes its profits, the failure to include a cost item that increases as output rises will cause the firm to choose an output level greater than the one they would have selected had they been forced to consider all costs. Some reorganization that would induce the firm to include all relevant costs in its calculations would increase total revenues accruing to all of society (although it might reduce those accruing to the firm), and it would pay those who now bear the cost of the smoke to innovate some new institution that would induce the manufacturing plant to include all cost items in its profit calculations.

Although it is always possible that a private side market will develop which will make it possible for some group to capture the potential external profit (i.e. to 'internalize' the profit), at times the costs of such private innovations are prohibitive. In this case, the reorganization is likely to occur outside the market – through the interposition of government. When the institutional rearrangement involves some political action, there are no longer any guarantees that the new arrangement is superior to the old. It may just be different.

In the case of the factory, if the plant had not already been built, it would be possible for the owners to buy all of the surrounding land and sell it at costs low enough to compensate for the loss of utility. The firm, by absorbing the differential in land prices, is forced to bear the cost of its smoke-generating activities. If, however, property rights are already vested, the solution becomes more complicated. On the one hand, the company might attempt to bribe the landowners to put up with the smoke. If production is dependent upon agreement, though, each property holder has a potential veto, and is therefore in a position to demand all the increase in income. Since *every* landowner has this potential veto, any time there is more than

[1] This preference is, of course, only an assumption. If people are indifferent, there is no difference, and if they prefer smoke to clean air, they will be better off and we are back to our 'interacting is more fun than typing' example.

17

The theory developed

one affected property holder the sum of the demands for possible profit exceeds the total profits available for distribution. Under these conditions, it is unlikely that any agreement could be reached – at least not without a long delay. On the other hand, if the law permits a firm to pollute the air, the property owners might join together to bribe the firm to desist or reduce its pollution. Since, however, it is impossible for the plant to reduce the pollution over some pieces of property but not over all, it would pay each potential member of the coalition to stay outside and get a 'free ride' from the payments of the others. Once again, it is likely that agreement would be impossible or at least long delayed.

When exclusion is difficult or when any potential member of a coalition has a potential monopoly veto, it is costly to organize the private side markets needed to effectively internalize the externalities. If these conditions do not exist, however, private reorganization is possible. In the case of employee training, it might be possible for the firm to tie training to some contractual obligation, but this solution is not without cost and may not be very effective. The reader should not forget that reorganization, although potentially profitable, must also be viewed as a resource-using activity. In this case, for example, contracts must be written and then they must be enforced.

Such costs often make private reorganization uneconomic. In these cases, it is common to turn to the government's coercive powers to effect an institutional rearrangement. In the case of the factory, strict zoning laws prohibiting pollution may be passed. In the case of labor training, the educational system may be socialized or an appeal may be made to courts to enjoin employees from taking their skills to competitive firms. Finally, in the case of the army and fire protection, the functions tend to be socialized and their costs spread throughout the body politic.

Nowhere, however, in these government solutions is there any guarantee that the resulting reorganization, although certainly profitable from someone's point of view, will be Pareto superior to the old.[1] Instead, they may make someone better off only by making someone else worse off. The zoning board's decision to prohibit smoke may be as far, if not farther, from an optimal solution as was the firm's original decision; the existence of a socialized educational system does not necessarily lead towards an optimal output of that product.[2]

Institutional reorganization aimed at internalizing externalities can,

[1] An economist would say that A is Pareto superior to B if a move from B to A would make someone better off and no one worse off.
[2] Certainly not all voluntary cooperative solutions lead to Pareto superior results either – in fact, in the redistributive case we will find many examples of arrangemental innovation that make someone better off only at the cost of making someone worse off.

18

therefore, increase total revenues to society, but it can also reduce them. This fact should be kept in mind throughout this entire analysis.

(c) *Overcoming risk aversion*

The prevalence of risk – the inability to be certain of terms on which future transactions can be made – is yet another factor that curtails economic activity.

We may assert that most persons are risk averters. In the absence of risk aversion, an individual would be as willing to risk a dollar for a possible return of a million if the odds were a million to one as he would to risk a dollar for a potential profit of a dollar when the outcome is certain. In fact, with the exception of the very poor, most people appear to prefer the certain to the uncertain outcome for large gambles. If, as appears likely, risk aversion becomes stronger as the odds increase, its presence tends further to bias activities toward those with more certain outcomes and away from those marked by a high variance of returns. Clearly, since the expected value of the profits is higher in the high variance activities that are not being undertaken than in the low variance activities that are, total profits could be increased if some mechanism could overcome the tendency towards risk aversion (i.e. by concentrating the risk among those who are not averters), or make risky outcomes appear more certain in regards to the income to be obtained. The former types of solutions are usually achieved through the development of some speculative side market (and are considered in this section under 'Market Failures'), but the latter can often be achieved through insurance.

Not all risks are insurable, but when they are, institutional reorganization aimed at innovating insurance schemes can frequently permit an increase in total profits. For insurance to be successful, however, there must be some basis on which to assess the risks accurately, and the insurance base must be broad enough to permit that the risks be spread. Moreover, the insurance cannot be so complete that all management risks are removed since such insurance would, by dulling management decisions, undercut the very basis on which the insurance was written. After all, if the only cost of a poor management decision is that profits are collected from the insurance company rather than from the customer, there is little incentive to make good decisions.

Insurance schemes can be intra-firm, but more often innovation produces firms specialized in supplying the requisite insurance. To be effective, however, someone must first be able to assess the risks. Thus, while the idea of life insurance dates back into the seventeenth century, it was almost the middle of the nineteenth before it was successfully innovated in the United

19

States. Innovation, in this case, awaited the construction of an adequate mortality table – the basis for risk assessment. Even then, however, firms refused to sell insurance in the South because for that subset of the population they did not have an adequate basis for rate making. Second, the insurance base must be large enough to adequately spread the risk. In the late nineteenth and early twentieth centuries, for example, a number of states passed bank insurance laws designed to protect depositors from bank failure.[1] Unfortunately, the plans were innovated in farm states where the primary cause of bank failure was bad weather. Since the weather tended to be region-wide, the state unit was insufficiently broad to provide the necessary insurance base (all banks tended to get into trouble at the same time), and the schemes were universal failures. Thirty years later, the innovation of a similar scheme with a nation-wide base (the Federal Deposit Insurance Corporation) made the insurance plan viable.

Insurance from the effects of fluctuations in the price of a single security is the characteristic of the services offered potential investors by a wide range of financial institutions. The goal of 'diversification' so revered in investment textbooks is nothing but a technical term for insurance. A diversified portfolio implies that an institution has invested in a wide range of activities and while not insured against general business failure (as the experience of the 1930s proved), is protected against individual (or even industry-wide) failure.

American development has been marked by the growth of a large number of firms specializing in some phase of insurance, and almost certainly these innovations have increased total revenues. They have not, however, been cost-free. There are organizational costs, there are costs in assessing risk, and there are costs in effecting the insurance contract. Despite these costs, innovation was still profitable.

(D) *Market failures and improvements in imperfect markets*

The implications of positive transaction costs have only recently been extensively explored by economists. The organization and improvement of the flow of relevant economic information (one of many types of transaction costs) has probably been the major area of arrangemental innovation. If

---

[1] Although the schemes were partly politically motivated, there was an economic rationale as well. It was hoped that by increasing the certainty of the returns from bank deposits it would be possible to increase the total volume of savings. While insurance would reduce the expected value of the return (the schemes were not cost-free) they would also reduce the variance. Insofar as the depositors were both risk averters and willing to save more at higher rates of interest, the reduction in variance could have increased the volume of deposits.

there were no costs to acquiring information, then prices in all markets would differ only by transport costs. In fact, information is costly and the widespread existence of purely local markets reflects in good part simply a lack of information about profitable trading opportunities in more distant areas. As information about prices in distant regions becomes available, merchants will send their products to markets where net price differentials (i.e. adjusted for transport costs) are highest.

Economists are wont to assume that all markets are perfect, and this assumption, by definition, rules out any possible potential profits arising from the failure of markets to operate. In the real world, however, information is not cost-free, and therefore, perfect markets (whose existence depends on perfect knowledge) do not exist. The lower the cost of information, of course, the better markets will operate. Even in developed countries they are far from perfect, and in an underdeveloped country the costs of information may be so high that the markets do not operate at all.

In general, not only is information costly, but it is subject to increasing returns. That is, one must frequently pay for information, but the cost does not change much whether that information is used to effect one, one hundred, or one thousand transactions. If information costs are substantial and if they are subject to decreasing costs, it is likely that substantial profits are to be earned from increasing information flows that reduce uncertainty. The arrangemental innovation that is most economical will likely be a specialized firm capable not only of supplying the information but also of achieving the potential economies of scale.

While there is no logical reason to assume that the high cost of information might not lead to market failure even if the market deals only with a single location and a single time period, the fact is that market failure most often occurs when the markets must reach across spatial or temporal barriers. In the absence of an adequate information network (and other things being equal) the discounts that entrepreneurs put on potential income because of the uncertainty tend to be higher the farther the potential buyer is (either in time or space) from the location of the transaction. In fact, these uncertainty discounts may be so high that the discounted equilibrium price may be below zero and the markets not operate at all.

Spatial or industrial relocation of economic activity involves the establishment of new markets for inputs and outputs. Most economic literature on foreign trade (where it has long been recognized that the world is characterized by more than one market for each commodity) tends to assume that only transport costs prevent complete intermarket arbitrage.[1] Thus, it is

[1] Arbitrage is another piece of economist's shorthand. To the uninitiated let it be said that it merely refers to the purchase of goods in a market with lower prices and their resale

frequently argued that price differences between two markets for the same commodity can never exceed the cost of transporting that commodity from the lower to the higher priced market.

Such a formulation, since it implicitly assumes that potential arbitragers exist and that they know with certainty the prices prevailing in each market and the potential transport routes between the markets, is largely irrelevant to a discussion of the process of economic growth. Historical experience suggests that the lower the level of economic development in any country and the newer the relevant markets, the less are such assumptions justified and the greater are the uncertainty discounts the potential arbitrager will make. Moreover, since different individuals stand in different relation to the markets, one would not expect that the same uncertainty discounts would be applied by all. Thus, it might be possible that discounts are so high no arbitrage takes place (the case of market failure); or, if an individual arbitrager's resources are limited, partial arbitrage may reduce the intermarket price differentials, but these differentials may still exceed transportation costs.

Given the fact that there are certain indivisibilities in search costs, that markets lack complete information flows, and that different people are differently situated in relation to those markets, one would expect the level of uncertainty to differ markedly between individuals. Thus one might expect a person located closer either spatially or geographically to the new markets to be more willing to engage in some arbitrage relation. Such was clearly the case in United States development. In the case of capital, for example, persons with specific knowledge of the West frequently were willing to lend in that area when others were not; similarly, men connected with the iron industry were more ready to lend to the incipient steel industry than were the bankers and the other more 'traditional' sources of loan finance. Thus it is possible that for some persons the uncertainty discounts are low enough that they recognize the potential benefits from arbitrage, although they themselves cannot move enough goods or factors to completely arbitrage the markets.

If such imperfect markets exist, it is possible that some institutional

---

in a market with higher prices. The result is to assure that the price of the same commodity in two different markets will never differ by more than the cost of transport between them. At the same time it is also possible to conduct arbitrage transactions between two markets that are temporally separated. In this case arbitrage will prevent prices from differing by more than interest and storage costs. If the prices should diverge by more than that amount (and if transaction costs are zero) then it will pay someone to engage in arbitrage. Needless to say, any legal barrier that prohibits (or interferes with) the arbitrage transactions can lead to 'overly large' intermarket price differentials. Here, however, we are considering the effect of certain transaction costs (e.g. uncertainty discounts) that have traditionally been ignored.

rearrangement can set them to operating more easily, and such an innovation can increase total income by permitting the movement of inputs and commodities to the market in which they receive the highest return. For example, while it pays no individual to accumulate up-to-date information on investment opportunities in some far distant place if he only wishes to invest a small amount, it does pay a brokerage house to make that expenditure since the costs can be spread over a large number of transactions. Again, a market service can provide price information from many markets to a large number of customers at very low cost, but any attempt by an individual shipper to get that information for himself would probably be prohibitively expensive.

Although the empirical problems are probably less and the implications for economic development fewer, many of the same problems that arose in the process of arbitrage between markets that are spatially removed appear also in contracts that have a time dimension. Just as prices in a market a distance away tend to be heavily discounted in the absence of information, so are similar uncertainty discounts applied to prices of future transactions. Moreover, as institutional changes can reduce the effective spatial distance between buyers and sellers, so a different set of institutions can reduce the temporal distance.

Total income can be increased by moving goods spatially to the activities of greatest return; similarly, resources can be redistributed through time to increase the stream of output or satisfaction. In the latter case, however, goods are not moved physically, but are redistributed between competitive activities today to achieve the alteration in the flow of output through time. For example, assume a businessman has the option of investing in a steel mill or of consuming some stock of resources. The investment is a long-term one, and he will compare the present value of that investment with the satisfaction he can achieve through present consumption. The present value of the mill, however, depends in part on his expectations about the prices he will receive in the future for his steel. Since the future is uncertain, he will tend to discount his price expectations, and, if the degree of uncertainty is high, the discounts, too, will be large. As a result, he may choose not to invest even though the 'expected value' of his price expectations might suggest that the investment was a profitable one (once again we find an example of the bias introduced by risk aversion). In theory, however, the innovation of a side market (in this case a market for future steel) could reduce his uncertainty (at least that relating to future steel prices) and he might find the investment a viable one. For such a market to develop, however, it is necessary that someone (a nonrisk averter) be willing to assume the uncertainty and that the uncertainty itself can be assessed with some

23

reliability.[1] That such a market has not grown up suggests that it is unprofitable to innovate a side market; but the question of why it is unprofitable remains an interesting one.[2]

While future markets for steel have not developed, such markets do appear in other intertemporal transactions. In both the securities and the agricultural commodities markets, side markets have evolved to overcome some of the problems of intertemporal market failure. In both cases the markets are essentially short term (and in this way they avoid the classic uncertainty of long-term transactions) and in both cases they depend on the existence of a class of speculators willing to take the uncertain side in the intertemporal transaction. The speculators are persons whose aversion to risk is less than the average and/or who specialize in speculative transactions and are able, therefore, to effect these intermarket exchanges at lower costs than the farmers or stock holders, just as a miller who specializes in flour milling can grind wheat more cheaply than the farmer who grows the grain. In the case of wheat futures, for example, a mill may want to function solely as production and sales units and to insulate its profits from the vagaries of the future price of wheat. Thus, its management will buy wheat for delivery in the future at the present price of future wheat. The 'speculator', on the other hand, will gamble that future wheat prices will be below the present quotation, and that the deliveries he contracts to make can be purchased at this lower price. The market, then, merely concentrates the risk in the hands of those who are willing to assume it, and those that are not, pay some 'certain' charge for the service.

The fact that markets have not developed in other areas suggests that the uncertainties in these transactions are subject to such large discounts that no one is willing to offer the risk-bearing service at a price the risk averters are willing to pay. Temporal uncertainties, like spatial uncertainty discounts, however, are partly a function of information costs. One may, therefore, expect that cheaper information would reduce uncertainty and permit a side market to develop. Unless there is considerable improvement in crystal balls, however, it appears unlikely that improvements in intertemporal markets will be as substantial as they have been in the spatial dimension. Still, the existence of futures markets in commodities and securities suggests that

---

[1] Alternatively, large inventories could be held to provide intertemporal price insurance; however, these stocks are costly.

[2] The steel example is drawn from Arrow, 'Political and Economic Evaluations'. It has been suggested that the example is not a good one, since the absence of a future market for steel may flow from the high degree of certainty about future prices that follows from the structure of the industry. This criticism may or may not be relevant but in general the Arrow point is a very good and important one.

it is possible to improve the temporal distribution of economic activity by improvements in these side markets.

(V) Conclusion

We have seen that the innovation of a new institution can permit the capture of potential increases in income arising from externalities, economies of scale, risk and transaction costs when this income cannot be internalized within the existing institutional structure. Moreover, we have argued that the choice between levels of institutions (individual, voluntary cooperative, or governmental) is dictated by the costs and revenues associated with each alternative.

Given these potential profits, it paid someone or some group to innovate a new arrangement to capture them. In each of these cases, successful innovation caused total income to grow and in principle made it possible for no one to lose in the process.

The model that we have outlined, when more precisely specified and when conjoined with a set of initial conditions relating to the economic environment, can be used to 'explain' this process of arrangemental innovation as it occurred in the American past.

CHAPTER 2

THE GOVERNMENT, COERCION, AND THE REDISTRIBUTION OF INCOME

(I) Introduction

While profit opportunities from institutional reorganization are not limited to the four types described in Chapter 1, each of those has played an important role in the institutional history of the American economy and thus had a significant impact on the shape and pace of the nation's development. That is, they were part of the process of improving productivity and output in the society. There is, however, yet another type of profit that can be captured by arrangemental innovation, although that profit comes not from an increase in the total but from someone else's share of the existing income. It is, of course, the profits inherent in any scheme that leads to a redistribution of income. Since successful capture means a loss to someone, the probabilities that such capture can be effected without reliance on some governmental coercive power are very small.[1] In these cases it is very likely that only a governmental (or partly governmental) arrangement can successfully capture the profits, although it is possible that it might be done by a non-governmental arrangement if an exogenous political event has effected some change in the rules of the 'political game' that govern economic behavior. In either case, however, some understanding of the political process is necessary if we are to predict successfully the course of arrangemental innovation leading toward income redistribution. Without such knowledge it would, for example, be very difficult to incorporate into any analytical history of American institutional development the widespread intervention of government in colonial America, the relative decline in the participation of government into the economy of the nineteenth century, and its resurgence again in the twentieth. In the succeeding sections of this chapter we shall examine in more detail the factors that make the government the 'preferred' sector for arrangemental change, analyze the relationship between politics

---

[1] The Mafia, for example, was able to effect an income redistribution by monopolizing the traffic in some illegal drugs. The monopolization, however, rested on considerable extra-legal coercive power – a power that is available to relatively few others in society.

and the 'rules of the game', and explore the factors that encourage groups to endeavor to redistribute nicome.

It appears important to distinguish between three different forms of government action effecting potential arrangements: a piece of specific legislation that proscribes or permits a particular institutional arrangement; a general enactment that proscribes or permits an array of possible institutional arrangements; a law that delegates authority to a secondary action group and permits that group to proscribe or permit a variety of actions. Since we can (in theory) estimate costs and revenues of each, the model should predict which will be selected in any given instance.

The analysis of change in individual and voluntary cooperative arrangements in the context of a market economy is susceptible to examination along traditional lines; that is, to analysis within the context of a price system. Examination of innovation and mutation of governmental arrangements, however, while still resting on the assumption of profit maximization, projects the analysis into the murky area of a theory of the state and requires an extension into as yet unresolved theoretical problems. Recent pioneering works in analytical political theory have made a beginning. We hope that the present study will extend our theoretical probing still further; however, we are still a long way from a satisfactory general theory of political change.[1] As a result, we take as given the degree of development of the government's structure at any moment of time and make no attempt to provide a dynamic theory of the state. Nor do we explain why changing norms of behavior lead to varying degrees of support for private property rights over time, but we do attempt to trace out the implications of such changes. Moreover, since attempts at redistribution often bring competing groups into conflict and since theory has not yet provided us with solutions to many of these game theoretical problems, our model often breaks down. It appears to work reasonably well when the gains are large and/or the competing groups not evenly balanced, but it appears to be at best almost useless when the potential gains are small and/or the competing groups fairly equally balanced.

(II) Government: the innovation of choice

Under what conditions will the government sector be the preferred vehicle for arrangemental change? The logic of our model suggests that the government will likely be the 'treatment of choice' when:

[1] A. Downs, *An Economic Theory of Democracy* (New York, 1957); J. Buchanan and G. Tullock, *The Calculus of Consent* (Ann Arbor, Mich., 1962); D. Black, *The Theory of Committees and Elections* (Cambridge, England, 1958); W. Riker, *The Theory of Political Coalitions* (New Haven, Conn., 1962).

27

The theory developed

(1) There is a relatively well developed structure of government, but private markets are not highly developed. Government organizations may yield substantial profits which cannot be realized under a fragmented market structure. For example, the early efforts of entrepreneurs to develop transport (particularly during the canal era) were hampered by a fragmented capital market. Given the embryonic state of these private markets and the lack of population in the West, the transfer of finance from East to West could be most cheaply accomplished by a change in institutional arrangements that permitted mobilization through the use of government credit. Under these conditions the government was a preferred alternative.

In terms of the productivity of government arrangements, however, the stricture about the degree of development and the control exercised by the government is very important; and in this regard the American experience is certainly not typical of many underdeveloped countries. In the United States, even at very early stages of economic development, there was fairly well established government control, and it was this degree of control that made it possible to innovate governmental arrangements in the early nineteenth century. A governmental arrangement is seldom superior to a private one unless it has the power to coerce the reluctant; and without effective political control, the government has no effective coercive power. The federal government (and frequently the state governments as well) had such power as early as 1787 and so, for example, did the Russian government some eighty years later. In many underdeveloped countries, though, the governments lack effective political control. In these instances, it is seldom worth the cost to enlist the services of the government, and one would not expect to find government arrangements emerging at an early state of economic development. In the recent unfortunate case of the Congo, for example, the withdrawal of the Union Miniere, a voluntary cooperative group, led to the total breakdown of the economy since no domestic arrangement, government or otherwise, had sufficient coercive power to provide protection for lives and for property rights.[1]

(2) Large external benefits are coupled with already existing property rights. Under these conditions voluntary solution is very difficult, since the

---

[1] We should note in passing that the well developed characteristics of American government in the early national period is in contrast to many underdeveloped areas today where the government 'infra-structure' is not well developed, and where efforts to undertake activities through the government are confronted with continuous frustration because of its ineffective organization; in this respect the degree to which America provides an example to be followed by underdeveloped countries is suspect indeed. On the frontier where government was less 'in control' the American experience may have been nearer those of the underdeveloped countries. The distribution of public lands and the problems of squatters and speculators is a case in point.

refusal of any one individual to join the cooperative venture may preclude the capture of the external gains. Every member is in a position to extract from the others the total profits, and therefore the possibility of any solution remains remote. In the absence of already vested property rights, it might be possible for a single cooperative organization (a large corporation, for example) to organize an entire area and thereby capture all the potential externalities. But once property rights have been vested in a number of individuals, the possibility wanes for recapture through voluntary association – and, other things being equal, the larger the numbers involved the smaller the chance of success. Thus, as we have seen in Chapter 1, a single land development company owning all of a large tract of land may find it profitable to prohibit industrial smoke; but once the land passes into the hands of individuals, that same prohibition probably cannot be effected without the coercive force of the government (this is, after all, the justification of zoning laws).

(3) The benefits derived from the reorganization are indivisible, and it pays each individual to pretend he is not interested in capturing them. If he does reveal his true preference he would be required to bear part of the organizational costs; but if he does not, he can avoid those costs but still reap the same benefits as everyone else. Under these conditions, unless one individual finds his share of the benefits worth the entire cost of organization, reorganization will not be undertaken except under the aegis of governmental coercion. Consider the example of a military defense force. Since it is almost impossible to defend some citizens of a political unit without defending all, it is necessary that the government have the power to tax or draft its constituents if that service is to be supplied at all.

(4) The benefits do not lead to a greater total but merely to a redistribution of the existing income, particularly if that redistribution is in the direction of greater equality.[1] Since any form of income redistribution involves making someone worse off, some coercion is almost always required to make the injured person accept the new solution. If the redistribution is from the many to the few, the costs of information and the organizational expenses involved in resisting the change may be prohibitive and, as a result, it may be possible to effect the change without explicit coercion. It may be possible for a few businessmen to form an effective cartel to redistribute income in their favor; but it is unlikely that members could be coerced in the other direction.[2]

---

[1] One would not, of course, expect a government that is totally elitist to be an effective agent for promoting equality in income distribution; in fact you would expect it to pursue a set of policies designed to achieve just the opposite redistribution.

[2] It has been suggested that the repeal of the Corn Laws in Great Britain provides a historical counterexample. Careful examination of the laws suggests that it was a weighing

The theory developed

These then are the general areas where one might expect a governmental arrangement to be the preferred innovation. Income redistribution is particularly important, so let us pause briefly and examine it in greater detail.

(III) Income redistribution

The efforts of groups to achieve gains by redistribution of income have not been limited exclusively to the employment of government. Voluntary organizations, in many instances, have been quite effective in accomplishing this end. As noted in Chapter 1, trade unions and the American Medical Association have been successful at redistributing income in their favor. However, we should note that the success of voluntary groups in redistributing income requires an ability to control supply effectively, and therefore implicitly or explicitly requires some coercive power. In many instances this power requires the approval (either tacit or explicit) of government. Government may condone some private form of coercion or it may enact enabling legislation to legalize the exercise of that power. Therefore, while we recognize the ability of voluntary groups to effect redistribution, we will treat the general subject under the heading of government because it is there that the source of coercive power most often lies.

There is probably no better place to begin this discussion than with Madison's *Federalist Paper No. 10*. That document represents the clearest and most precise statement of the need to organize the government in a way that will prevent 'factions' (whether majority or minority) from using government to further their own interests. Madison is quite explicit in describing the ways such factions may be able to use government to succeed in 'a rage for paper money, for an abolition of debts, for an equal division of property, or for any other improper or wicked project'. In order to forestall redistribution by faction (i.e. from the rich to the poor) – a basic danger of representative government – Madison argues for a system of indirect representation and checks and balances. Such a system raises the political cost of redistribution and thereby reduces its profitability. As we will note in our subsequent analysis of costs and benefits, Madison's concern was based upon shrewd political observation, and our history suggests his concern was well founded.

---

of the alternatives (violence v. reform) rather than benevolence that led to their passage; however, the general point is still a good one – that decision makers are concerned with maximizing someone else's utility. Nowhere do we argue that money profit maximization is society's only goal. When another criterion is relevant, the model is clearly inapplicable. In the present day, society's concern about poverty reflects a willingness to redistribute income in the face of economic self-interest narrowly defined.

The government, coercion, redistribution of income

The potential benefits of redistribution to any one group – a loss, of course, to another – rest upon the coercive ability of government to appropriate wealth and income. Anything that changes the government's ability to appropriate wealth and income will change the potential benefits. An increase in the taxing power of government, an extension of its regulatory powers, or a widening of its authority to exercise eminent domain, all may increase the potential net benefits of redistribution.

Several basic factors influence the costs of using government to effect income redistribution:

(1) The total cost of organization varies directly with numbers and heterogeneity of the persons organized, and the organization of *any* large segment of society is very expensive.[1] In qualification we should note, however, that if existing organizations can be appropriated or utilized, these costs may be significantly reduced. In subsequent analysis we shall particularly explore this aspect of cost reduction (the use of existing political parties or other groups already formed whose costs of organization therefore are not borne by the groups desiring income redistribution).

(2) Legislation aimed at redistributing income in favor of a segment of society will benefit all members of that segment whether or not they have been involved in achieving the passage of that legislation. It is therefore to each individual's advantage not to incur the costs of involvement (i.e. the dilemma of the 'free rider'). In consequence, the most effective organizations for redistributing income are those involving small numbers, or where belonging confers additional benefits from which outsiders can be excluded.[2] It follows that producer groups have been more effective in redistributing income (as by tariff legislation) than have consumer groups, and organizations that offer their members exclusive benefits not open to outsiders (such as trade unions and the American Medical Association) have been more effective than those which did not.

(3) The political process involves the election of agents (representatives, senators, etc.) who actually enact legislation. The goal of the agent is to remain in office (i.e. to receive the approval of more than 50 percent of the electorate at voting time). Since the behavior of the electorate is uncertain, he must cater to many and conflicting interest groups. Under these circumstances, a 'passionate minority' will have more leverage than an

---

[1] Given the increasing returns in printing and advertising, the statement is less true in the modern world, and it may not be true when the numbers are very large. However, the most likely effect would probably be a U-shaped curve relating cost to the numbers recruited. (The cost per unit of effort declines because of the scale economies, but the amount of effort per recruit rises as numbers increase.)

[2] See M. Olson, *The Logic of Collective Action* (Cambridge, Mass., 1964).

31

The theory developed

indifferent or unorganized majority, and the winning coalition is likely to be unstable.[1]

That a subgroup is only one member of a coalition, however, greatly increases the cost of organizing an activity through the political process. Most voters distribute themselves more or less normally around some middle position; a party platform tends to be all things to all people, and almost any subgroup can persuade the platform committee to insert some statement about their particular project. When the legislative stage is reached, though, some substantial compromises usually must be made among the various subgroups constituting the party (i.e. the winning coalition). As a result, the probability that one subgroup can effect exactly its desired legislative goals declines as the size of the coalition increases. Thus the very system that permits subgroups to have a voice raises the costs of their completely achieving their objectives.[2]

The motivating force that pushes persons and groups into a political coalition is a desire to gain some benefit through winning an election and therefore effecting (or preventing) some change by appropriate political action. The desire to gain some tangible benefit from political action implies something about the size of an efficient political coalition, and this size in turn affects both the costs of political action and the structure of the political institutions that emerge. Since most redistribution schemes can be at best a zero sum gain, if winning is to be worth anything, it is necessary that something be won. And if something is won, someone must have lost. If the winning coalition encompasses everyone, membership has no value, since by definition there can be no losers (and therefore no winners). In fact, if gains per coalition members are to be maximized, the winning coalition should be no larger than the minimum required to win the election, or, if there are long-run considerations, to guarantee stability.[3] It is this desire for gain from the political process that, in part at least, explains the emergence of American political parties – parties that have often been criticized for their lack of ideology and whose only element of cohesion is an ability to capture (at least sometimes) more than half of the vote.

In 1932, the Democrats under the leadership of Franklin D. Roosevelt were able to put together a new winning coalition made up largely of those who up to that time had been or who because of the depression had become the 'have nots' in the economy. Over the next decade, while the record was far from perfect, the coalition did manage to effect some legislation which,

[1] See Downs, *Economic Theory of Democracy*.
[2] The probability of success has decreased and therefore the cost of achieving any given probability has gone up.
[3] This point is very nicely made in Riker, *Theory of Political Coalitions*.

32

The government, coercion, redistribution of income

in the long run, brought about income redistribution. By 1936, though, the coalition had been broadened to include almost everyone, and the benefits from membership began to decline. As a result, the coalition lost strength in each succeeding election and finally broke up in the late 1940s over the question of civil rights for Negroes. Within the coalition Negroes could gain only at the expense of the southerners (also members); and the unionized blue collar workers in the cities, only at the expense of the white collar workers in the suburbs. In each case one group was forced out of the coalition. Fifteen years later Lyndon Johnson was able to put together another 'grand alliance' in the face of a threat from the far right, but since the desires of some member subgroups could be satisfied only at the expense of other members, that coalition, too, broke down once the threat had passed.

(4) In theory at least, the 'rules of the political game' as practiced in the United States in the 1960s, give each citizen one (and only one) vote and prohibit buying and selling those votes. Although the definition of a citizen has changed and indirect trading of votes is not strictly prohibited, these restrictions have set some limits on the ability to organize activity through the government. In addition, changes in this rule have altered the costs of the government alternative. Since political parties are interested in winning, unless the coalition is already larger than minimum size, the tendency is to favor programs that shift income from small groups of voters to larger groups – other things (including taste) remaining equal. Such a shift, while losing votes in the small group, will gain votes in the large one. In a case where losses to the small group are greater than gains to the large, this transfer could be prevented if members of the small group were permitted to buy votes. As it is, all they can do is attempt indirectly to influence enough votes to prohibit the transfer.

Over time, substantial changes have occurred in the kinds of activities the government could be expected to assume. In part this refocusing came from changes in the nature of the electorate and in part from changes in the rules of the political game. Property requirements for voting were abolished by the end of the third decade of the nineteenth century; the principle of universal white male suffrage was not effected until the Civil War; women were not given the vote until the second decade of the present century; the right of Negroes to vote is still not established in all political units; and the rights of Spanish-speaking voters are established in only a few places.

At the same time, although the principle of 'one man, one vote' is still more an ideal than a reality, in the recent past there have been decisive movements in that direction. Until 1911, United States senators were chosen by indirect vote, and the upper house was more responsive to the desires of those who controlled that process than to the electorate at large.

33

The theory developed

Only in the past decade has the Supreme Court forced state legislation to reapportion themselves in conformance with changing population and economic patterns; before that time they tended to reflect the views of a nineteenth century electorate far more than those of current day political distribution.

Under these conditions, one would expect that United States senators would support legislation furthering the interests of the oligarchy that elected them, that state legislatures would support policies of farm rather than city groups, and that no one would have much interest in policies affecting groups without the franchise. With changes wrought by the Seventeenth Amendment, the extensions of the franchise, and the redistricting requirements of the Supreme Court, these constraints have been drastically altered; and the types of activity organized through the government have changed accordingly. Income taxes have become more progressive, a part of the income redistributed to producers through the high tariffs of the nineteenth and early twentieth centuries has been returned to the consuming sectors, and subsidizing urban transport has become of concern to state legislatures.

Anthony Downs has used a diagram similar to that in Figure 2.1 to explain the political effects of the extension of the franchise to the British working class. It appears an equally useful way of illustrating the American political experience. Assume that it is possible to array all citizens along a scale on the basis of their attitude toward some economic activity (a method of redistributing income from the rich to the poor via a progressive income tax, for example). This array is shown by the white area under the curve in Figure 2.1. Assume further that one can also array voting citizens (or the group that selects senators) along the same scale. This group (represented by the shaded area) is both smaller than the group of citizens and also tends to be farther to the 'right' on the scale. If the two political parties were interested in maximizing votes, one would expect that their positions on the issue would tend to converge on the center of the shaded distribution

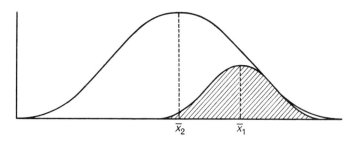

Figure 2.1

34

$(\overline{X}_1)$ – if a party chose any other point, it could never command a majority as long as the other party made the appropriate response. If, however, the franchise is extended to include all citizens, both parties would tend to move to the left and their positions would close on $\overline{X}_2$. One would not expect the government to have assumed a rich to poor income-redistribution role in the initial period, but it is very likely it would do so after the change in the franchise broadened the electorate.

(5) The increase in the size of the electorate (accompanied as it was by a broadening of the composition of the enfranchised) has made income redistribution from rich to poor politically possible, but at the same time by increasing the costs of organization, it has made political action more expensive. These tendencies have been in part offset by the development of the power of the legislative, judicial, and executive branches to effect policies without reference to the electorate. An important part of this process has been the growth of quasi-legislative bodies empowered to enact and administer policies without recourse to the legislative process. Very frequently these boards and regulatory agencies have been created for one set of purposes but have come to be used for a quite different one. Whether they operate as they were intended to do or not, the result of their growth has been a reduction in the cost of political action since interested groups need influence only a small number of individuals rather than having to influence half of the electorate or their representatives. Moreover, since membership tends to be appointive rather than elective, the agency members are shielded from any political response to their actions. The classic case is the Interstate Commerce Commission. Promoted by farm groups and city merchants to lower railroad rates, it ultimately led to a regulatory agency utilized by the railroads themselves to cartelize an industry – a cartel which would have been prohibitively expensive had it required the passage of legislation through the entire United States Congress.[1] The ICC is one of a vast array of regulatory quasi-legislative bodies that have grown up in American society that have drastically lowered the costs of redistributing income despite the concurrent expansion of the franchise.

(IV) A digression on game theory[2]

Ever since Von Neumann and Morgenstern published their pioneering work in game theory, social scientists have felt that work in that area should hold

[1] See P. MacAvoy, *The Economic Effects of Regulation* (Cambridge, Mass., 1965).
[2] The material in this section has been drawn from R. Luce and H. Raiffa, *Games and Decisions* (New York, 1967); and W. Baumol, *Economic Theory and Operations Analysis* (Englewood Cliffs, New Jersey, 1965).

The theory developed

the key to the solution of a number of problems that have not proved amenable to more traditional analysis.[1] The problem of predicting the outcome of a political bargain is one of those. Unfortunately, most political bargains belong to the class of '*n* person' or 'non-zero sum games' or both, and for them, recent extensions of game theoretic analysis, while suggestive, have yielded few concrete results.

As to non-zero sum cooperative games, Von Neumann and Morgenstern argued that the equilibrium bargain could not be inferred from theoretical analysis and the most that the game theorist could hope for was the delineation of a set of possible equilibrium bargains (a set they termed the negotiation set). Assume, for example, that the shaded area in Figure 2.2 represents the set of potential outcomes that could be achieved by some cooperative bargain between the two players and that the point v_1v_2 represents the level of satisfaction that players 1 and 2 can guarantee themselves should they choose to play the game in a non-cooperative fashion (the point could, therefore, represent the *initial* distribution). Since we assume that more is better than less, any preliminary negotiation should produce a point in the outcome space that is jointly undominated (i.e. a point is said to be jointly dominated if there exists another point yielding a greater level of utility to both players). In Figure 2.2 the heavy line *aebcfd* encompasses the set of all jointly undominated outcomes. Since, however, player 1 can assure himself an amount v_1 and player 2 an amount v_2 by refusing to cooperate, the line segments *ae* would be excluded by 1 and *fd* by 2. Thus the negotiation set

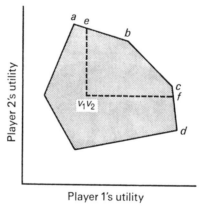

Player 1's utility

Figure 2.2

---

[1] J. Von Neumann and O. Morgenstern, *Theory of Games and Economic Behavior* (Princeton, New Jersey, 1947).

36

The government, coercion, redistribution of income

consists of all points on the line *ebcf*, but the particular point will be determined by non-mathematical considerations that underlie the bargaining strengths of the two players.

Since Von Neumann and Morgenstern, a number of authors have attempted to push the analysis further, but these extensions have been largely in a direction that is of little interest to us. What work has been done has been aimed at producing a 'just' solution (i.e. one that might result from arbitration) rather than at an analytical method of predicting actual outcomes.

As to *n* person games, again the new work has been more suggestive than useful. It has suggested that there will be a tendency to form coalitions; that the pay-offs to any single members of the winning coalition cannot be less than that member would receive should he decide to leave the coalition; and that the total amount received by all players is equal to the amount that would be realized from a 'grand coalition'. Moreover, the work recognizes the fact that side payments (i.e. bribes) may be one method of reaching the actual bargaining equilibrium. However, it has yielded no operational theory that could lead us to specific predictions about the actual equilibrium solution.

Until the tools of game theory (or some alternative analytical formulation) are able to engender better predictions, our model of institutional change is less than we might like. As a result, when the government solution involves bargaining between competing groups (i.e. has the characteristics of an *n* person zero sum game), we can expect coalitions to emerge, we can say something about the minimum profit distribution to each group, and we can, perhaps, outline the feasible negotiation set. Beyond that we can do no more than suggest that some cooperative solution is apt to be found if the increase in total profits from cooperation are large and that the solution is most likely to favor the group with the greatest bargaining strength.

(V) Conclusions

Since governmental institutional arrangements rest on the coercive power of government, they stand on a somewhat different footing than individual and voluntary cooperative organizations. It is impossible to discuss such governmental organizations without bringing up the subjects of law and politics, to say nothing of the constitutional base on which both rest. Unfortunately, the theory of politics is not as well developed as economic theory, and as a result, there is more room for 'slack' in this part of the analysis. Despite these reservations, it appears worthwhile to attempt to include governmental arrangements in our discussion of change. For that matter, it is fairly obvious that any attempt to eliminate them would likely

37

yield a model of institutional change no more useful in the growth context than are the present models with their *ceteris paribus* assumptions about institutions. Moreover, as shall become apparent in the second part of this volume, the model (as lacking as it may be) does yield some useful and interesting predictions about the course of institutional change in the governmental level as well as those that relate to the private and voluntary cooperative levels. Still, we readily admit that we are unable to explain all (or perhaps even most) aspects of politics, government, and law. Therefore changes in the 'rules of the political game', modifications in the constitutional base on which the economy rests, and shifts in the political utility functions of the citizens of the economy are all assumed to be determined outside the model. Of course the implications of such changes for the endogenous variables are a part of the analysis presented in Sections II and III. Chapter 3 specifies our general model in more detail as it applies to governmental as well as individual and voluntary cooperative groups; and Chapter 4 enumerates the most important 'exogenous' political and legal changes in the economic environment that have marked American history and that we take as 'given' in the remainder of the volume.

A THEORY OF INSTITUTIONAL INNOVATION: DESCRIPTION, ANALOGY, SPECIFICATION

(I) Introduction

The sources of external changes in techniques and structure that, if exploited, *could* lead to greater total income and certainly *would* lead to greater income for the action group that effected the exploitation were examined in Chapter 1. In addition, it was suggested in Chapter 2 that a change in the 'rules of the political game' can permit one person's (or group's) income to be increased at the expense of another's, if the former can find a way of taking advantage of (or perhaps even of initiating) the change. If these 'increases in profits' can be realized within the structure of existing institutional arrangements, few problems result and the desire for more income should lead to their exploitation within a relatively short period. In that case, present theory with its assumptions of a fixed institutional environment is adequate. If, however, the increased income cannot be realized within the existing arrangemental structure, existing theory is much less useful.

It is the possibility of profits that cannot be captured within the existing arrangemental structure that leads to the formation of new (or the mutation of old) institutional arrangements. To do no more than assert a relationship between income changes and arrangemental innovation is hardly a significant step; however, it is our intention to offer a theory that helps predict (or explain) the emergence of these new or mutated arrangements. In particular, the theory predicts the level (individual, voluntary cooperative, or governmental) of the new institutional arrangement and the length of time that passes between the recognition of the potential profit and the emergence of the new arrangement.

Why is it profitable to form new economic arrangements at one time in history and not at another? While there are potential external profits to be gained under a number of given circumstances, a new arrangement will emerge only when changes in the expected benefits from innovation or the costs of that innovation will make such an arrangemental modification worthwhile. Thus, while at any moment in time, there may be a state of institutional equilibrium (no advantage to be gained from arrangemental change), alterations in costs and revenues can create a disequilibrium in the system and thereby induce arrangemental change.

Although most economic models take the state of existing institutional arrangements as given, and while it is the object of this book to turn that constant value into a variable one, traditional theory still offers important support for the present work. In accordance with traditional theory, our basic assumption is that the motivating factor in arrangemental change is the desire to gather the greatest amount of all possible profit. Also, the type of model used here is a variant of the 'lagged supply' type, one frequently employed in more traditional economics. In a lagged supply model, a change in demand in one period of time produces a supply response in a later period of time.[1] In this model an increase in the potential profits from arrangemental change induces after some delay (or lag) the innovation of a new arrangement capable of capturing those profits for the innovators.[2]

(II) The model: introduction

Assume an initial equilibrium. That is, a state where, given prevailing conditions, no change in existing institutional arrangements could yield additional income to any individual or group of individuals in the economy. Such a condition could exist if: (1) all potential income increments arising from the sources enumerated in Chapter 1 had been captured by arrangemental adjustment; or (2) such potential profits exist but the cost of altering the existing arrangements exceeds those profits; or (3) there is no chance to

[1] The most common use of lagged supply models has been in the explanation of agricultural behavior. In these models an increase in price after one harvest induces increased production at the next planting. The increased production, in turn, drives down prices and induces a reduction of the quantity supplied in the third period. The Cobweb models are, of course, of this type, as are the models of investment in plant and equipment in the Marshalian long run. It is the latter type that appears most analogous to what we have in mind.

[2] To further clarify the definitions of invention, new innovation, and innovation, consider the following example: John D. Rockefeller invented the trust form of industrial organization when he realized that operational control of a number of companies could be exercised through that particular organizational arrangement. It was a new innovation when he applied it to the Standard Oil complex. Its application to other industries (the Sugar Trust, for example) illustrates the spread of innovation (there the application was an innovation, but not a new innovation). Finally, the return to informal cartel arrangements (the Gary dinners, for example) after 1890 reflects induced innovation as a well-known organizational form was applied in response to a change in relative prices (the cost of the trust rose substantially when it became illegal). For a further discussion of these historical episodes see Chapter 8 on manufacturing.

effect any income redistribution without some change in the institutional environment. The equilibrium is not necessarily permanent, since pressure for arrangemental innovation could be engendered by any of three types of exogenous events.

(1) Potential income from arrangemental innovation might increase because some exogenous change led to the emergence of an externality where none existed before, to a restructuring of risks, to a shift in transaction costs, or to the application of a new technology subject to increasing returns.[1]

(2) The costs of organizing and/or operating a new institutional arrangement might change because of the invention of new arrangemental technology, of arrangemental change in the non-economic sector, or because the price of the factors used in the new or in competing arrangements may have changed.

(3) Some legal or political change might alter the institutional environment and make it possible for some group to effect a redistribution or to take advantage of an existing external profit opportunity.

We assume that businessmen are profit maximizers and that entrepreneurs are as willing to take advantage of profit opportunities arising from arrangemental reorganization as they are willing to exploit new markets, technologies (in the narrow sense), or changes in relative factor prices. Thus the profit potential inherent in any of the three types of exogenous changes would lead to attempts to capture it through arrangemental reorganization. Let us first examine the process through which changes in external profit potential, costs, or ground rules are transmitted to the potential entrepreneurs and then let us examine the conditions that determine the level and timing of the innovation.

Although almost innumerable events might produce profits external to the existing arrangemental structure, three have been particularly important in the American context. They have contributed greatly to the 'demand' for new institutional arrangements in the past and appear likely to continue in that dominant role in the future.

(1) Changes in market size can alter the benefits and costs of particular institutional arrangements: the cost of acquiring information or of excluding nonparticipants does not grow proportionately with the volume of transactions. Both exhibit the characteristics of decreasing-cost activities. For example, when the volume of western farm mortgages was small, it was not worthwhile for eastern financial interests to establish branches in the West to take advantage of the much higher interest rates. As the volume of such mortgages grew, however, it became worthwhile for these eastern financiers

[1] Let us remind the reader that, as we have pointed out in Chapter 1, this list does not exhaust the sources of potential external profits.

to send representatives out to organize allied financial institutional arrangements in western markets. The cost of organizing these arrangements had not changed, but the revenues had. In like fashion, the cost of establishing new arrangements or secondary action groups designed to police markets, spread risks, etc., will not increase proportionately with the volume of transactions.

(2) Technology has had a pervasive influence in altering the benefits of arrangemental change. First, in general, over the past two centuries technical change has resulted in increasing returns to scale over a substantial range of output and thereby made it profitable to form more complex organizational forms. Second, technological change has produced, as a by-product of scale economies, the factory system and the agglomeration of economic activity which has led to the urban, industrial society of today. These in turn have produced widespread externalities that have induced still further change. The massing of people in vast urban complexes, together with their propinquity to productive activity, has led to 'neighborhood effects' on a scale simply unimaginable in the agrarian society of the eighteenth century. Air and water pollution and traffic congestion are but three of the more obvious consequences of this agglomeration revolution.[1] While some of the neighborhood effects have been internalized by voluntary organization, some have not, and the existence of these uncaptured profits has been a major force leading to the intervention of government in the economy in the recent past.

(3) A change in the income expectations of groups in a society will lead to a general revision of their appraisal of the benefits and costs of forming institutional arrangements. Generalized market failure in the form of depression which persisted long enough to alter people's expectations about their income prospects was an essential part of the wholesale attempt to employ government to improve on the performance of a market economy in the 1930s. Similarly, particular groups – farmers, for example – have shifted from using volunteer organization to achieve their ends to supporting widespread government reform and intervention in the 1870s, to abandoning such policies (1896–1920), to again pressing for governmental solutions (after 1920) as farm income has expanded or stagnated (or absolutely declined).

---

[1] In turn it might be noted that the so-called population explosion itself has triggered substantial arrangemental change. On the one hand individual and voluntary cooperative groups have pushed for national family planning, and at times even the government has seen fit to make birth control information available to the poor. On the other hand, the existence of extant institutional arrangements (the Catholic Church, for example) has certainly slowed the process of arrangemental change.

As in the case of the 'demand' for new institutional arrangements, many things could have reduced the costs involved in innovating and operating certain of these arrangements. Because of their marked impact on American development, however, four appear particularly worthy of mention. In addition, the four provide good illustrations of the way changes in costs affect the process of institutional rearrangement.

(1) The costs of arrangemental innovation can be markedly reduced if an arrangement whose organizational expenses have been underwritten for one purpose can be used to effect a second. Organizational expenses can be a major element among the costs involved in launching almost any organization. If those costs have already been paid, the marginal cost of redirecting the arrangement toward a new goal may be low enough to make innovation profitable. In the 1870s the costs of organizing a large fraction of the American farm sector into an effective political lobby were very high, but once these costs had been paid by the Grange (a social organization) the much smaller costs of redirection made the innovation of the economic arrangement appear profitable. History is marked by any number of examples of institutional arrangements that became profitable only after redirection costs were substituted for organizational expenses.

(2) Technological change has not only increased the potential profits from arrangemental change but also has reduced the costs of operating certain arrangements. In particular, technical developments that have radically reduced the cost of information (the telegraph, telephone, radio, and computer, to cite four) have made it profitable to innovate a series of arrangements designed to improve markets and to facilitate the flow of goods between markets. Without the fast, cheap and accurate information of security prices that the stock ticker makes available in almost every broker's office, it would be impossible to support a national securities market centered in New York City and serving savers and investors from Portland, Maine to San Diego, California. Similarly, the technical improvements that have led to mass communications have greatly reduced the costs of organizing institutional arrangements based on the participation of individuals spatially removed from each other. Without the radio, for example, there would have been no fireside chats and without them it would have been more costly for Franklin D. Roosevelt to put together the coalition of laborers, Negroes, and the poor that dominated American politics for the three decades after 1932.

(3) The accumulation of scientific knowledge, the development of an educational system that has led to the widespread dissemination of social and technical information, and the growth of the stockpile of recorded statistics that has gone hand in hand with the growth of business and the government have reduced the costs associated with certain arrangemental innovations. No

43

insurance scheme is viable unless there is some method of assessing the risks to be insured. In the case of life insurance, it was the improvement in the collection of vital statistics that provided the basis for an adequate mortality table and made innovation of such insurance schemes possible. In the more recent past, it is the increased knowledge of population characteristics that can be garnered from the census, coupled with a knowledge of statistical sampling techniques and certain behavioral propositions drawn from psychology, that has made innovation in the advertising field 'pay off'.

(4) The steady increase in the power of the federal government and its penetration into ever more aspects of American life have drastically reduced the costs associated with innovating governmental arrangements and made it profitable to launch such organizations today while a century ago their innovation would have involved costs far in excess of the potential profit. For example, it appears likely that an attempt to organize a political coalition to effect an income redistribution through some form of governmental social security scheme would have been almost infinitely costly in 1890. Such an arrangement was innovated during the 1930s, but only at very high costs. Today, however, the innovation of similar arrangements, for example, Medicare, can be effected at substantially lower cost. There are two aspects to this point: that once a government arrangement has been accepted, the political costs of extension decline; that an existing bureaucratic infrastructure built for one program frequently can be extended to other programs at relatively low cost.

Exogenous changes have also affected the institutional environment, and these, too, have altered the profits to be garnered from institutional innovation. Two in particular appear to illustrate the process of arrangemental change induced by environmental events.

(1) Formal organizations and legal rights are either supported and reinforced or else they are circumvented and sometimes neutralized by the norms of behavior and the values of a society, and when these norms change, arrangemental adaptation may follow. It is the general support of the community for property rights which reinforces the use of police power in protecting those rights, and a decline in community support for such rights will lead to decline in the value of those assets and a consequent disequilibrium.[1] Society's support for property rights has changed sharply at many moments in the past and has led to such results as, for example, an increased use of police power (public, or sometimes private, as in the case of the Pull-

---

[1] We do not mean to imply by this statement that there is no causal relationship between institutional arrangements, society's norms of behavior, and the feedback from these norms to the institutional arrangements. It is not, however, a unicausal relationship and cannot be discussed in any existing model.

man strike and many other instances of labor strife) or the modification of property rights (as in the passage of the Pre-emption Law of 1841, that gave squatters first rights of purchase of newly surveyed public lands on which they had already illegally settled).

(2) Changes in the costs and benefits from arrangemental innovation can also be induced by changes in the size, composition, or the rules of government. For example, reduction in property qualifications for voting, the enfranchisement of women and Negroes, and the redistricting of legislatures to conform to population changes illustrate respectively the above three changing factors in the government sector. Each is exogenous to our model, but each alters the costs and revenues associated with government arrangemental innovation and may therefore induce arrangemental change.

As we have seen, an institutional change may involve only a single individual, it may involve a group who are held together by a voluntary agreement, or it may involve a group who are held together and/or whose power to effect decisions rests on the involvement of government. While at any moment the state of arrangemental technology may reduce the 'menu of choice', in principle an arrangemental innovator could be faced with choosing between arrangemental alternatives drawn from any (or all) of the three levels. If the model is to be useful, it must predict which level he will turn to, or if no existing institutional technology will suffice, on which level he will search for a new invention. The choice rests, as we have seen in Chapter 1, upon the benefits and costs of each, and on the relative market and non-market power of the affected groups.

In the 1830s, for example, large blocks of capital were required if the economies of scale inherent in the new railroad technology were to be captured. Individual institutional arrangements were ruled out since no private fortunes were large enough to underwrite projects like the Pennsylvania Railroad. While voluntary cooperative arrangements (corporations) tended to be innovated, given the state of the private capital markets, those arrangements were unable to acquire sufficient capital to underwrite the size required to realize the economies of scale. The arrangement of choice, then, was a form of private–government partnership, since only the government could command the requisite capital resources at a price that made the transport enterprises profitable. There were, however, costs involved in government participation. In particular, the government demanded a voice in railroad operations and the road itself was made quite vulnerable to political attack. By the 1850s, the private capital markets had improved and finance could be raised without government's participation. Abandoning the public–private partnership that had been the most economical arrangemental form two decades previously, a new arrangemental form was innovated that depended solely on the voluntary participation of private parties.[1]

Not only is the level at which the arrangement emerges not a random event, but also the length of the lag between the appearance of the profit and the innovation of an arrangement capable of internalizing that profit depends on certain distinguishable factors and can (it is hoped) be predicted with some degree of accuracy. Although many factors may affect the length of the lag, the most important relate to the state of existing laws and institutional arrangements. Among this latter group, three seem particularly important.

(1) At any moment of time, existing laws (both common and statute) circumscribe the range of institutional arrangements that can evolve. Although laws can be changed, in the short run at least, they limit arrangemental choice. Thus, since the passage of the Sherman Anti-Trust Act, it has been difficult, although not impossible, to innovate a cartel-like arrangement that derives its coercive power from the government. Other things being equal, therefore, one would expect that, when such cartel-like arrangements do appear, they are either based on some specific legal loophole or that they are an extra-legal voluntary arrangement with no legal coercive power. Thus, the Interstate Commerce Commission can act like a cartel because of a legal exception to the general law, and the Mafia could cartelize the illegal drug industry because their coercive power was extra-legal.

Again, since some arrangemental innovations are based on already existing institutional arrangements, the presence or absence of these 'basic' arrangements will have an effect on the shape of the 'second level' ones. As long as commercial banks exist, for example, a commercial paper market represents one alternative arrangement that could emerge to arbitrage interregional short-term capital markets. Since commercial banks act as both buyers and sellers in the paper market, an absence of such banks would force the arbitrage arrangement into a different mold.

The existence of prior legal and other arrangemental structures affects not only the shape of arrangemental innovation, but its period of gestation as well. If laws must be changed or primary arrangements developed before a new innovation can be adopted, one would expect that the period of arrangemental gestation would be lengthened.

(2) The state of existing institutional technology also affects the lag in the

---

[1] The costs and benefits of voluntary organization versus the use of government are discussed in detail in J. Buchanan and G. Tullock, *The Calculus of Consent* (Ann Arbor, Mich., 1962), Chapter 6.

supply response in another manner. A firm will not innovate a new technological process in the short run as long as the average variable cost of the
old technique is less than the average total cost of the new. It will, of course,
replace its old capital equipment with the new technology when the old
capital equipment wears out. A similar rule appears to hold for institutional
arrangements. Like capital equipment, arrangements can earn quasi rents
and do have scrapping costs even if the counterpart of depreciation (but not
obsolescence) is difficult to conceive.[1] Frequently the life of the arrangement
depends on the personnel of the potential innovating group, but people do
die and retire just as capital equipment wears out.

An example of the effect of existing institutional technology on the process
of change can be seen in the relatively slow penetration of commercial
banking into the South. In other areas there were no existing institutional
arrangements capable of effecting intra-regional capital transfers, but in the
South the cotton factors underwrote such transfers, as well as their primary
business of interregional mobilization. Although commercial banks were more
efficient intra-regional mobilizing agents than the factors, the existence of
factors meant that the profits from the innovation of commercial banking
were lower in the South than in other areas. The result, as one might expect,
was that banks were innovated in the South much more slowly than elsewhere. When the existing arrangemental structure (the cotton factors)
declined (as they did after the Civil War) the pace of arrangemental innovation quickened – profits from innovation in the South were now comparable
to those in other regions.

(3) Invention is a difficult process, and if innovation must await the
invention of a new arrangemental form, the lag is apt to be long. If, however,
an arrangemental form that has proved itself viable in one situation can with
little change be applied in another, the lag is likely to be shorter. A government regulatory agency (the Interstate Commerce Commission) became the
secondary institution through which the cartel of long-distance railroads
effected its decisions. In that instance there was no technology that could be
borrowed, and the gestation period was almost twenty years. Later, however,
when airlines faced the same problem, they were able to draw on the existing
institutional technology, and the Civil Aeronautics Board was established
and effectively enforcing cartel decisions almost before the profits were
recognized.

The model, then, suggests that profits appear outside the existing arrangemental structure and new arrangements are formed to internalize them.

[1] Since sunk costs are sunk, the firm is only interested in its return above operating (as
opposed to total) costs when it has already made the investment. These returns economists
(for who knows what reason) call quasi rents.

The theory developed

The profits are, of course, the product of events exogenous to the model, but the model predicts the level and the timing of the new arrangements.

(III) Digression: a technological analogy

Traditional theory offers some useful analogies for the present work and among these it appears that an analogy drawn between the theory of technical and arrangemental change is particularly useful. While economists do not commonly assume that institutional arrangements change, they do assume that technology, although fixed in the short run, is subject to change over some longer period. In this regard, they have distinguished (and we believe, usefully) between two types of technical change.

(1) Technical change induced by a shift in some economic variable that forces the firm to alter its technical configuration by selecting some new technical process from among a menu of known alternatives.

Induced innovation can come from either one of two sources: a change in relative factor prices or a change in the scale of operation. In the first instance, firms faced by the relative decline in the price of a factor will, if given time, alter their productive process to use more of the relatively cheaper input and less of those whose relative prices have risen. Alternatively, if the capital input to some process is not infinitely divisible, then an increase in market size may cause a firm to alter its factor mix to use more capital and less labor.

(2) Technical change can also be the product of the innovation of a new invention, and, to the layman, this is probably the most common use of the term.

Finally, one might examine a third intermediate type of technical change, although in fact it does not represent a logically distinct class. In this instance, an innovation of a new technology in one industry induced by, for example, a change in factor prices, may focus research interests on a similar problem in other industries, and yield new inventions and innovations there.

Arrangemental change appears to be subject to analysis similar to that employed in the explanation of technical change. An arrangement is, after all, nothing more than a set of formal arrangements that permits resources to be combined in a particular way. In this sense they are nothing but another form (although perhaps a more general one) of a technical process. Most would agree that the introduction of the assembly line (an innovation attributed to either Henry Ford or his production manager, Sorenson) is an example of a technical change, but it involved only a rearrangement of existing labor and machines. If the assembly line is an example of technical change, then the development of a set of corporate controls that involve an institutional rearrangement of existing functions must be, if not identical, at least very similar.

48

If the reader is willing to accept this view, the analysis can proceed along lines similar to those employed in the discussion of changes in technology. That is, the response to a disequilibrium that has made it profitable to reorganize economic activity may be realized by a simple reorganization based on existing known alternatives or it may require the innovation of a new form of institutional organization.

As an example of the first variety of change, take the financial subsidies paid by the government to many canal and railroad companies during the 1820s and '30s.[1] The known alternative institutional arrangements included private operation and government control. Firms could select total private operations, but the costs of capital to such firms (particularly if the project were a large one) were very high. On the other hand, the costs of capital mobilized through the intercession of the government were much lower, but government ownership involved the sacrifice of control and therefore profits. In the 1820s and '30s, given these alternative net revenues, it paid the transport companies to adopt an institutional arrangement that, while forcing them to surrender a portion of their profits, gave them access to low cost government mobilized finance. In the case of the Pennsylvania Railroad, for example, state and local governments underwrote a portion of the firm's construction expenses and were permitted to appoint some directors to the railroad's board. By the 1850s, however, the cost of private capital had declined relative to government finance, and now when faced with the same finance versus control decision, the railroad's management moved toward total private control. The subsidies would not have been less productive, but their net revenue had fallen (i.e. the alternative cost had declined), and at this new set of prices, it was no longer profitable to retain the old institutional arrangement.

Not all institutional arrangements are government ones, and the history of the corporation (a form of voluntary cooperation) yields an interesting example of the adaptation and modification of an arrangemental form induced by both changes in net revenues and by increases in the size of the market. As early as the eighteenth century, the corporation was recognized as a possible arrangemental alternative to the then organizationally dominant partnerships and sole proprietorships. However, corporate charters could be granted only by a state or federal legislature, and the costs of obtaining such legal sanctions were very high. In terms of our analogy, the corporate charter represents a piece of indivisible capital and only large firms could profitably innovate this arrangement. As the model would suggest, private corporations were largely concentrated in interregional transportation and in those few manufacturing activities displaying substantially increasing

---

[1] These subsidies are more fully discussed in Chapter 7.

The theory developed

returns to scale (Massachusetts-type textile mills, to name one). Elsewhere costs appear to have outweighed the revenue. Other enterprises, although recognizing the usefulness of unlimited life and limited liability, found it too costly.[1]

By the 1870s, however, conditions had altered markedly. On the one hand, the growth of a national market and technical change in a number of manufacturing industries had greatly increased optimal firm size (economies of scale now existed over wide ranges of economically feasible production). This fact was reflected in the growth of the number of corporate charters issued to manufacturing firms in the period from 1850 to 1870 even in states that retained legislative chartering provisions. On the other hand, by the 1870s, many states had adopted general incorporation acts, and this procedure markedly reduced the cost of corporate innovation.[2] The response to this change in 'factor prices' was a widespread abandonment of partnerships and proprietorships and the innovation of corporate organization in parts of the service and manufacturing sector where there were no obvious scale economies but where the other aspects of corporate organization engendered smaller but positive revenues.

Like their technological counterparts, some arrangemental innovations are the results of invention and do not depend on changes in factor prices or in the size of the firm. Their innovation depends entirely upon the diffusion of knowledge about the new arrangement and the longevity of the existing arrangements. The growth of a national market in the nineteenth century broke down many historic local monopolies and threw firms into fierce oligopolistic competition with each other. Not too surprisingly, in an attempt to protect themselves against the effects of this competition, firms searched for effective ways of cartelizing their markets. Informal cartel arrangements were in every firm's list of alternative arrangemental techniques, and the emergence of the national market altered relative net revenues to induce some such form of organization. Given the legal system, however, traditional techniques were not too effective, and solution awaited the invention of new arrangemental forms: forms that would permit a greater degree of cartel control at the same resource cost.[3]

The trust, invented – or at least first innovated – by the Standard Oil Company, was such an innovation, but one that depended only on voluntary

[1] The innovation of the corporate form is discussed in more detail in Chapters 6 and 7.
[2] General incorporation legislation may have been exogenous to the model. The evidence, however, suggests that those laws were the political response to potential profits that were positive but too small to make special incorporation appear profitable. If they were, they, too, can be explained. See Chapter 8.
[3] Cartelization in manufactures is discussed in greater detail in Chapter 8.

cooperation. Its costs were no more than those of the informal arrangements that had dominated organization in the earlier period, but because of its structure, there was no possibility of cheating on the cartel decisions. Moreover, although entry was voluntary, the coercive power of the law prevented a member from withdrawing unless a majority of the trust's stockholders agreed. Again, the Interstate Commerce Commission became an effective government-underwritten cartel device in the railroad industry, although it had been invented for quite a different purpose. The cost from the point of view of the railroads was probably substantially less than they had paid for the loose cooperative rate associations of the earlier period, but the revenues in terms of effective cartel rule were much larger. In these two examples, inventions are innovated, but their innovation did not necessarily depend on changes in factor costs or upon increases in the size of the market.

Like the third type of technical developments, institutional arrangements also have an 'external' category. Once an arrangement has been innovated in one sector (perhaps for reasons of net income), there tend to be similar inventions made in other related industries. Thus there was a twenty-year delay between the rise of severe interregional rail competition and the innovation of the ICC as an effective income redistribution arrangement, and another thirty-three years before cartelization was complete.[1] The airline industry, however, had hardly been launched before the arrangement for cartelization had been innovated. Students of the industry date the emergence of a viable passenger service from the introduction of the DC-3s in 1937, and the Civil Aeronautics Act of 1938 gave the Civil Aeronautics Board effective control power. Assuming any positive period of political gestation, the arrangemental innovation almost antedates the emergence of potential profits from effective cartelization.

(IV) A theory of arrangemental innovation

The theory was briefly sketched in Section II, and in Section III an analogy was drawn between arrangemental and technical change. In this section that analogy is used as the basis for a more precise specification of the theory we intend to utilize throughout the remainder of this study. As we have seen, the model attempts to predict both the level of the new arrangement and the length of the lag between the emergence of the external profit and the innovation of the new arrangement. The theory of the profit maximizing

---

[1] This is not to argue that the railroads invented the ICC (or even supported its initial establishment), but that they did redirect its aims from consumer protection to cartelization once it had been established. See Chapter 7.

firm and its choice of technology provides the basis for predicting both, but the two remain distinct. Let us first examine the question of level.

If only a single type of institutional arrangement is capable of capturing the external profits, the decision rule is simple – you innovate that arrangement. If, however, there are several choices, the decision can best be examined in terms of a slightly modified investment model. For the remainder of this analysis let:

(1) *PV* be the *present value* of the net income that the decision-making unit expects from the innovation of some particular organizational form. The subscripted letters i, v, and g refer to the level of organization (individual, voluntary cooperative, or governmental, in that order) and the numbers 1, 2 ... m to the particular arrangement.

(2) *R* be the *returns expected* by the primary action group from the new arrangement, the subscripts 1, 2 ... n refer to the years in which the return is expected, and the superscripts i (1, 2 ... m), v (1, 2 ... m) and g (1, 2 ... m) refer to the level and name of the arrangement.

(3) *r* be the *rate of discount* appropriate to the decision-making unit involved in the selection.

(4) *Co* be the expected costs of organizing the new arrangement with superscripts referring to level and name.

(5) *Cs* be the expected *costs of being 'stuck'* with an undesirable decision with similar superscripts.[1] Stuck costs are, of course, the dollar cost of the adverse decision multiplied by the probability that they shall be incurred.

(6) Cr_n that portion of the arrangement's expected *operating costs* that are borne by the decision-making unit in *year n* with identification superscripts.[2]

In the case of individual arrangements, the array would look like:

$$PV_{i1} = (R_1^{i1} - Cr_1^{i1})/(1 + r) + (R_2^{i1} - Cr_2^{i1})/(1 + r)^2 + \cdots + (R_n^{i1} - Cr_n^{i1})/(1 + r)^n$$
$$PV_{i2} = (R_1^{i2} - Cr_1^{i2})/(1 + r) + (R_2^{i2} - Cr_2^{i2})/(1 + r)^2 + \cdots + (R_n^{i2} - Cr_n^{i2})/(1 + r)^n$$
$$\vdots \qquad \vdots \qquad\qquad \vdots \qquad\qquad\qquad \vdots \qquad\qquad\qquad \vdots$$
$$PV_{im} = (R_1^{im} - Cr_1^{im})/(1 + r) + (R_2^{im} - Cr_2^{im})/(1 + r)^2 + \cdots + (R_n^{im} - Cr_n^{im})/(1 + r)^n$$

The relevant costs and revenues for the calculation of the present value

---

[1] The 'stuck' costs are assumed to be equal in each future year. A change in that assumption, however, does not alter the analysis in any significant fashion.

[2] To be perfectly general one should realize that operating costs are the sum of labor, land, and capital costs and that the choice between competing arrangements might turn on relative factor prices or on relative factor requirements. However, throughout most of the historical epoch that is the subject of this volume, labor represented the only important operating cost for most economic arrangements. Thus, the assumption of fixed proportions greatly simplifies the analysis and does no great damage to the facts. In the very recent past the emergence of a new computer technology may open up the possibility of factor substitution in arrangemental innovation.

A theory of institutional innovation

are those expected by the action group. These expected values are arrived at by multiplying an estimate of the costs or revenues by some factor (p) reflecting the likelihood that the estimated level will in fact be realized. One could, therefore, reformulate the revenue cost term for year n in the above equation as:

$$[(R_n^{im} \cdot P_r) - (Cr_n^{im} \cdot P_{cr})]$$

where P_r is the probability that R_n^{im} will be realized and P_{cr} the probability that Cr_n^{im} will be realized. The addition makes the exposition very difficult, and for this reason we have not included it explicitly. However, the reader should be aware that the present value of some particular arrangement could be changed either by a change in the estimate of the relevant costs and revenues or by a change in the likelihood of their realization.

As is the case in any model where costs and revenues are deferred in time, the present values of those streams are discounted to allow for the fact that future dollars are worth less than present dollars. In the case of costs, if the bill need not be paid until next year, the money can be earning interest throughout this year so the present value of that cost is its dollar value less the earnings that could come from investing that sum until the bill is due. In the case of revenues the opposite logic applies (they are worth less than present revenues because you forego the interest you could have earned had you invested that sum from the present to the date of accrual). The appropriate rate of discount is, of course, the rate of interest at which the decision-making unit can borrow or that rate that they can expect to earn on alternative uses of their resources.[1]

The present value of a particular individual arrangement (PV_{i1}), for example, is equal to the discounted value of the expected returns in each year less the costs of operation of the arrangement borne by the action groups and accruing in that year summed over the expected life of the arrangement. The present value of any other individual arrangement alternative ($PV_{i2} \ldots PV_{im}$) is calculated in the same fashion, although of course the costs and returns are those appropriate to the particular arrangement. In the case of individual arrangements, since there are no organizational costs and one does not face the prospect of 'getting stuck' with a decision one does not like, the only costs that must be considered are those incurred in the operation of the arrangement.

---

[1] For example, if the appropriate rate of discount is 6 percent, the present value of $100 one year from now is $100/1.06 or $94, while the present value of the same $100 two years from now is $100/(1.06)^2 or $100/1.12 or $.89. In short, if I were to invest $89 at 6 percent compound interest for two years, at the end of that time it would be worth $100.

The theory developed

In the case of voluntary cooperative organizations, the formulation must be changed slightly. Although the cost and revenue streams appear in the same order (they are, of course, not necessarily the same) there is an added term, the cost of organization. Moreover, that cost must be borne now so it is not subject to any discount:[1]

$$PV_{v1} = -Co^{v1} + (R_1^{v1} - Cr_1^{v1})/(1 + r) + (R_2^{v1} - Cr_2^{v1})/(1 + r)^2 + \cdots + (R_n^{v1} - Cr_n^{v1})/(1 + r)^n$$
$$PV_{v2} = -Co^{v2} + (R_1^{v2} - Cr_1^{v2})/(1 + r) + (R_2^{v2} - Cr_2^{v2})/(1 + r)^2 + \cdots + (R_n^{v2} - Cr_n^{v2})/(1 + r)^n$$
$$\vdots \qquad \vdots \qquad \vdots \qquad \vdots$$
$$PV_{vm} = -Co^{vm} + (R_1^{vm} - Cr_1^{vm})/(1 + r) + (R_2^{vm} - Cr_2^{vm})/(1 + r)^2 + \cdots + (R_n^{vm} - Cr_n^{vm})/(1 + r)^n$$

Finally, the formulation of the returns from possible governmental arrangements must include not only organizational costs, but also the costs of getting 'stuck' with decisions you do not like. These latter costs are spread over the life of the organization, and therefore, are subject to discounting; however, we *assume* that such costs are likely removed at least one period into the future. Moreover, in the case of governmental organizations, not all operating costs are necessarily borne by the innovating group; it is sometimes possible to pass them along to the body politic. In this case, only those costs that must be borne by the innovating unit are relevant. The formulation then looks like:

$$PV_{g1} = -Co^{g1} + (R_1^{g1} - Cr_1^{g1*})/(1+r) + [R_2^{g1} - (Cr_2^{g1*} + Cs^{g1})]/(1+r)^2 + \cdots + [R_n^{g1} - (Cr_n^{g1*} + Cs^{g1})]/(1+r)^n$$
$$PV_{g2} = -Co^{g2} + (R_1^{g2} - Cr_1^{g2*})/(1+r) + [R_2^{g2} - (Cr_2^{g2*} + Cs^{g2})]/(1+r)^2 + \cdots + [R_n^{g2} - (Cr_n^{g2*} + Cs^{g2})]/(1+r)^n$$
$$\vdots \qquad \vdots \qquad \vdots$$
$$PV_{gm} = -Co^{gm} + (R_1^{gm} - Cr_1^{gm*})/(1+r) + [R_2^{gm} - (Cr_2^{gm*} + Cs^{gm})]/(1+r)^2 + \cdots + [R_n^{gm} - (Cr_n^{gm*} + Cs^{gm})]/(1+r)^n$$

* refers to that part of total operating costs that is borne by the decision-making unit as opposed to total operating cost.

To select the most profitable arrangement the decision maker compares the present net values of each of the competing organizational alternatives, and chooses the form with the largest positive present value. If all are negative there will be no innovation until revenues rise or costs fall sufficiently to produce an economically viable alternative. Although this formulation is overly simplistic, several interesting results emerge.

(1) Because of the discount applied to returns and costs deferred in time, the time structure of payments and receipts may have important implications for the level of arrangement chosen. Three in particular appear to have been important in the determination of the structure of institutional arrangements

---

[1] As should be clear, the procedure for determining the present value of any particular voluntary cooperative arrangement (PV_{v1}, for example) is the same as that employed in evaluating the present value of an individual arrangement, with the exception that the costs of organization of that arrangement (to the action group that engenders it) – Co^{v1} – must be deducted from the summed and discounted net revenues.

in the American past. First, since organizational costs cannot be deferred, the period of time that elapses between organization and the realization of the first returns is particularly important when interest rates are high. Since agreement between members of a voluntary coalition often depend upon extensive and lengthy bargaining, the government is apt to provide the arrangement of choice in the early stage of development when interest rates are high. Moreover, a similar line of reasoning explains, in part, the benefits that can be accrued by voluntary cooperative groups if they are able to redirect the goals of an existing organization rather than having to incur the entire organizational cost of a new one.

Second, the higher the rate of discount the less likely that the expectation of a small but steady income from the arrangemental change will induce an organizational innovation. At the same time, an expectation of large initial returns, even if their duration is quite short, is likely to induce innovation even at high rates of discount.

Third, while organization costs must be incurred at the moment of innovation, the costs of 'getting stuck' with unwanted decisions are spread out over the life of the arrangement. Other things being equal, one would expect, therefore, that, during the early stages of development when interest rates are high, there is a tendency to choose governmental arrangements, a portion of whose costs are long delayed because the present value of those costs appears quite small.

(2) The costs of operation of a government arrangement are not always entirely borne by the decision-making unit. If society does share the costs in proportion to the benefits received, no problems arise. The costs and revenues of a zoning board, for example, may be spread reasonably equally among the property owners in a community if the activity is financed by a property tax. If, however, the group that receives the benefits can pass a portion of the arrangemental operating costs along to others, the present net value of a government level alternative may rise above the 'best' private and voluntary arrangements even if organizational costs and revenues are identical. Under these conditions, there is a tendency for the governmental alternative to become the arrangement of choice. This fact probably provides at least a partial explanation for the apparent preference among certain business groups for regulation effected through the decision of quasi-legislative governmental commissions (the ICC and the FCC are two cases in point) rather than through the voluntary cooperative alternatives.

(3) Since individuals and groups of individuals have different implicit rates of discount, the arrangements of choice may vary with the access to the capital market commanded by the relevant decision-making unit. The higher the rate faced by the group, the larger organizational costs will bulk

The theory developed

in the decision-making mechanism and the more likely the action group will choose arrangements with streams of returns biased toward the present. The model, therefore, predicts that large business firms with easy access to the capital markets will be more likely to organize voluntary cooperative arrangements while small business, labor and consumer groups will prefer institutional arrangements drawn from the governmental level.

Investment theory, then, appears to provide a model of arrangemental choice, but it is to the theory of technological change and to modern political science that we turn for an explanation of the lag between the recognition of profits external to the existing institutional arrangement and the innovation of an arrangement capable of effecting their internalization.

Unfortunately, neither the theory of technological change nor the modern work in political science is as closely specified as investment theory. As a result, we have been unable to 'squeeze out' of the analysis the predictive (or explanative) implications that we managed in the case of 'level' decisions. Instead we view our work on lags as largely theory suggestive. We have drawn a number of *a priori* constraints from politics and technology and to a large degree have used history to test their usefulness rather than using the theory to explain the history.

From the viewpoint of exposition, it appears useful to separate the total lag into four parts and to formulate the model in a fashion designed to predict each independently. However, the reader should bear in mind the fact that the total lag is not necessarily the sum of the parts; it may be less (i.e. it is possible that the activities involved in one lag can be carried on at the same time as those involved in another).[1] First, there is a 'perception and organization' lag – the time that is required to perceive the external profits and organize the primary action group. Second, additional time is required to invent a new 'technology', if no known arrangements can internalize those external profits or if they can be internalized only at costs that absorb the entire potential gain. Third, there is a 'menu selection' lag; the time committed to searching the list of known arrangemental

---

[1] For example, consider the following scenario. Joe perceives that changes in arrangement *A* could increase his profits, and the profits of other people with characteristics similar to his own. He talks it over with Harry, and they decide (*a*) what general reforms are necessary, and (*b*) that a primary action group is needed. Joe is appointed membership chairman and Harry takes on the tasks of policy planning chairman. The former recruits members to the primary action group; the latter works out the details of the desired institutional arrangement. As the group grows, more people are added to the policy planning committee and the group-compromise institutional rearrangement reflects the greater heterogeneity of the new committee. Eventually the group constitutes (or joins) a winning coalition, and evolution of the rearrangement ceases. The current version is 'institutionalized'. Thanks to Professor Roger Noll of the California Institute of Technology for this example.

56

alternatives and choosing the one that maximizes the profits of the primary action group. This delay is equivalent to the lag involved in the spread of best practice techniques in the theory of technical change. Fourth, there is a delay between the selection of the best arrangemental alternative and the commencement of actual operations aimed at capturing the external profits. This delay we call the 'start up' lag. The work of J. Schmookler has provided some useful insights into the analytics of the second lag and that of W. Salter into the third.[1] The work in modern political science (particularly that of Buchanan and Tullock, A. Downs, and W. Riker) suggests something about the nature of the fourth, and both the work in political science and that in technological change provide us with a set of working hypotheses about the length of the 'perception and organization' lag.

From this work in other fields, then, we have produced the following set of *a priori* constraints on the four lags and these are the basis for our 'explanations' of the actual institutional lags incurred in the course of American economic development.[2] In each case, we assume *ceteris paribus*.

Lag 1: Perception and organization

(1) The lag will be shorter the greater are the potential profits that might be realized from an arrangemental innovation and these profits will be greater the larger and closer (in point of time) are the revenues and the greater is the degree of certainty with which the expected costs and revenues are known.

(2) The lag will be shorter the longer is the menu of known and legal arrangemental alternatives. The longer the list the more likely that some innovation will realize the profits and therefore the more reason to speed the organization of an action group. At the same time, if the institutional environment rules out some potential choices, those items on the menu

[1] W. E. G. Salter, *Productivity and Technical Change* (Cambridge, England, 1960); J. Schmookler, *Invention and Economic Growth* (Cambridge, Mass., 1966)
[2] We have not tried to specify the form of the lag model with any particular precision. However, for those of a mathematical bend it may be useful to suggest that a formulation of the form:

$$L = X_1^a X_2^b X_3^c$$

has much to recommend it. In this case the parameters a, b, and c can be viewed as lag elasticities. Our constraints are all of the form $a > 0$ or $a < 0$, but further work might make those predictions more precise ($0 < a < 1$, for example). In the case of Lag 1, for example, X_1 could refer to the size and certainty of profits and the assumed a is less than zero, X_2 to the length of the menu and the assumed b is less than zero, X_3 to the number of persons in the relevant action group and the assumed c is greater than zero. It might be noted that when size and certainty move in opposite directions, and risk aversion exists, lumping together produces ambiguous results. In the American experience the two have tended to move together.

will have less impact on the lag than will those that are not so constrained. However, it may well be true that the existence of illegal alternatives may tend to yield shorter lags than cases where there are *no* known alternatives.

(3) The lag will be shorter the smaller is the number of persons who compose the relevant action group. Organization is both costly and time consuming. The costs are included in the profit calculations, but the time involved is not, and the more people that must be organized the longer will be the length of time required.

(4) The lag will be shorter if there already exists a prototype organization of the persons who constitute the relevant action group. The argument here is similar to (3). If such a group exists, it is likely to be less expensive to redirect (that cost consideration is already included in the present value calculation), but also it probably takes less time than would have to be committed to organizing the same group from scratch.

(5) The lag will be shorter the better are communications and transportation. Organization involves bringing the action group 'together' so that some consensus decisions can be made, and, other things being equal, this can be done more quickly the better are communications and transportation.

Lag 2: Invention

(1) As Schmookler has found for inventors in the more narrow sense, it appears useful to assume that arrangemental inventors are also profit maximizers, and the invention lag will be shorter the greater and more certain are the profits to be realized from the innovation of the new arrangement. The greater are these profits, the higher the potential return to the successful inventor and the more inventive activity it pays to devote to that as opposed to other potential inventions.

(2) The lag will be shorter the greater the number of analogous arrangements currently operating in other industries or economies that can be 'borrowed' in their entirety or in some modified form. Just as technology in the narrow sense can be transferred from society to society, so can arrangements, and when such borrowing is possible, the invention lag will be shorter.

(3) The lag will be shorter the more solidly are economic arrangements based in the legal and political environment and the larger is the number of existing arrangements that can provide the base for further arrangemental extension. Other things being equal, the larger and more firm the arrangemental base the less complex must be the 'new' parts of the arrangement since the inventor can draw on that base for some 'sub-assemblies' in the solution.

58

(4) The lag will be shorter the less the economic environment constrains the choice of alternative solutions. The larger is the area of illegal solutions the greater the probability that any given invention will fall into that area and, on the average, the longer it will take to produce an invention that is outside that area or to change the menu of 'legal' alternatives.

Lag 3: Menu selection

(1) The lag will be longer the larger are the number of arrangemental choices available on the known menu. Just as a long menu produces delays in selection at a restaurant, so a long list of legal arrangemental alternatives increases the time required to evaluate and perform comparative tests of the potential choices.

(2) The lag will be shorter the greater is the spread among the present values of the alternatives appearing on the menu. If some are clearly superior to others, the period of choice will be reduced, but, if all bunch closely together, the time needed to make a selection increases. It does not take long to choose between steak (which I like) and stuffed green peppers (which I can't stand) on a restaurant bill of fare; it takes much longer to choose between steak and lobster (both of which I like) or between the stuffed peppers and a New England boiled dinner (neither of which I like).

(3) The lag will be longer the greater is the element of fixed costs in the total costs of existing arrangements that can effect at least a partial internalization of the external profits. While existing arrangements will be replaced by newer and 'more efficient' ones, that substitution will take place in the short-run only if the variable costs of operating the old arrangement are greater than the total costs of the new. Organizational costs are the arrangemental counterpart of sunk capital costs, and, since investment in organization frequently doesn't depreciate, the short run may be very long indeed.[1]

Lag 4: Start up time

(A) *Individual arrangements*

(1) The start up time will be shorter the greater and more certain are the potential profits. The larger are the profits the more it is worth for the action group to devote its time to the problems inherent in the innovation of the new arrangement.

[1] There are, of course, some exceptions. If the organization expense has taken the form of a political bribe, then a change of government may bring about rapid 'write-off'. Similarly, if the organization is closely identified with a single individual, the lifetime of the organizational investment may be the same as the lifetime of the person in question.

The theory developed

(B) Voluntary cooperative arrangements

(1) The start up time will be shorter the greater and more certain are the potential profits, for the same reasons given in 4(A)(1).

(2) The lag will be shorter the greater is the degree of unanimity among the members of the primary action group and the more equal is the distribution of potential profits among that group. If there are wide areas of disagreement among the group, negotiation will take time, and if some members expect to receive much less than others they may 'drag their feet' in an attempt to 'bargain up' their share of the gains.

(3) The lag will be shorter the smaller is the membership of the primary action group. The smaller is the number the less time it should take to work out some type of compromise in the areas where opinions differ.

(c) Governmental arrangements

(1) The start up time will be shorter the greater and more certain are the profits for the same reasons given in 4(A)(1).

(2) The lag will be shorter the greater is the frequency of elections. If the choice involves some necessary legal change, it may be necessary to pass new legislation by means of initiative or to elect new representatives who will effect such legislation indirectly. In either case, the shorter the time between elections the sooner such alterations in the legal structure can be effected.

(3) The lag will be longer the more evenly are the opposing political coalitions balanced and the less passionate are the representatives influenced by the primary action group about this particular issue. When the political issues are resolved in some form of indirect election and when those indirect bodies (state legislatures, for example) are faced by a number of issues (of which arrangemental innovation is only one), we would expect more rapid decisions if the opponents to the plan are few in number and when the proponents are very passionate about the issue and the opponents are relatively dispassionate. A balance of political forces and a reverse of the strength of feelings should lead to a lengthening of the lag.

Just as a more precise formulation of the choice problem permitted us to make certain predictive statements, so this specification of the determinants of the lag (although less specific than we might like) permits us to make certain predictions about the effect of certain exogenous variables on the length of the total arrangemental lag: an examination of the structure of lag four leads us to expect that the total lag for individual arrangements should be less than that for voluntary cooperative arrangements and those in turn are shorter than for governmental alternatives; since the size of the 'menu' enters with opposite effects into two different lags it is not possible to predict the net effect of changes that increase menu size (alterations in the institutional environment that make previously unacceptable solutions legal or socially desirable, for example); anything that increases the size or certainty of the potential profits acts to reduce the total lag; and anything that increases the size of the relevant action group probably yields a longer total lag. Only an examination of the American historical experience will, of course, tell us whether our model helps explain the timing of arrangemental innovation or whether our *a priori* theorizing will have to be modified in light of actual experience.

(V) Conclusion

Figure 3.1 is a flow diagram that attempts to provide a visual summary of the theory of arrangemental change that we have outlined in these first three chapters. Certain exogenous changes (in technology, market size, relative prices, income expectations, the flow of knowledge, or in the rules of the political and economic game) make it possible for someone's income to increase. However, because of some inherent economy of scale, externality, aversion to risk, market failure, or political pressure, it is impossible to realize those gains within the existing arrangemental structure. As a result, there are potential profits that can be harvested by anyone (or any group) who can innovate new institutional arrangements that will overcome those barriers.

Some person or group of persons perceives these potential profits and after some lag organizes a primary action group of the affected parties or redirects the activities of some already established action group towards the capture of these profits. The length of the 'perception and organization' lag depends to a large extent on the size and certainty of the profits and on the availability of an arrangemental technology that might allow the profits to be captured by the primary action group. If no technology exists that can effect the capture at a cost less than the profits, a further delay occurs while attempts are made to invent a new or modify an old arrangement to that end. If one or more economically available arrangements do exist, the action group selects the one that yields them the highest returns. In making their choice they must consider the potential revenues, the organization costs, the operating costs, the costs of 'getting stuck' with unwanted decisions (if their choice involves the government), and the time distribution of these costs and revenues. If there is more than one possible choice, it may take some time to select the one that is, in fact, 'best'; this 'menu selection' lag

61

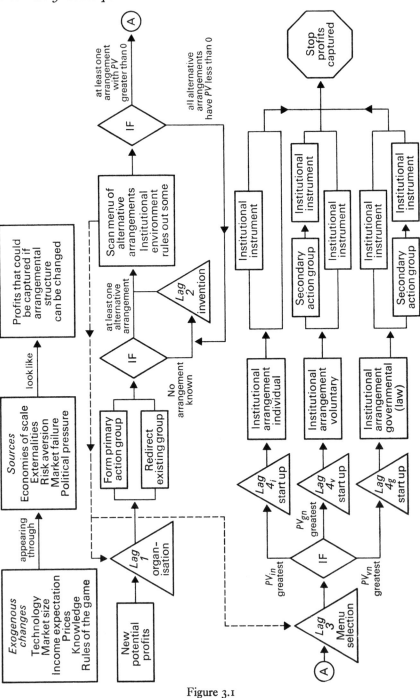

Figure 3.1

then depends to a large extent on the number and the diversity of choices that are available. Moreover, it should be clear that the institutional environment at any moment in time can rule out some potential alternatives (i.e. there may be a difference between the number of items on the menu and the number that are legally and/or socially acceptable). In this regard it becomes obvious that a change in the environment can lead to a new search through the menu even in the case of arrangements that have long been in operation.

Once the new arrangement has been selected, it must be innovated, and since the arrangement sets new rules for intergroup cooperation or competition, the process of innovation may also take time. Likely this 'start up' lag is shortest in the case of individual arrangements, more lengthy if the choice involves a voluntary cooperative group, and longest when the change involves the government. Finally, the capture of the profits can sometimes come directly from the new arrangement, sometimes only through the application of an institutional instrument engendered by the new arrangement, sometimes only indirectly through the action of a secondary action group established by the new arrangement. Once captured, however, the system returns to equilibrium and there is no pressure for further arrangemental change until some exogenous event produces new external profits and the equilibrium is again upset.

CHAPTER 4

CHANGES IN THE INSTITUTIONAL ENVIRONMENT: EXOGENOUS SHIFTS AND ARRANGEMENTAL INNOVATION[1]

(I) Introduction

In the first three chapters we have outlined a theory of institutional change. We have argued that it is the emergence of potential profits outside the existing arrangemental structure that provides the impetus for such change; we have enumerated the sources of those profits; and we have specified a model that, we suggest, is useful in explaining the type and timing of arrangemental innovation. Theory can never be predictive, however, unless the model is conjoined with a set of initial conditions (i.e. a model is a set of logical relations of the form A implies B, and the initial conditions say that A exists).[2] In this case, the process of innovation takes place within an institutional environment, and the environment helps to shape the course of innovation. One would, for example, hardly expect that the same external profits would produce the same innovational response in twentieth century America (where the environment is characterized by a fair degree of political democracy, a high level of sophistication among the private business community, and the rule of law) as in eighteenth century Russia (where the environment was quite different).

Certainly, therefore, the institutional environment must be specified, but in the context of an evolving American nation, the problem is even more urgent. The initial conditions, far from remaining constant over the past

---

[1] The legal history in this chapter is based on C. Swisher, *American Constitutional Development* (Boston, Mass., 1954); E. Corwin, *The Constitution and What it Means Today* (Princeton, N.J., 1948); M. Shapiro, *Law and Politics in the Supreme Court* (Glencoe, Ill., 1964); J. Weaver, *Warren, the Man, the Court, the Era* (Boston, Mass., 1967); D. Lunt, *The Road to the Law* (New York, 1962).

[2] Again, this statement is nothing but a very complicated way of saying that if a model is to make any kind of useful predictive statements about the real world, the model has to have something to do with the world.

175 years, have been in an almost continuous state of flux. While such changes might (or perhaps 'should' is a better word) be endogenous to a more general theory of institutional change, they are not in the context of our present work (we assume that they are exogenous to the model). Since changes in the environment will, however, alter the model's predictions, it is necessary that those changes (as well as the initial environment) be specified. This chapter, then, attempts to specify the institutional environment as it existed in 1790 and sketches the 'exogenous' changes that have altered the environment over the course of American development.

The relevant institutional environment has three dimensions: the political ground rules that govern the extent and the weighting of the franchise; the legal basis for private property; and the expectational weights that the community chooses to apply to the future costs and revenues of particular arrangemental innovations – weights that are the product of experience triggered by events exogenous to the model.[1] The sources of change in these three aspects of economic life lie in changes in the Constitution (the written document that spells out the legal basis for economic decisions), the court decisions that provide the interpretation for that document, the common law that governs day-to-day business transactions, and the external changes in the political and economic life of the nation that affect the people's attitudes toward government.[2]

(II) The rules of the political game

The history of the United States has been characterized by a fairly continuous and largely unidirectional trend away from restricted suffrage and differentially weighted votes towards a universal franchise with equal political weights. The nation's political structure as it emerged from the Constitutional Convention in 1787, while perhaps quite liberal by eighteenth century standards, could hardly be called egalitarian. The federal government had no power to set voter qualifications in federal, let alone in state or local elections, and almost every state restricted the franchise to propertied (or sometimes taxpaying) adult white males. Nor was the structure of political weight designed to give each voter an equal voice in the nation's political affairs. Both the United States Senate and the electors who were to choose

---

[1] As we indicated in Chapter 3, the costs and revenues relevant to arrangemental choice are the products of some estimate of those costs and revenues and some probability weight. That probability weight, in turn, is in part a function of past experiences that are endogenous to the model and in part a function of events totally exogenous. Insofar as the latter are important, the initial conditions at any point in time must be specified. That specification permits us to reestimate the probability weights and, therefore, predict the new institutional arrangements.

[2] Changes in statute law are assumed to be endogenous to the model.

The theory developed

the executive officers of the federal government were to be selected by the state legislatures in any manner they saw fit. Over the past century-and-three-quarters, however, this elitist political structure has been undermined by changes in local laws, by constitutional amendment, and by the interpretation placed on the Constitution by the Supreme Court.

While the phrase 'taxation without representation is tyranny' may have provided the rhetoric for the Revolution, the constitutions of only two of the original thirteen states gave all male taxpayers the right to vote and none provided for universal manhood suffrage.[1] Although it is difficult to assign relative weights, the pressure for change appears to have come from three sources. First, the 'new' French republic (although short-lived) was a living example of the democratic ideal and provided a rallying point for a growing intellectual support for an extended franchise. Second, the new trans-Appalachian states granted almost universal manhood suffrage (since land was nearly free, property requirements were largely meaningless), and the threat of emigration provided further impetus to reform. Finally, and probably most important, the emergence of modern political parties – parties committed not to an ideological position but to getting certain politicians elected to office – hastened the process of franchise expansion still further. It has been a fact of American political life in our competitive system that the party in power has always attempted to extend the franchise to any group that they feel will support them, and since, because of the ground rules, voting rights are hardly ever taken away from a once-enfranchised group, the long-term implication was an ever-broadening electorate.[2]

The last decade of the eighteenth century saw Georgia, South Carolina, Delaware, and New Jersey extend the franchise to all taxpaying adult males, and New Hampshire, Kentucky, Maryland, and Vermont adopt universal manhood suffrage. Outside the South and West progress was slower. Madison was not alone in his concern for the impact of universal suffrage on income redistribution. In New York, for example, where the battle for an extended franchise was fought twice during the 1820s, the same sentiments were echoed by the jurist Chancellor Kent: 'Now sir, I wish to preserve our senate as the representative of the landed interest . . . I wish them to be always enabled to say that their freeholds cannot be taxed without their consent . . .'[3] Still, by 1830 broad (although not universal) suffrage had

[1] The two states were North Carolina and Pennsylvania.
[2] The decision to expand the electorate is logically a question of coalition costs and benefits, but in the American experience these economic considerations have most often led to expansion.
[3] Chancellor Kent to the New York State Constitutional Convention of 1821: in H. Carter, W. Stone, and M. Gould (eds.), *Reports of the Proceedings and Debates of the Convention of 1821*, secs. 219ff.

66

Changes in the institutional environment

been acquired by the male citizens of almost every state. The exceptions were Rhode Island, North Carolina, and Virginia, but only in Rhode Island did it take a revolution to effect the change. Moreover, by the end of the Civil War the principle of universal manhood suffrage had been established for all whites.[1]

Constitutional amendment has also altered the 'rules of the political game', although only one of the three relevant amendments had much impact on the innovation of institutional arrangements before World War II. The Fifteenth Amendment (1870) supposedly enfranchised the Negro, the Nineteenth (1920) did the same for women, and the Seventeenth (1913) provided for the popular election of United States senators. The Fifteenth was largely circumvented in the South (where most Negroes lived) until a series of court decisions in the very recent past. The Nineteenth was rapidly effected, but that extension has apparently underwritten few obvious shifts in the economic balance of power. The Seventeenth, however, has been the source of important changes in the pattern of arrangemental innovation.

As long as senators were appointed by state legislatures, they were not very responsive to the wishes of the general citizenry, but they were very responsive to the needs of the special interest groups that had a strong voice in those legislatures. While direct election has not changed the character of the Senate completely, it is interesting to note that, in the recent past, it has been the Senate that has provided the chief support for policies aimed at effecting a redistribution of income from the few to the many. As a result of the Seventeenth Amendment, the costs of certain kinds of political action have risen while those of others have fallen substantially.

The process of constitutional amendment cannot, however, affect the political ground rules if the courts are unsympathetic. For example, although it took a long time for women to win the franchise, the victory was quickly effected once the Nineteenth Amendment was ratified. Such was not the case for the Negro. The century since 1870 has seen the southern states raise successive stumbling blocks to the Black franchise, and the courts only gradually forced their removal. It was not until 1915 that the Court held that grandfather clauses violated the Fifteenth Amendment.[2] As late as 1935, the Court held that the Fifteenth Amendment did not guarantee the right to vote in a primary election, and, since the South was a one-party

[1] For a more detailed account of the emergence of universal suffrage, see C. Seymour and D. Frary, *How the World Votes* (Springfield, Mass., 1918).
[2] *Gunn & Beal* v. *U.S.* (1915); *Myers* v. *Anderson* (1915). The grandfather clauses in the electoral laws of some states restricted the franchise to those persons whose grandfathers had had the right to vote. Since the typical Negro's grandfather had been a slave, the law disenfranchised the black citizen.

67

state, Negroes were effectively precluded from the democratic process.[1] It was only with the *Classic* decision in 1941 that the Fifteenth Amendment was extended to cover federal primaries, and it was yet another three years before it was further expanded to include the primaries of state and local elections as well.[2] Finally, the use of the poll tax to bar Negro voters has only recently been declared unconstitutional.[3]

In other areas, too, the courts have often proved themselves at least as important as the written Constitution in establishing the rules of the political game.[4] In 1803, Chief Justice John Marshall enunciated the power of judicial review of legislative and executive enactments, and since then the Court's power to examine the constitutionality of legislation has produced the basis for 'judicial (as opposed to legislative or executive) supremacy'.[5] This redistribution of political powers has, in turn, had important effects on the costs of arrangemental change. Seldom used before 1860, the power to declare laws unconstitutional has been used progressively more frequently since that date with quite ambiguous but nonetheless substantial effects. With judicial review and an unsympathetic Court the costs of action at the governmental level rise substantially, but with a sympathetic Court, the reverse is true. The Court was unwilling to apply the Sherman Anti-Trust Act to manufacturing companies in the 1890s, but enunciated the 'rule of reason' in 1911, and this rule covered manufacturing firms.[6] It held that minimum wage laws were unconstitutional in 1923 (and again in 1936), but gave its approval to such legislation in 1937.[7] Judicial review in a very fundamental sense makes the 'rules of the game' depend not on the written Constitution but on the views of a simple majority of the justices presently on the federal Supreme Court, and unquestionably it induces considerable uncertainty into the process of institutional rearrangement.

While the Constitution says nothing about judicial supremacy, it is very explicit about the separation of powers between the executive, legislative and judicial branches of government. The court has tended to respect this separation, and until recently has refused to rule on 'political questions' – matters that are clearly under the jurisdiction of the legislative or executive branches of the government. This doctrine has had important effects on the

---

[1] *Grovey* v. *Townsend* (1935).

[2] *U.S.* v. *Classic* (1941); *Smith* v. *Allwright* (1944).

[3] *Harper* v. *Virginia Board of Election* (1966).

[4] When we speak of the 'courts' we refer to the entire hierarchy of state and federal courts, although because of its position at the peak of the review procedure, it has been the federal Supreme Court that has been the most influential single body.

[5] *Marbury* v. *Madison* (1803).

[6] *U.S.* v. *E. C. Knight Co.* (1895); *Standard Oil Co.* v. *U.S.* (1911).

[7] *Adkins* v. *Children's Hospital* (1923); *West Coast Hotel* v. *Parrish* (1937).

nation's political institutions and through them on the fundamental ground rules. Recently the Court has somewhat modified the doctrine, thus changing the rules and again altering the costs of arrangemental innovation.

The 'political question' doctrine was first enunciated in *Cherokee Nation* v. *Georgia* (1831), but it was the Court's refusal to decide which of the two competing Rhode Island governments was the legal one that established the principle of judicial non-interference in questions relating to the legality of the government (as opposed to the actions of that government).[1] This principle was extended to the issue of legislative reapportionment in 1946 when the Court refused to force the Illinois legislature to reapportion itself despite the stricture in the Illinois constitution.[2] That decision locked the political structure into the established mold, and set relative costs for arrangemental innovation via the route of state government (it kept the costs low for the over-represented rural areas and high for the under-represented cities and suburbs). Sixteen years later, however, the Court entered the 'political thicket', forced the state legislatures to reapportion themselves, and in so doing once again altered the rules substantially.[3] In the short run, the decision obviously has altered the costs of arrangemental innovation, but their long-run implication is less clear. If the principle is expanded into other political questions, the legal rules may be continually modified by judicial action. Combining the power of judicial review with the right to rule on political questions could drastically alter the nation's political structure.

By this point it should be obvious that the actions of the courts can have an important effect on the costs of arrangemental innovation. For example, until the 'one-man-one-vote' decisions, the costs inherent in any attempt to redistribute income from farm to city via the mechanism of a state government instrument or secondary action group was in some states nearly infinite, but after those decisions the costs fell substantially. Again, until the Supreme Court held that minimum wage and hour laws were constitutional, the present value of most arrangemental innovations aimed at raising wages or reducing hours and depending on the government's coercive power was negative and the only viable alternatives lay in some bargain between voluntary cooperative groups.

(III) The rules of business behavior

The common law, the Constitution, the legislature, and the courts establish the rules that govern the operation of private business, the transactions

---

[1] *Luther* v. *Borden* (1849).
[2] *Colegrove* v. *Green* (1946).
[3] *Baker* v. *Carr* (1962); *Reynolds* v. *Sims* (1964).

between businesses and the relation of business to the government. As these rules change, the relative profitability of alternative institutional arrangements also changes. The cease and desist order issued at the behest of the zoning commission alluded to in Chapter 1 would not have been effective if the laws had not permitted the abridgment of the rights of private property in those instances when the present use of that property creates a public nuisance. Since most of the rules governing business behavior lie rooted in either the Constitution or the common law, the courts have played a particularly important role in determining this part of the institutional environment.

While changes in statute law are properly considered as endogenous to this model, changes in the common law (dependent as they are only on a long series of legal precedents and the feelings of the jurist) are not. Furthermore, many of the day-to-day rules that have governed the relationship between businesses and between businesses and their suppliers and customers are a part of the body of common law.[1] It would be impossible here to spell out all aspects of those rules, but there are a few areas where the courts have acted to redefine private property that are particularly relevant to our discussion. For these it appears useful to mention the changes that jurists have written into the institutional environment. In terms of American history three questions of common law appear particularly important: the laws governing the accession of property, the confusion of property, and squatters' rights.

Taking Blackstone as the source of most American common law, it follows that if one acquires the property of another by accident or fraud, the owner's rights to reclaim it are sometimes limited. For example, if accession (an increase, change or improvement of property through some natural means or by the intervention of a human agency) changes the property enough to make identification impossible, it causes the title to pass, the original owner to lose his property, and limits his relief to reclaiming the value of the good at the time of its acquisition.

This strain of law was accepted by most American courts, and its application is illustrated nicely in an 1851 Illinois case, and later in an 1871 Michigan case.[2] In the first, the Court held that the owner could recover his property (in this case trees) even though they had been taken quite by accident and had in the meantime been cut into lumber. In this case identification was possible. Such a decision can, of course, result in a grave injustice, if every owner is allowed to recover his property without regard to the way that property has been altered by the person who acquired it. Blackstone recog-

---

[1] Recently, courts have tended to base judicial decisions on what they determine to be 'reasonable economic behavior' more frequently than they did in the past.
[2] *Davis* v. *Easley* (1851); *Wetherbee* v. *Green* (1871).

nized this problem and went on to hold that, if the property is grossly transformed, the owner is entitled only to his prorata share of the total value of the new asset. In an American case in point, trees worth $25 were unknowingly logged by one man off the land of another and turned into barrel staves and hoops worth $700.[1] The Court held that in this case recovery was limited to $25 – the value of the trees when they were cut.

American courts have modified Blackstone substantially in the case of assets that have accessed after fraudulent acquisition. As early as 1850, the courts held that title can never pass when accession has been achieved through fraud (intentional accession) no matter how far the assets are later transformed. In this leading case (the transformation was from corn to whiskey) the Court held that the owner was entitled to the entire value of the transformed assets.[2]

Hand in hand with the questions of accession go those that arise from confusion (the mixing of the property of one with that of another). In the United States, the courts have held that if mixing has occurred without intent to defraud and if the property mix is of substantially equal value, then each owner is entitled to his fair share of the now mixed property.[3] In the case of bad faith, the courts have been split; about half follow the Michigan decision in the case of *Stephenson* v. *Little* and about half, Judge Campbell's dissent in that case.[4] The majority held that the wrongdoer lost all rights to his property; the dissenters held that he retained some rights. When, through fraud, assets of poorer are mixed with those of better quality, the courts have not been ambivalent. In these instances they have ruled that since severance is impossible, the wrongdoer loses his property.[5] Finally, the courts have held that even when mixing occurs without fraudulent intent, the mixer must bear the costs of determining his share of the total and any questions of doubt must be resolved against him.[6] This, then, is the state of common law of the subjects of accession and confusion.

Given the large unoccupied areas in the United States of 1800, it is not difficult to understand why questions of squatter rights have loomed large in American history. As early as 1850, the courts recognized that a squatter could acquire title to unowned or abandoned land if he 'exercised control over and enjoyment of the land, if his act of control and enjoyment are in harmony with its appropriate use and adapted to the particular land, its

---

[1] *Wetherbee* v. *Green* (1871).
[2] *Silbury* v. *McCoon* (1850).
[3] *Pickering* v. *Moore* (1893).
[4] *Stephenson* v. *Little* (1862).
[5] *The Idaho* (1876).
[6] *Great Southern Gas Co.* v. *Logan Natural Gas Co.* (1907).

The theory developed

condition and locality, and if the acts proclaim to others that the person doing them claims the land as his own'.[1] The courts have held that enclosure and improvement are acts that are indicative of such a claim.

It is within this framework of the common law rights of property that arrangemental innovation must take place, and changes in these rights have altered the costs of such innovation.

In terms of American development, if we want to understand the rules that govern business behavior, it also appears useful to examine court decisions that relate to: (A) property rights; (B) the commerce clause of the Constitution; (C) the police powers of the states and the due process clauses of the Fourth and Fourteenth Amendments; and (D) some special rules that have been established to govern the operation of corporations.

(A) *Property rights*

Private property was important to the framers of the Constitution, and in Section 10 of Article 1 they wrote: 'No state shall ... pass any ... law impairing the obligations of contracts.'

The history of the relationship between business and the government could in large part be written in terms of the Court's interpretation of that clause. In the early years of the Marshall Court, those words were interpreted very stringently, but gradually the interpretation has been softened to permit more and more impairments of contract. From 1810 to 1819, the Court in a series of important decisions spelled out the hard line on the rights of contract. In the Yazoo land fraud case, the Court held that even evidence of fraud was not sufficient grounds for a state to abrogate a contract, since such action might cause loss to innocent third parties.[2] Two years later the Court held that once a state gives tax exemption to a piece of property, that exemption attaches itself to the property regardless of changes in ownership, and, once granted, it cannot be withdrawn by later legislative action.[3] In 1819, the Court ruled that a charter granted by a state was a contract and like any other contract was protected from arbitrary legislative action.[4] In the same year it held that state bankruptcy laws passed after a contract was written were unconstitutional under Article 1.[5] It is interesting to note that this decision not only represented the high water mark in the strict interpretation of Section 10, but that Chief Justice Marshall wanted to go further and declare

[1] *Brumagim* v. *Bradshaw* (1850).
[2] *Fletcher* v. *Peck* (1810).
[3] *New Jersey* v. *Wilson* (1812).
[4] *Dartmouth College* v. *Woodward* (1819).
[5] *Sturgis* v. *Crowninshield* (1819).

all state bankruptcy laws unconstitutional. Since then, however, while the courts have often held that certain kinds of government action abridged the rights protected by the contract clause, they have refused to extend that protection into a number of new areas and they have weakened its application even in some areas that were close to the heart of Justice Marshall.

In 1827, the Court held that states could pass bankruptcy laws that would affect contracts written after the law went into effect.[1] Ten years later in the *Charles River Bridge* case the Court held that state charters to private companies were based on the public interest and that the act of charter does not imply any surrender of the state's power to charter unless such surrender is explicitly written into the contract.[2] In 1899, the Court held that the constitutional protection of the freedom of contract does not extend so far as to protect contracts that would be in violation of otherwise valid acts of Congress.[3] Although the Court vacillated on the question, in a series of decisions between 1907 and 1937, the Court finally held that minimum wage and hour laws do not impair the rights of contract as protected by Article 1.[4] Finally, in two decisions made during the depression of the 1930s, the Court touched at the very heart of the 'sanctity of contract'. At that time it held that laws outlawing gold clauses in contracts were legal as was a state law granting debtors a moratorium on mortgage payments.[5] Clearly, the menu of permissible governmental arrangements has expanded markedly between the retirement of Marshall and the outbreak of World War II, and this expansion has in many cases tipped relative profits away from private towards governmental alternatives.

(B) *The commerce clause*

Section 8 of Article 1 of the United States Constitution gives Congress the power to 'regulate commerce . . . among the several states'. As the clause was originally interpreted by the Supreme Court, it would have biased the selection of transport related arrangements toward the federal government, but it probably would have had little application outside of that field. In *Gibbons* v. *Ogden* (1827), the Court preempted the regulation of interstate

---

[1] *Ogden* v. *Saunders* (1827).
[2] *Charles River Bridge* v. *Warren Bridge* (1837).
[3] *Addyston Pipe and Steel Co.* v. *U.S.* (1899).
[4] *Bunting* v. *Oregon* (1917); *Stettler* v. *O'Hara* (1917); *Lochner* v. *New York* (1905); *Adkins* v. *Children's Hospital* (1923); *Morehead* v. *New York* (1936); *West Coast Hotel* v. *Parrish* (1937).
[5] *Norman* v. *Baltimore and Ohio Railroad Co.* (1936) and *Nortz* v. *U.S.* (1935) ruled on the gold clause, and *Home Building and Loan Assn.* v. *Blaisdell* (1934) approved the moratorium.

The theory developed

commerce for the federal government, a decision that was confirmed in the *Wabash* case sixty years later.[1] But even by that later date they had done little to expand the definition of commerce, and in so doing they had displayed an unwillingness to let the commerce clause become the basis for an extension of federal regulation. In 1895, for example, the Court ruled that manufacturing was not a part of interstate commerce, and even as late as 1918, they held that the commerce clause could not be the basis for federal laws regulating child labor.[2]

Nevertheless, by the first decade of the twentieth century, the Court had begun to broaden its definition of commerce, and this reinterpretation had important implications for the relative profitability of alternative institutional arrangements. In a decision reached in 1903 (and reaffirmed in 1905), the Court moved from the narrow view that commerce was limited to the movement of goods across state lines to the much broader concept of 'the current of commerce', a definition that brought all of the processes of the production and distribution of goods within the review of the federal government.[3]

The impact of this redefinition was only gradually felt, but during the 1930s, it became the basis for an extension of federal regulation into a large number of economic activities that previously had been untouched by governmental interference.[4] In the ten years after the election of Franklin D. Roosevelt, the commerce clause became the basis for upholding federal regulatory laws in such diverse areas as radio communication, non-navigable rivers, child labor, minimum wages and maximum hours for adults, union activity, and output restrictions in agriculture.[5]

(C) *Police powers and due process*

The Constitution granted the federal government police powers over certain types of activities, but it reserved for the states the policing of all those that were not enumerated. The Fifth and Fourteenth Amendments prohibited

[1] *Wabash, St. Louis, and Pacific Railroad* v. *Illinois* (1886).
[2] In *U.S.* v. *E. C. Knight Co.* (1895) the Court held that the Sherman Anti-Trust Act was not applicable to manufacturing concerns. In *Hammer* v. *Dagenhart* (1918) they ruled that a federal child labor law was unconstitutional since the police powers were reserved for the states.
[3] *Swift and Co.* v. *U.S.* (1905); *Kelley* v. *Rhoads* (1903).
[4] In 1923 the Court used the new interpretation in defense of its decision to bring the commodities futures markets under federal regulation, *Board of Trade* v. *Olsen* (1923). Although this decision was an isolated one, it set an important precedent.
[5] See *Federal Radio Commission* v. *Nelson Brothers Bond and Mortgage Co.* (1933); *Arizona* v. *California* (1931); *U.S.* v. *Darby* (1941); *Opp Cotton Mills* v. *Administration* (1941); *Jones and Laughlin Steel Co.* v. *NLRB* (1937); *Consolidated Edison Co.* v. *NLRB* (1938); *Wickard* v. *Filburn* (1942).

Changes in the institutional environment

federal and state governments from depriving any 'person of life, liberty, or property without due process of law'. And, over the course of the nineteenth century, the Court's definition of property was broadened from physical assets to 'all the valuable elements of ownership' including the right to use the property to make money. There are clearly areas where these three legal strains could come into conflict, and as the Court has attempted to resolve these problems, the costs and revenues inherent in alternative institutional arrangements have changed.

In the late seventeenth century, Sir Matthew Hale ruled that when private property was 'affected by the public interest, it ceases to be *juris private* only', and this thread of common law, when combined with the police powers of the states, has been the legal basis for much of the government regulation of business. Any attempt by a state legislature to regulate the use of business property opens the possibility of depriving that business of its property (or at least the right to use that property to make money) without 'due process', and sets the stage for a clash between property owners and the government: a clash that sees each party supported by a fundamental plank in the structure of the institutional environment. As late as 1873 in the *Slaughter House* cases, the Court still held to a narrow definition of property, and the conflict was not apparent.[1] Within a very few years, however, the Court had changed its mind about what constitutes property, and the conflict was joined. Since that time the Court has vacillated considerably over the questions of 'legal regulation' and the definition of the set of businesses that are 'cloaked in the public interest'. As a result, the process of arrangemental innovation has been subject to exogenous change.

In 1877, the Court held that the common law doctrine of the public interest did apply in the United States, and the next year they held that railroads, since they derived their monopoly power from a government charter, were subject to regulation.[2] Ten years later the Court began to set limits on regulations. At that time it held that 'the power to regulate is not the power to destroy', and, in the last decade of the century, it provided for judicial review of regulatory rate making and laid down the concept of 'reasonable rates'.[3]

The ground rules for regulation had been established by the turn of the century, but the question of which firms are subject to such regulation is still undecided. The decision in the *Munn* case was very broad (any firm that

[1] 16 Wallace 36 (1813).
[2] *Munn v. Illinois* (1877); *C. B. & Q. v. Iowa* (1878); *Peik v. C & NW RR* (1878); *C. M. & St. P. RR v. Ackley* (1878); *Winnona and St. Peter RR Co. v. Blake* (1878); *Stone v. Wisconsin* (1878).
[3] *Stone v. Farmers Loan and Trust Co.* (1886); *C. M. & St. P. RR v. Minnesota* (1890); *Smith v. Ames* (1898).

75

vitally affected the public), but in little more than a decade the definition had been narrowed to include only businesses that had incurred obligations to the public in return for concessions made by the public.[1] Since the 1920s, the Court has been moving back toward their original view. In two cases emerging from World War I, the Court held that activities not normally in the public interest could be placed in that category because of a wartime emergency.[2] In 1923, the Court enumerated three classifications of business that it felt fell within their definitions of the public interest:

' 1. Those which are carried on under a public grant of privileges which . . . imposes the duty of rendering a public service . . .

2. Certain occupations regarded as exceptional, the public interest attaching to which, recognized from the earliest times, has survived the period of arbitrary laws . . . for regulating all trades and callings . . .

3. Business which though not public at their inception may be fairly said to have risen to such in consequence of some government regulation.'[3]

Even this list proved too small within a few years. In 1932 the depression was added to the list of emergencies that the Court considered serious enough to warrant regulation of businesses that fell outside the list, and two years later the Court appeared to remove almost all limitations by holding that ' " Affected with the public interest " could mean no more than that an industry for adequate reasons was subject to control for the public good.'[4] In that case, for example, the public interest was extended to firms engaged in the distribution of milk. In the 1930s and '40s, even agriculture found itself subject to regulation as the Court held that it was not a violation of due process for the government to regulate those industries that it subsidized.[5] Clearly the revenues from arrangements designed to redistribute income through the interposition of governmental regulation has altered markedly between 1877 and 1971.

(D) *Corporations*

Finally, the rules governing the regulations between governments and corporations have changed, and this shift, too, has had its impact on the process of arrangemental innovation. As early as 1839, the Court held that states could not prohibit 'foreign' corporations from doing business within their borders; they were, however, permitted to regulate them.[6] In 1922, the Court went a

---

[1] *Munn* v. *Illinois* (1877); *Georgia Railroad and Banking Co.* v. *Smith* (1888).
[2] *U.S.* v. *Ford* (1920); *Block* v. *Hirsch* (1921).
[3] *Wolff Packing Co.* v. *Court of Industrial Relations* (1923).
[4] *New State Ice Co.* v. *Liebmann* (1932); *Nebbia* v. *New York* (1934).
[5] *Wickard* v. *Filburn* (1942); *Secretary of Agriculture* v. *Central Roig Refining Co.* (1950).
[6] *Bank of Augusta* v. *Earle* (1839).

step further and placed severe limits on the states' ability to exercise these regulatory powers.[1] In 1844, the Court held that a corporation was a citizen and entitled to access to the federal court if suing or being sued by a foreign person, and in 1886, they held that corporations, like any citizen, were protected from arbitrary state action by the due process clause of the Fourteenth Amendment.[2]

(IV) Shifts in the community's probability weights

Attitudes toward the costs and revenues associated with government and private business can be changed by events that have nothing directly to do with the process of arrangemental innovation, but these changes can and do affect that process. A change in an individual's attitude towards government may change his estimates of the expected value of the costs and revenues he assumes will be incurred and/or realized by the innovation of some governmental arrangement. Similarly for private arrangement. In terms of the model, the probability weights have been altered by events totally exogenous to the model and these changes have, in turn, affected the choice among arrangemental alternatives. Over the past two hundred years it appears that events have caused marked changes in the attitudinal preference of the American community, and we have witnessed first a shift in preferences away from the government toward the private sector and then, full circle, back to a preference for governmental institutional arrangements as the probability weights have changed.

Despite the vocal anti-mercantilist protests that set the tone for the American revolution, the colonies had experienced a long period of reliance on government, and the view that government intervention – particularly state and local intervention – was a useful way of effecting certain economic decisions was widespread.[3]

The pro-governmental attitudes, however, appear to have undergone a fundamental change over the course of the first three decades of the last

[1] *Terral* v. *Burke Construction Co.* (1922).
[2] *Louisville, Cincinnatti, and Charlestown RR* v. *Letson* (1844); *Santa Clara County* v. *Southern Pacific Railroad Co.* (1886).
[3] This attitude has been documented in studies by Oscar and Mary Handlin, Louis Hartz, and Milton Heath, as well as a large quantity of work by Carter Goodrich and his students. See O. and M. Handlin, *Commonwealth: A Study of the Role of Government in American Economy* (Cambridge, Mass., 1947); L. Hartz, *Economic Policy and Democratic Thought: Pennsylvania, 1776–1860* (Cambridge, Mass., 1948); M. Heath, *Constructive Liberalism: The Role of the State in the Economic Development of Georgia to 1860* (Cambridge, Mass. 1954); C. Goodrich, *Government Promotion of Canals and Railroads* (New York, 1960).

century. Frontiersmen have long tended to manifest an intense dislike for government and governmental control, and the relative importance of the frontier increased greatly after the Erie Canal opened the Upper Midwest to trade and commerce. The financial debacle of the period 1839–42 also appears to have contributed to this change in attitude. The psychic costs of government are one thing, but money costs that must be paid are quite another. Throughout most of the 1820s and '30s, it appears that most people felt that the government could initiate and underwrite vast public improvement schemes without incurring any monetary liabilities that might have to be met out of the public revenues. The widespread failures of these projects in the late 1830s threw the contingent liabilities back onto the public rolls, and the necessity of raising taxes to meet these obligations seems to have caused a fundamental change in the public's attitude toward government – a change that was manifested in their estimate of the expected net returns on government arrangement far removed from those effected by the depression. The reaction was reflected in the initial refusal to meet the obligations, but more fundamentally it was reflected in attempts to prevent reoccurrence by any legal means – despite the costs that these attempts placed on future generations. New state constitutions were the order of the day. Indiana's, for example, went so far as to prohibit any borrowing by a state or local government; and Michigan's placed a $25,000 limit on state debt. Taken together, the growth of frontier areas and the experience of the late 1830s mitigated against governmental arrangements and tended to cause people to look toward individual and voluntary cooperative solutions.

In the past three decades, preferences appear to have once again shifted in favor of governmental solutions. This recent shift can almost certainly be attributed to: the depression of the 1930s; World War II and the Cold War; and the extreme complexity of living in a modern industrial society marked by large agglomerations of population and a high degree of specialization implying, in turn, an equally high degree of mutual interdependence.

Granted there were depressions in the eighteenth and nineteenth centuries, these earlier slumps certainly were shorter, affected fewer people, and produced substantially less unemployment than the breakdown of the 1930s. That depression was an unprecedented phenomenon that persisted through an entire decade. Long-lived and almost totally pervasive unemployment undermined people's confidence in the mode of economic organization, creating doubts that a laissez-faire economy could resolve the economic problems of society. As a result, the depression years were marked by a demand for an increase in government activity aimed at increasing employment and bolstering the market economy, and the 'look to government' attitude persisted long after the depression had disappeared.

78

Any war involves a rapid expansion of the government relative to the private sector, and because of the persistent reduction in the effective isolation of the United States from the rest of the world, this bias has apparently become a permanent part of the American economic structure. Moreover, the expansion is not solely quantitative, but almost always carries the government into areas where it had not been before. For example, wages and prices became subject to government regulation during World War II, the draft (never before more than a wartime phenomena) has persisted in peace as well as war, and military expenditures now underwrite a substantial portion of the development costs of goods and services that are not limited to military use. In such a world it is difficult to avoid concluding that the government is capable of solving almost any problem, and such a conclusion certainly affects the people's attitude toward governmental institutional arrangements.

Finally, our highly integrated specialized society has spawned incredible agglomerations of people whose lives and activities are hopelessly inter-twined with each other's. In such a society it is easy to conclude that no individual or group of individuals can contribute significantly to the solution of social problems. After all, what can mere men do about the anger in the ghettoes, the urban decay, the polluted environment, and cyclical unemploy-ment. This attitude often leads to the choice of a governmental arrangement – a choice that may turn out to be unprofitable because the 'perceived revenues' of governmental innovation have been inflated (relative to other alternatives) by the apparent hopelessness of private solutions.

(V) Conclusion

These, then, have been the changes that the institutional environment has undergone over the course of the past 175 years. A survey of the changes suggests that they have probably led to a gradual reduction of the cost with a corresponding increase in the benefits of government when compared with private arrangements. These relative changes appear in voting rights, in the rules governing private property and the relations between government and business, and in the satisfaction citizens receive from public and private arrangements. These changes must be taken into account if our model is to provide a satisfactory explanation of the process of arrangemental innovation. Let us now turn to the record of history to examine our theory of arrange-mental evolution in the context of American development.

PART TWO

THE THEORY APPLIED

CHAPTER 5

LAND POLICY AND AMERICAN AGRICULTURE

(I) Introduction

The history of American agriculture not only covers three-and-a-half centuries in time but also the spatial movement of settlers across an entire continent. It equally is a history of an agriculture which gradually evolved to become the most productive and efficient that man has ever known. It is not surprising, therefore, that this lengthy history should have provided a bewildering and seemingly endless variety of potentially profitable new institutional arrangements.

At least from the era of independence the fundamental institutional arrangements have changed very little. Perhaps the most basic of all, the ability to own and dispose of land freely, was an early achievement in the American colonies despite some abortive and brief efforts to hold land in common. This property right gave the colonists and then the independent farmer the ability to receive all of the benefits from whatever productive efforts he undertook and was an initial and important impetus to the successive histories of the institutional arrangements which we shall examine. Another important underpinning was the set of decisions arrived at during the era of confederation to dispose of the public domain in such a way that it would shift from public to private hands. The series of acts between 1784 and 1787 laid out the basic ground rules in which the survey units were defined and specified and the original decisions about land sales and distribution were made. While it is true that successive policies by government modified and changed the way by which the land was disposed with respect to the minimum size unit, the cost per acre, and the credit terms, these did not alter the fundamental decision that was reached. Even the Homestead Act was simply a further extension of this basic decision.

Given the fundamental institutional environment, the profitable opportunities for *arrangemental* innovation largely stemmed from three main lines of opportunity in the history of American agriculture. These have been described by one leading student of agricultural history as: (1) the expansion

83

The theory applied

into new lands with unknown conditions of soil, terrain and climate; (2) adjustment of regional specialization to growing markets, transport improvements, and geographically more perfect factor markets; and (3) incorporation of new practices, genetic materials, and mechanical equipment into the productive process.[1]

(1) The transformation of the American wilderness into producing farms spawned a myriad of arrangemental innovation. First, there was the whole process of disposal of public lands and the profits that could be garnered from taking advantage of the government's land policy. These arrangements have been the subject of a lengthy, voluminous and contradictory literature which can be illuminated by our model. It was one thing to dispose of the public domain, that is, to shift it initially from public to private hands; it was still something else to transform the wilderness into working farms. Here the basic obstacle was ignorance, simply a lack of information; not only about the risk of Indian attack – an early and persistent worry of colonial settlers and those who moved out onto the plains in the newly independent country – but, equally, a lack of information about insects, plagues, climatic variations, the composition and fertility of soils. Second, were those arrangements that were designed to improve and pool information in order to reduce the risk associated with moving out to and beyond the frontier and settling and developing new land.

(2) The dynamic and competitive character of the growth and spread of American agriculture contributed heavily to the number of arrangemental innovations. As new areas came into production and produced new crops, they competed with older existing areas. As transport innovations occurred, they led to a dramatic fall in costs and continuous disequilibrium with one region competing against another, with consequent shifts in crops and new production patterns emerging. The result was a continually changing location of agricultural production throughout the century. With surging movement of supply, there were periods of local and national distress and low prices and still other periods of bonanza and booming times. Caught up in these tides of relative low prices and income or alternatively of prosperity, the farmer's attitude towards the market or governmental intervention changed. Farming was a competitive industry, one in which there were typically no individual sellers who could significantly influence the market, and the *product was usually undifferentiated*. This fact, together with the vast available land and the uneven flow of this new land into production, produced a cyclic pattern of depressed prices followed by eras of expansion and good times. This continual alternation was endemic to the structure of agriculture and played a major

[1] See W. N. Parker, 'Outlines of American Agrarian History' in *American Economic Growth: An Economist's History of the United States* (New York, 1971).

84

role in the changing attitude of the farmer in regard to the efficacy of the private market as compared to government involvement.

(3) The evolving techniques of American agriculture were still a third source of disequilibrium that led to arrangemental innovation. The history of changing agricultural techniques involved the development of mechanical inventions, partly a direct result and indeed a handsome payoff of the farmer's tinkering with machinery, equipment and tools. But gradually, and partly in association with other industries such as construction, a farm implements and machinery industry evolved outside of agriculture as the potential market grew to permit such specialization. Throughout the nineteenth century these advances in techniques, the harvester, the combine and the reaper, were associated with the application of animal power. It was not until the twentieth century that the transformation from horsepower to the internal combustion engine revolutionized the source of power and thereby released some 90 million acres which had heretofore been used to feed the animal source of power. A striking feature of this history is that throughout the eighteenth and most of the nineteenth century, the efforts to improve productivity were primarily mechanical. In part, this bias was a function of the relatively laggard state of pure chemical and biological sciences; in part it reflected the variable character of soils and climate that made generalization in terms of biological or chemical changes difficult to apply; and in part it reflected the inability to raise the private rate of return on pure and/or applied developments to make it privately profitable to undertake research. It was in this connection, therefore, that we see the gradual evolution of efforts to devise institutional arrangements at the federal, state, and local levels that would undertake research along these lines. The consequent development of the Department of Agriculture at the federal level (and subsequent expansion of its functional departments) with the Land Grant College and the Agricultural Extension Agent at the state and local level, ultimately combined to produce a revolutionary breakthrough in agricultural productivity in modern times.

In the succeeding sections of this chapter we shall see a wide array of institutional arrangements devised to take advantage of the profitable opportunities associated with this growth of American agriculture, but as with the other chapters in this book it will in fact represent only a small sample of the many institutional arrangements that developed. In the organization of the early land companies, we shall see some remarkable similarities to the corporation: devices designed to enable groups of speculators to reap profit from engrossing large amounts of the public domain; at a later time, with the claims clubs we see efforts by squatters to use coercion to redistribute wealth; and still later, a variety of illegal institutional arrangements structured to take advantage of potential profits from acquisition of the public domain.

Beyond these, there was the array of voluntary organizations which grew up to improve information on specific crops, to prevent depredation by wolves, to coalesce sheep herders or cattlemen in their individual interests (frequently in opposition to one another). And still further, the efforts of farmers to overcome the problems of isolation in space by the development of organizations for improved communication, often gradually coalesced into arrangements aimed at influencing government and, at times, transforming and redistributing income on a substantial scale.

Yet with all these institutional arrangements, we note that one potential source of disequilibrium is of far less significance than elsewhere in the American economy – that is, the basic production unit in American agriculture has remained, throughout most of our history, the family farm. The family farm, which begins with colonial settlement continues right down to the present day as the most typical production unit of American agriculture. It is not that we don't see variations and permutations such as the plantation system in the South, the bonanza farms of the Dakotas, or the large-scale farms in California at the end of the nineteenth century. But these were the exceptions until the twentieth century. Nor, indeed, was the family-size farm always able to make efficient use of changes in technology. The family farm was simply an inappropriate unit for exclusive use of the farm machinery which developed in the nineteenth century. But voluntary institutional arrangements evolved to permit the family farm to make efficient utilization through the development of cooperative arrangements or through the creation of independent harvesting companies that moved from farm to farm and region to region as the harvesting season progressed. As William Parker has said, the family-size farm was an efficient production unit in the nineteenth century and appears to have remained so even into the twentieth century. While the family-size farm survived the vicissitudes of change that we have described above, vertical disintegration occurred as that farm shed many of the self-sufficient functions and specialized in production for the market. Whether the family farm will survive into the future remains a more difficult point since it appears that the optimum scale of farms recently has been growing very rapidly. However, this increase remains something which, while it is affecting institutional arrangements in very modern times, is largely peripheral to our historical investigation.

In subsequent sections of this chapter we shall first examine some of the institutional arrangements that evolved to take advantage of the profits that were available in the disposal of the public domain. While some of these institutional arrangements were legal and some were on the borderline between legality and illegality, we shall explore, as we have not done elsewhere in this volume, the profit potential inherent in deliberate evasions of the legal structure.[1] Second, we will explore the development of voluntary farmers' organizations, their shift back and forth between private solutions and appeals to government. Third, we will examine some of the institutional arrangements that evolved at the governmental level that were designed to improve farmers' information and eventually led to develop more efficient agriculture via systematic and scientific experimentation.

(II) From Yazoo to Teapot Dome – land policy in American history

The history of land policy does not belong alone in the chapter on institutional arrangements in agriculture since many of the innovations were devised by ingenious Americans who were concerned as much with the alienation of timber and mineral lands as they were with lands which ultimately moved into agricultural production. In general, the arrangemental innovations were set within the basic framework of the land ordinances and system of division of land, enunciated in the acts of 1784–7. Gradually the system was changed from the wholesaling to the retailing of land. Initially whole townships and sections were sold, but successive land acts reduced the minimum size of the purchaseable unit. The Homestead Act, of course, marks the end of sale of land as formal United States policy (although it should be noted that still much if not most of the land was sold after that date). Some of the specific laws that changed the size, cash and credit terms can be explained in terms of our model. Certainly, the early decision to distribute land in large units can be traced to the pressure applied by primary action groups interested in large-scale land speculation. Acts related to railroad land grants are also obviously consistent and interpretive within the model we have described. Yet, we must confess that some acts are not so easily explained; they represent in part the long ideological effort on the part of reformers to institute a Jeffersonian democracy of small landholders in America. While the initial efforts of these reformers were seldom guided by personal profit and cannot be predicted, the support from the electorate for these changes is explicable. The continuous pressure for smaller minimum units was explicitly designed to give the individual settler, the homesteader, the family-size farmer, a stake and indeed a dominant role in America's agrarian picture. The efforts of Evans and his followers in the mid-nineteenth century to institute a policy of free land for settlers, an effort which culminated in the passage of the Homestead Act, was of similar origins. Undoubtedly the whole movement toward smaller units of sale was promoted by the extension of the franchise. The

---

[1] It is probably correct that quasi-illegal institutional arrangements have been equally prevalent in other factor and product markets and that our model could be a useful framework in examining them; therefore our neglect does not mean to imply that they were uniquely prevalent in public land policy.

The theory applied

institutional arrangements devised to achieve profitable opportunities within the framework of the act (sometimes legal and sometimes, as we shall see, extra-legal) are eminently explainable, and our model would appear to shed a substantial amount of light upon them.

The sources of profits from institutional rearrangement were varied. In the case of the early land companies, large profits could be garnered if sufficient capital could be raised and an efficient marketing system could be designed. As we shall see, both the problems and the solutions had remarkable similarities to the later development of the long term capital market and the problems attendant to the risk of security 'indigestion'.

The costs of information were reduced by a number of institutional arrangements. The railroad colonization schemes, for example, were arrangemental innovations in which agents circularized the eastern United States and Europe with information about settlement opportunities. Probably the most important was the western land agent. Paul Gates provided a thumbnail sketch (albeit a somewhat jaundiced one) of his role in western settlement.

'These western land agents rank with the registers and receivers of the land offices as among the most important people on the frontier. They dealt in land warrants and script, ran a local note shaving business, purchased exchange, sometimes operated a bank of issue with funds provided by eastern capitalists, loaned eastern funds to squatters at frontier rates ranging from 20 to 60 per cent, bought and sold land, paid taxes for absentee owners and undertook to protect their lands against depredations. At a later date, they arranged for renting land, made collections, and sold produce received in payment of rent. Small investors in the East were obliged to work through these agents, to submit to their exactions, and to suffer from their inefficiency, and could not effectually protest against their obvious neglect. The agent could take his commission from rents or sales before any money was remitted to the owner, could sell his own land to prospective purchasers, rather than that of the owners he represented, could neglect tax payments and get the title involved, or could pay taxes on the wrong land. In numerous cases western agents took advantage of their clients, used the prestige which their contacts provided for personal interests, and constantly minimized the value of the land they represented in order to increase sales and thereby commissions. In this way, absentee investors whose eastern responsibilities did not permit them to give personal attention to their possessions in the West were imposed upon and victimized.'[1]

The borderline between legality and illegality was tenuous where policing was rudimentary and therefore government coercive power could be ap-

[1] P. W. Gates, 'The Role of the Land Speculator in Western Development', in *The Public Lands*, ed. Vernon Carstensen (Madison, Wis., 1963), p. 353.

propriated by voluntary groups. Squatters' organizations were one such extra-legal group who could redistribute wealth by means of their own coercive organization. They will be described in more detail in our sketch of claims clubs.

The capturing of externalities (of which the railroad land grants were an important example) was still another source of profitable institutional arrangement. It is evident that the distribution of the public lands provided for a wide variety of profitable opportunities and, as we would expect, primary action groups devised a large number of arrangemental innovations to capture them. In the pages that follow, we shall explore in more detail the character of the early land company, the claims clubs, and then turn to a more general survey of the nature of illegal institutional arrangements.

The land companies that developed in the years after the Revolutionary War were formed to make profits from the acquisition and subsequent resale of large blocks of land, primarily on the western frontier. The primary action groups typically were made up of individuals or groups who had special and superior knowledge of the complicated structure of land holdings that existed between states and the federal government, and who more often than not, were well placed in government and thus able to persuade public officials to sell or grant them large blocks of land. In the case of the states, problems of fiscal revenue had become increasingly burdensome and the almost endless amounts of land available for sale appeared to be an easy source of revenue. In addition, problems of clear title greatly increased the uncertainty of these transactions. Uncertainty was particularly apparent in the case of the Yazoo land, but to one degree or another, was involved anywhere that there was more than one claim to lands or where the United States had appropriated lands from another power.

The primary action group not only had to acquire and finance large blocks of land, but had to develop a market for this land. It is well known that these early land companies were large-scale speculators, but it is less well known that they innovated a series of institutional arrangements which were strikingly parallel to subsequent developments in the corporate field. It is primarily this aspect of their development which interests us here. The problems these primary action groups faced were in many respects similar to those faced, much later, by transportation companies or large-scale organization in the capital markets, and the simple partnership was not suited to these needs. These land companies evolved a structure of organization similar to the corporation without the formal legal underpinnings.[1] These early land companies had no special legislative charter. They were formed with legal

[1] The subsequent part of this section of the land companies is based on a study by Shay Livermore entitled *Early American Land Companies* (New York, 1939).

advice, and the articles of association specified the structure of meetings, reports, voting powers, status of shareholders, etc. Despite the existence of a large number of shareholders, powers in the company were delegated to a small group of managers. Transferability and marketability of shares were specified so as to make the shares attractive as a capital investment. The one thing that was lacking throughout, of course, was limited liability, but this lack does not appear to have been a significant concern to the organizers of land companies.[1] The North American Land Company, formed in 1795, might be taken as a fairly typical example of such companies. The primary action group were three men of whom Robert Morris is by far the most famous. The other two were John Nicholson and James Greenleaf. As individuals they had acquired a large number of parcels of land and substantial amounts of debts incurred in acquiring the land. The North American Land Company was formed to take over this land and to create one very large-scale organization and sell stock in it and to use the realized funds to satisfy creditors. In this sense it was different from other land companies which were formed to purchase government land. In this case, the objective of the primary action group was to underwrite a more efficient capital market to sell land to pay off creditors and to make a profit. Six million acres were to be turned over to the company at a flat valuation of 50 cents an acre. Thus, there were 30,000 shares of stock of $100 par value. The articles of agreement drawn up the 20th day of February, 1795, specified that the assets were to consist of 6 million acres of land for which legal title would rest with three trustees. In the case of title disputes, the fourth article in the agreement provided that suits to quiet title should be filed in the name of Board of Managers. Upon actual settlement, the board would direct the trustees to convey titles. The Board of Managers was to be elected annually on 30 December. Proxies were permitted and the form of a proxy was given. The board was to consist of a president and four others chosen from among the stockholders, and any three would constitute a quorum. In the case of the death of a trustee, the Board of Managers could select a new trustee and have all deeds transferred. Article 22 provided that a dividend was to be declared annually to include all income from sales except that of a contingent fund of not more than $4,000. Article 23 specified that the three originators agreed to guarantee at least 6 percent dividends annually. Despite an absence of legal sanctions, this company looked and acted like a modern corporation.

The subsequent history of the North American Land Company is of less interest to us. The total number of shares was never issued, but the company continued in existence for seventy-five years largely as a result of litigation

[1] See Livermore, *Early American Land Companies*, p. 236.

during which time it ran through innumerable suits. But the structure of organization, the problems of evolving an institutional arrangement capable of large-scale financing of land and its wholesaling and retailing were worked out in these early land companies and undoubtedly provided a source of information which was later applied to the development of corporate organization.

Squatters' associations have been a source of controversy in American history. Frederick Jackson Turner saw them as symbolic associations reflecting democratic ideals on the frontier. Subsequently historians have argued that the squatters' associations were as frequently involved in speculation and, if not fraud, at least extra-legal activities. From our viewpoint, the controversy is less interesting than the emergence of the institutional arrangement itself. Essentially, the claims club was a voluntary group of squatters whose expressed objectives were to thwart claim jumpers and large speculators. While they possessed no legal sanction the members acted in concert to forcibly eject or dispossess those thought to be in violation of the club's objectives. These clubs appear to have been particularly numerous in the Midwest. Allan Bogue's study of the Iowa claims clubs presents the best detailed study of the way by which a voluntary association can assume coercive power in the absence of an effective governmental structure.[1]

The claims clubs are but one illustration of institutional arrangements that were extra-legal, that is, voluntary organizations that could effect a redistribution of wealth through their own coercive power in the absence of effective policing by governmental agencies. The whole history of the disposal of public lands includes many illustrations; some, like the claims clubs, were extra-legal and some, clearly illegal. We shall examine some of these institutional arrangements and in particular we will explore a perplexing but critical question for our model: when do extra-legal and illegal institutional arrangements become profitable?

One major source of institutional arrangements that often bordered on the illegal stemmed from the complicated questions of who in fact had authority to dispose of public lands. One of the earliest and most famous controversies was connected with the Yazoo land grants. In the era of confederation, it was not clear whether state or federal government had the authority to dispose of land. The state of Georgia, perpetually in financial difficulties and undoubtedly encouraged by the interests of a number of its legislators in the proposed land disposal, granted lands in what it claimed to be its territory. The first of these grants by the legislature was made to the South Carolina Yazoo Company in December 1789 and consisted of a 10 million acre tract bordering the Mississippi River. The Virginia Yazoo Company received a

[1] A. Bogue, 'The Iowa Claims Clubs: Symbol and Substance', *Miss. Hist. Rev.*, 45, 231–53.

grant north of that containing approximately 11.4 million acres and the Tennessee Company received an additional 4 million acres. Altogether, 25 million acres were disposed of by the state without clear title. In this case the primary action group was made up of land speculators, and some members of the legislature. There ensued a controversy between Georgia and the federal government over title, and it was many decades before the resultant suits were actually settled. This is an illustration of a set of institutional arrangements that were devised in the face of uncertainty over clear title, and for the most part were unprofitable to the primary action group.

A somewhat similar problem continually confronted the federal government whenever it acquired tracts of land from a foreign power and was forced to deal with the claims granted by that power. In most instances, treaties specified that prior legitimate claims would be recognized. Even explicit recognition left room for innovational profits. In the case of the Louisiana Territory, for example, news of the sale induced public officials to make last-minute grants of land. These grants became known as ante-daters, as the date of the claim was moved back to before the treaty. Frequently, the Louisiana official did not even know the location of the claim. Presumably, suitable side payments were made. Similar voluntary groups attempted to acquire land in Texas and California, and as in the case of the ante-daters, these attempts were ultimately settled in the courts.

The innovation of still another institutional arrangement was encouraged by the provisions of the Homestead Act. That Act was intended to aid settlers in taking out and operating farms, but it was employed in acquiring mineral and timber land which had no real farming value. The Minnesota iron district was a famous case in point.[1] The Homestead Act could be used to acquire mineral land without any intention of farming the property. Since it was well known that these lands were not suitable for agricultural use, collusion was required. To serve this purpose, there evolved a primitive institutional arrangement involving nothing more than individuals and groups and the clerks in the Duluth land office.[2] A report to the general land office in 1884 pointed out that in this district there had been 2,361 homestead entries, but that only 273 of these had proven up an actual homestead. A similarly collusive agreement developed in the timberland region of the Pacific coast where dummy entrymen were employed to file under the Homestead Act and to turn the land over to the timber companies. It should be noted that these illegal institutional arrangements arose because of the inappropriateness of the land law to the conditions that existed; that is, that

[1] F. P. Wirth, 'The Operation of the Land Laws in the Minnesota Iron District', reprinted in Carstensen, *Public Lands*, pp. 93–108.
[2] Wirth, 'Operation of Land Laws', p. 98.

the size of the units of land that could be acquired were simply too small to realize the economies of scale inherent in the industry.

But why should fraud be widespread in these circumstances? We can get some suggestion of an explanation for bypassing the legal disposal systems by looking at the case of timber companies who cut timber on public lands in the Great Lakes area. Here, timber companies simply cut timber on public lands. The agents of the public land office attempted to force them to desist. The result was a period of high tension between the land agents and the timber companies, even leading to an attempt to reenact the Boston tea party at Barlake, Michigan.[1] In this case, the timber company brought pressure on Washington, the agents were withdrawn, the investigations dropped, and any further protective efforts were for the most part hamstrung. When we examine the operations of the general land office in Washington, D.C., we get a better picture of the explanation for such widespread fraudulent activity.[2] It was understaffed, the workers low-paid, and therefore, the potential returns on bribery and side-payments to agents were so great that it would be unlikely that it could effect a policing of the various disposal systems. In effect, the public land office was a battleground in which the interests of action groups concerned with such fraudulent exploitations were at least as powerful as and frequently more powerful than the interests from those who wanted a disposal system without fraudulent activity. Occasionally, there were powerful interest groups on both sides and the result was indeterminate. Most often, however, those who were organized into voluntary action groups were arrayed against individuals whose losses were small and whose information was poor. Under these conditions we would expect that the public land office would serve as the instrument to subvert land policy in the interests of these action groups.

(III) Politics and the market: the farmer's dilemma[3]

Farmers' movements and their long flirtation with the political process offers an interesting exploration of the changing policies of voluntary organizations which can be illuminated with the general model we have advanced in this study. The general contours of the ebb and flow of farmers' protest movements

---

[1] L. Cane, 'Federal Protection of Public Timber in the Upper Great Lakes' in Carstensen, *Public Lands*, pp. 439–60.
[2] H. H. Dunham, 'Some Crucial Years of the General Land Office, 1885–1890' in Carstensen, *Public Lands*, pp. 181–204.
[3] The basic sources for this section were: F. A. Shannon, *The Farmer's Last Frontier* (New York, 1963); J. D. Hicks, *The Populist Revolt* (Minneapolis, Minn., 1931); M. Benedict, *Farm Policies in the United States 1790–1950* (New York, 1953); C. Campbell, *The Farm Bureau and the New Deal* (Urbana, Ill., 1962).

The theory applied

can be understood if we keep two specific parts of our theoretical model continually in mind. First, that the costs of organizing a large number of people spatially distributed over a wide area are extremely high but may be reduced if initial organizational costs are borne by local groups originally formed to achieve locally desirable goals. Second, as a result of changing relative economic position, farmers may abruptly revise their view of benefits to be expected from arrangemental innovation. Such revisions are most likely to come at times of falling or stagnant agricultural income because the value of political action remains the same while the value of economic alternatives substantially declines.

The first national organization of farmers began in 1867. It was not organized from within the farming sector but rather by a government clerk, Oliver Kelly, for social and cultural purposes. Its beginnings were not particularly auspicious, and in 1868, only six Granges were formed in Minnesota; in 1869 there were thirty-seven. Then came hard times in the 1870s. Grange organization was abruptly vitalized: 1,105 were formed in 1872; 8,400 in 1873; and 4,700 in the first two months of 1874. While the early objectives may have been social and cultural, the gatherings of farmers very rapidly took on political and economic overtones. Thus while the initial organizing force does not fit within our model, once these organizing costs had been undertaken, farmers soon began to use the organization as an action group to innovate institutional arrangements designed to increase their incomes.

The Grange pursued its policies in two directions. The first encouraged the growth of voluntary organizations to reduce transactions costs by cutting down on the 'unnecessary middleman'. With this in mind Granges appointed state agents to deal directly with manufacturing firms and large wholesalers; indeed, Montgomery Ward was started in Chicago in 1872 for the specific purpose of such direct negotiation. The Grange's efforts in this regard had mixed results.

A dramatic example of the failure of a voluntary institutional arrangement was that of a producers' cooperative organized by the state Grange of Iowa in 1873. The cooperative acquired a harvester factory, three plow factories, and some other instrument factories. Harvesters were sold at half the usual price and these cuts provoked price wars from other farm machinery producers. The management of these producers' cooperatives was inept and simply unable to compete with the private firms, and by 1875, this institutional innovation had failed. Similar experiments by the national Grange met like results.

On the other hand modest success was achieved by some cooperative stores organized along the lines of the original Rochdale principle. The most successful voluntary arrangements by farmers were in grain elevator coopera-

94

tives. The first of these cooperatives, formed in Wisconsin in 1857, ante-dates the Grange. But even this type of cooperative had a slow development, and by 1907, there were no more than one thousand such grain elevator cooperatives. They did manage to lower marketing costs by providing competition with private elevators and in some areas by forcing railroads to lower rates and guaranteeing that freight cars would be available.

A second aspect of the Grange effort was political and was frequently only indirectly associated with the Granges themselves. What were called the granger movement and granger laws were so named simply because the Grange had undertaken the organizing costs of getting farmers together. The actual political movements were only incidentally (if at all) the direct and explicit policy of the Granges themselves.

Farmers' clubs in Illinois had already inaugurated efforts to regulate railroads before the Grange. But the Grange, which achieved a membership of 759,000 in 1875, became a potent political force in states along the upper Mississippi River. The farmers, early enthusiasts of railroad development, felt that the gains from lower cost transportation should accrue to them, and accordingly the behavior of the railroads became a major source of their discontent. Railroad regulation to redistribute income to the farmer through lower rates became a major source of political activity of the Grange, as well as other farmer groups. Maximum rate regulation and efforts to prevent rate discrimination were passed in Illinois, Minnesota, Iowa, and Wisconsin. In each case the legislation was challenged in the courts. In the case of *Munn* v. *Illinois* (a grain elevator rate case) the Supreme Court ruled that the state did have regulatory power, although ultimately in subsequent Supreme Court cases, it was made clear that railroads that engaged in interstate commerce were subject to federal regulatory legislation which had priority over state legislation. These later decisions ultimately encouraged farm groups to focus their attention on federal regulatory legislation and, eventually, the Interstate Commerce Commission (although, as we shall see in Chapter 7, the long-run results were quite different).

Still another direction of farmers' efforts, with respect to governmental institutional arrangement, involved continual lobbying on the part of the Grange (and other farm organizations as well) to expand the activities of federal government with respect to reducing the cost of information, developing new knowledge, and forcing uniform quality control, quarantining, etc. While the Grange was not alone in these, but was accompanied by other farm organizations, it did provide leadership during the 1870s and attempted to expand the role of the Department of Agriculture and help the department achieve cabinet status. We shall have more to say about the efforts of farm organizations to have the government undertake the cost of producing

The theory applied

information and research in the next section. As a leader of farm organization, the Grange's history is really quite limited. It had a spectacular rise in the 1870s associated with the depression. Thereafter, its membership fell dramatically and then began a slow rise again which continued for the next forty or fifty years. The sharp rise and fall is associated with depression, prosperity, and the failures of Grange efforts through cooperative and political activities to provide much in the way of success in alleviating problems that the farmers saw.

In many respects, however, the main problems of the farmer were local in character and were reflected in the local institutional arrangements which evolved to solve the diverse problems. These were many and varied, but as we have noted above, once they were established they provided a base for larger scale political action. In Arkansas, the Agricultural Wheel started as an early debating society. It evolved into a major political force in the Southwest, and by 1887 had 500,000 members with separate divisions for white and colored farmers. The Grand Alliance in Texas, founded in the 1870s to promote joint efforts to capture rustlers, to round up stray stock, and to provide quarantine information, gradually also expanded from these locally profitable types of activity into promoting general agricultural policies and efforts to influence and guide governmental institutional arrangements. By 1889, the various alliances attempted to form a united front. The process, however, posed dilemmas which have haunted national farm organizations ever since. There were clearly divergences of interests among the farm groups. Northeastern farmers who specialized in dairying and poultry used feed as an input, and wanted low grain prices, while western farmers who produced the basic grain as their agricultural activity had a different set of interests. Nevertheless, these differences were submerged sufficiently to allow the formation of a 'people's party' and by 1892 the Populists, as they became known, had put up a candidate for president. In that year they polled one million votes, almost 9 percent of the total. The issues were similar to those we have described above: they included the high price of middlemen and therefore policies to reduce transaction costs by means of railroad and grain elevator regulations, and the creation of a bimetallic standard to increase the money supply and thereby (in the farmer's view) increase agricultural prices. So popular, indeed, was the issue of making silver a part of the monetary base that the Democratic party adopted this plank in 1896, and in so doing stealing from the Populists a major source of their support (a common characteristic of political parties in American history). However, it was not so much this plank and the election of 1896 that submerged the Populist party as it was the prosperity of agriculture. In fact, from 1896 until World War I the farmers' political group declined and almost disappeared, at least on a national scale. Farm income was growing rapidly and a period of prosperity for agriculture continued until the end of that war.

Predictably, the revival of the farmers' movement in the 1920s was ushered in by falling farm prices and income resulting from a decline in demand for agricultural goods coupled with a sharp increase in supply as a result of the vastly increased acreage that farmers put into production in war time. The end of the war saw an imposition of European tariffs and a slowdown in American population growth. Together these led to a fall in the demand for farm products. As a result, the '20s were a period of extremely low agricultural prices and depressed farm income.

The rise of the Farm Bureau in the 1920s represented still another case in which the organizing costs were underwritten for other purposes. The agricultural extension agent system had led to the growth of local advisory boards to assist in planning and organizing agricultural improvements. These local boards were a natural basis for farmer organizations; local county boards gradually unified into state boards and finally into the American Farm Bureau. Here we have an interesting example of a governmental policy which had the effect of subsidizing the organizational costs of a voluntary cooperative group.

As in the earlier period of farmer organization, lowered organizing costs together with a sharp downward revision of farmers' expectations with the disastrous fall of prices in 1920 and 1921 led to the emergence of the Farm Bureau as a political force. However, its characteristics differed from the Grange. The Farm Bureau was dominated by commercial farming; while small farmers, subsistence farmers, and Negro farmers were members, they did not play a major part. Its policies were directed toward the market-oriented farmer and his products. Its organizational structure paralleled that of the government – that is, it was organized at local, state, and federal levels and as a consequence was politically effective at all levels As with earlier farm organizations, the Farm Bureau did not concentrate solely on political objectives, but was equally concerned with voluntary arrangement aimed at accruing economic gains directly.

The Sapiro movement instigated by a California lawyer, Aaron Sapiro, encouraged the growth of producers' cooperatives and was a major factor in Farm Bureau activities in the early 1920s. The Sapiro movement, however, could not have been successful without the passage of a cooperative marketing bill in 1922, a bill designed to exempt producers' cooperatives from anti-monopoly restrictions. Sapiro envisioned cooperatives in a different fashion than those of the Rochdale principle. Specifically, he advocated strongly centralized producers' cooperatives able to enter into binding contracts with their members so that each member producer was required to deliver his produce to the cooperative. If a member failed to make delivery, he was subject to a heavy fine for nonconformance to the contract. The idea of these producers' cooperatives was to take over the entire structure of terminal markets, wholesaling, warehousing and commission work, elevator companies, centralized creameries and so forth. Then the producers' cooperative would be in a position to effectively control supply. However, in order to be able to set and maintain the prices that they wanted, they had to be able to dispose of the excess supply. The plan was to store whatever percentage of the commodity was necessary to maintain monopoly prices and then dump the excess abroad so that a two-price system would prevail.

Sapiro's enthusiasm and evangelism led to efforts to develop producers' cooperatives along this line through the agricultural influence of the Farm Bureau. In livestock marketing, grain producing, cotton and other major crops, these efforts were attempted. However, in most cases the producers' cooperative was a failure as our model would predict. A voluntary association which includes large numbers faced insurmountable problems of policing and enforcement since it was always to the advantage of some individuals to cheat, and the result was that bickering and internal fighting made it impossible to achieve the unanimity necessary for success. Where producers' cooperatives worked successfully, again, was where our model would predict – that is, in specialty crops such as citrus where a small number of producers in a relatively localized area could be organized at small costs and where the problems of internal dissension were reduced because they were a largely homogeneous group.

Their success can, in large part, be traced to the homogeneity of the primary action group – a homogeneity that tends to minimize differences of interest. Even here, however, there is a tendency to cheat, and these groups frequently turned to government to provide coercive power for their activity. Thus, in the citrus industry, the producers established a marketing quota which is enforced by government.

Yet the Sapiro movement and other producers' co-op movements were important antecedents to what followed. The basic intent was to control supply by holding the crop off the market to achieve a price which would increase the income of producers. It was this philosophical intent which gets carried over into the political arena where political coercion substitutes for voluntary association. It is not surprising, therefore, that the Farm Bureau and other groups turned to the political arena to achieve a coercive structure to accomplish what a voluntary structure could not do. It was the Agriculture Department that initially drew up the bill, persuaded McNary and Haugen to introduce it, and ultimately encouraged the Farm Bureau to back it. The

Land policy and agriculture

basic principle behind the McNary–Haugen bills (and there were many of them) was that the government would buy agricultural commodities and sell them on the world market at world prices, thereby sustaining the domestic price of agricultural goods on a parity ratio with the prices of other goods – or what we would term in economics as the 'terms of trade' ratio. The first bill was defeated in 1924; two subsequent bills met the same fate. In 1927, the McNary–Haugen bill was passed by Congress but vetoed by Calvin Coolidge, and a later bill was vetoed by Herbert Hoover. But, with the depression of 1929 and a still further revision downward in expectations, a fundamental change occurred in farm policy.

Now that it had received congressional support, the Farm Bureau decided as its basic task in the election of 1932 to give backing to a candidate sympathetic to the notion of parity. In Franklin Delano Roosevelt they felt they had such a candidate; indeed, the relationship between the Farm Bureau and the early New Deal was so close and intimate that it is frequently hard to distinguish the Department of Agriculture from the American Farm Bureau itself in policies and in the intertwining of economic and political activities. The Farm Bureau looked on the first Agricultural Adjustment Act as its own creation and as fitting its needs exactly, yet some of its repercussions created problems for the Farm Bureau itself. While the Agricultural Adjustment Act as initially created was clearly designed to support the commercial farmer, there were sharp regional variations in its effect. The northeast Farm Bureaus were soon in near revolt because far from realizing any benefits from the Act they found it a burden. It provided no support for milk prices, but instead it levied on eastern farmers a processing tax which went to pay farmers in the West. The price of feed grain for eastern dairymen went up by $4 per ton while the price of dairy products remained constant. Eventually, unity was restored to the Farm Bureau by the internal process of implicit agreement known as 'log-rolling'. the Northeast could have the support of the Farm Bureau for a milk-marketing agreement, and in return the Midwest could have higher grain prices. This proposal was basic to achieving harmony again within the Farm Bureaus.

The Supreme Court invalidation of the first Agricultural Adjustment Act led to lengthy argument and discussion over the second identically named act. And, here, *as one would expect from our model*, it was in the Senate that the Farm Bureau received its strongest support for a tough parity program. A much weaker bill enacted by the House was stigmatized by the Farm Bureau as of little benefit, but the Senate–House conferees did ultimately emerge with a bill acceptable to the Farm Bureau. It is interesting that in the New Deal period explicit support for the Farm Bureau program and the price-support program was received from organized labor. It was accorded in return for

The theory applied

promised support by the Farm Bureau for labor's legislative efforts – minimum wage laws (as long as agricultural workers were exempt) and legislation legalizing union activity, to name two. Thus another 'log-rolling' process in the 1930s made for a congenial partnership between agricultural interests and urban organized labor interests which enabled both to achieve some of their ends. By the end of the 1930s the agricultural price-support program, the basic program desired by the farmer, had become institutionalized into the American political structure, and has continued so in one form or another since that time.

(IV) The farmer turns to government

In the previous section we observed the close inter-connection between voluntary organization and governmental organization in the history of land policy and American agriculture. We saw that the initiating force came from voluntary organizations which evolved for locally profitable purposes, but which in turn became action groups for broader purposes; the farmers had the choice of creating voluntary organizations or appealing to government to undertake some institutional arrangement to solve their problems. At one time or another, they went in one direction or the other; thus the Sapiro movement of the 1920s was an effort to use voluntary organization to limit supply and raise prices. And in like fashion the farm stabilization programs of the '30s were an attempt to get government to undertake the same thing. Government had a clear advantage in two areas that were continually susceptible to cost reduction through institutional rearrangement. One of these was the uncertainty and lack of information wherever farmers faced different and new problems. Typically, it would be difficult for voluntary associations to be profitable because of the public goods character of some of the kinds of information – information about climate, soil, statistical data about crops, prices. In short, the dilemma that we posed in the beginning of this chapter – the problem of uncertainty in the face of new conditions – was one that continually faced the farmer and for which governmental resolution was clearly a more practicable institutional arrangement than any form of voluntary organization. (Although, if the farmer had wanted only these objectives without the redistribution of income involved in the general tax payer's bearing the burden, he would have suggested a tax whose incidence fell on the farmer alone.)

The second major area of government's advantage was in undertaking research so as to stimulate an increased output of agriculture. You will remember at the beginning of the chapter we noted that the major sources of productivity increase in the nineteenth century, aside from the move to

100

better land, were mechanical implements which by and large had been manufactured outside of the farm firm; increasingly, toward the end of the nineteenth century and particularly in the twentieth century, the main underpinnings for productivity increase have been biological and chemical (in addition to the shift from the horse to the internal combustion engine as a source of power). The chemical and biological bases of agricultural efficiency were areas of research that were hard to patent, were not practicable for the individual farm to undertake, and which typically involved adaptation to regional and local variations of soil and climate. In short, they were activities which were most practicable and could be most profitably undertaken by government. And, as with reducing the costs of information and uncertainty, the farmer was not averse to these costs being borne by the whole society.

Early voluntary organizations had made efforts to reduce uncertainty, to develop new knowledge by various experimental farm organizations, and to spread existing knowledge, by informing farmers of the state of existing knowledge, but of necessity there were elements of a free rider problem in each of these associations. Voluntary associations of this type, by their nature, are unlikely to survive, and these did not. The gains from improved information in these associations cannot be captured completely, and therefore there is not the correct incentive for their sustained survival. As long as altruists covered the cost of the free riders, they survived even if they were not economically viable. Increasingly farmers turned to appeals to the government to take over and expand such functions.

The United States Department of Agriculture was an early result of the efforts of voluntary organizations and particularly those of the United States Agricultural Society. In 1859, the government invited farmers to Washington to examine the role the patent office played in agricultural activity. The farmers promptly demanded a separate department devoted to agriculture alone and appealed to the Republican party to create a Department of Agriculture. This was done in 1862. The two earliest functions of the department were the collection of statistics and the distribution of seed. However, we should note that the latter function quickly became embroiled in congressional patronage and, for example, for the year 1890, almost all of the 4.4 million seed packages that were distributed went to senators and members of Congress who used the seed for patronage purposes in their own district. Nevertheless, in spite of these typical side-benefits the Department of Agriculture did expand its functions, and a simple reading of the chronology of the development of different divisions is eloquent testimony to the department's movements in the direction of reducing risks and developing new information about basic problems that faced the farmer. In 1863 it began a Division of Entomology to study and do research on insect pests and their eradication; a Division of

The theory applied

Statistics was started in the same year for the purpose of gathering data to provide farmers with better information; in 1865 a soil analysis section began research on soil problems; in 1868 a Division of Botany was developed; in 1877 forestry investigation was undertaken; and in 1880 a Division of Forestry was created. Veterinary services, animal husbandry, and pomology divisions were but a sample of additional areas that the Department of Agriculture moved into both on its own and at the insistent prodding of voluntary organizations who appealed to government to solve problems that they faced in the new areas, crops, livestock, soils, etc. While it is possible that some of these departments that evolved from the pressure of farm groups might have been done by voluntary organizations, most of them had a public goods character to them which made it unlikely. The Weather Bureau, for example, which was taken over from the army in 1891 in order to forecast conditions to help reduce crop damage was of this character. While the research activities of each of these divisions of the Department of Agriculture would lead to expanded output and total income to the society, we should also note that they were paid for from general tax revenues. Since the agricultural industry was essentially competitive, the gains should have been passed on to the consumers, but it is almost certain that there was also some income redistribution in the process.

A second, and quite different strand in the development of governmental activity in agriculture, related to the growth of research in agriculture and the dissemination of knowledge to farmers with special emphasis on the regional character of research problems. A major beginning was made with the Morrill Act of 1862 which set up land grant colleges with the explicit objective that they should promote the development of agricultural knowledge and its dissemination. These colleges were to play a major role in agricultural research with special emphasis on chemistry, biology, entomology, and animal husbandry.

Another major step in this direction was the enactment, again at the insistence of local voluntary organizations of farmers, of the Hatch Act of 1887 which provided for the establishment of agricultural experiment stations in every state in the Union and funding each in the initial year with $15,000 for research. This modest beginning was expanded over time; once the initial costs of creating this organization had been incurred, it was easy then for subsequent pressure from farm action groups to expand the appropriations. The state experiment stations in collaboration with the United States Department of Agriculture and the land grant colleges became the coordinating organization for developing research, dovetailed to specific problems of local area, soils, and crops. The result was that each state with its own county agriculture agents not only focused on the local research needs but on the spreading of knowledge of improved agriculture techniques to farmers. With improved information, uncertainty was reduced and total income increased.

The result of this public expenditure of research, undertaken at the behest of farm groups and paid for through tax money, has been what most leading students of agriculture consider a very high rate of return upon research. Certainly, the astonishing growth of productivity in agriculture which began in the 1930s appears in good part to be a delayed response to the initiation of systematic research. That research initiated at the end of the nineteenth century finally began to bear fruit in the 1920s and '30s, and has produced a rate of productivity increase in American agriculture of unparalleled proportions. Professor Theodore Schultz, a leading scholar in American agriculture, has estimated that the rate of return upon such research between 1910 and 1950 was of a magnitude of something like 30 percent per year.

(V) Conclusion

Both the disposal of the public domain and the history of agriculture present unique challenges for our model. The transformation of millions of square miles of land and accompanying resources from public to private hands has no close parallel in the rest of American economic history. While our model sheds no light upon those altruistic reformers who envisioned this transformation as leading to an agrarian utopia, it does shed light upon the support they would get for changes in the disposal system; the variety of institutional arrangements devised to profit from this disposal system; the form of quasi-legal or illegal institutional arrangements which would emerge; and finally the relative disadvantage of the government disposal agencies in dealing with such illegal institutional arrangements.

In the light of our model, it is interesting to raise the question of the historian: Could we have done better? Some of the institutional arrangements, including many that were illegal (the dummy entrymen, for example), clearly were designed to realize economies of scale, or to reduce transactions costs and could, in short, increase total income. Others were primarily designed to redistribute wealth and income, but on balance it is not altogether clear which way. We would expect upper income groups to have better information and, consequently, to have an advantage in perceiving the potential profitability of new institutional arrangements. It is probably also true that they had more political influence to subvert the efforts of the Public Lands Office both locally and in Washington, D.C. The subject bears further investigation.

The farmers' efforts in many respects are similar to those of labor. Many of the institutional arrangements were designed to redistribute income. In

103

both cases they were something more than factors of production. The farmers were a people who developed an ideology in which they could justify to themselves (and frequently a wider electorate) that they were entitled to a larger share of the pie. But, beyond that, the farmer also promoted profits for himself (albeit from public sources) by inducing governmental organization to undertake the research necessary for a revolutionary change in agricultural productivity. Labor organization has no clear parallel for such institutional developments. Both did promote investment in human capital, but the farmer's interest in agricultural experiment stations and the Department of Agriculture's research promised directly increased returns to the farmer, an activity that has no exact parallel in the case of organized labor. Farmers, in common with labor groups, were more successful where they were homogeneous in economic interest and internal conflicts were minimized. On the other hand, both frequently failed to implement their objectives when conflicts of interest existed.

We should also note in conclusion that as the farmer became a smaller and smaller minority in other industrialized societies, he has pressed for institutional arrangements to redistribute income in other countries with a vigor that has paralleled the American experience.

CHAPTER 6

ORGANIZATION AND REORGANIZATION IN THE FINANCIAL MARKETS: SAVINGS AND INVESTMENT IN THE AMERICAN ECONOMY, 1820–1950

(I) Introduction

The first commercial banks were organized in the United States during the Revolution, and the New York Stock Exchange can, with some slight stretch of the imagination, trace its lineage back into the eighteenth century. Despite these examples of early capital market arrangements, the financial market was largely unorganized at the beginning of the nineteenth century. Even in the relatively static economy of the first years of that century, there were gains to be realized from more effective institutional arrangements, and with the geographic expansion and economic growth of the succeeding century-and-a-half, these potential profits increased enormously. A meaningful history of finance in the United States can only be told in terms of the rearrangements that resulted from the innovation of new institutions to capture and recapture the profits that, in 1810, were external to any institution. The result of this process is, in the 1970s, an economy marked by a myriad of financial arrangements. The process of organization and re-organization still continues, but even the history to the present is far too much to summarize in so short a chapter. Instead, we will draw from that history a few illustrations to indicate how the search for profits led to arrangemental innovation. For every example that we cite, there are a hundred that are slighted, but the outlines of the tests of the theory are certainly there. Moreover, as manufacturers who shifted to Hula Hoop production will attest, not all arrangemental innovations are successful; however, some mention must be made of the false starts well as as the successful ones, if we are ever to understand the process of institutional change.

It appears useful to distinguish two separate aspects of the problem of

The theory applied

capital market evolution, although the reader should remember that in reality the two are closely related and empirically intertwined:

(1) *Capital accumulation* – problems related to the total size of the savings stream.

(2) *Capital mobilization* – problems arising from the economy's attempts to transfer savings from surplus to deficit savings units.

If the level of savings is positively related to the rate of interest (as economic theory suggests) the innovation of financial intermediaries will increase the total volume of savings. By bringing borrowers and lenders together, any lender who previously was not in contact with at least one of the new potential borrowers finds additional demands for his savings. In addition, each lender makes his savings–consumption decisions on the basis of rates of return net of uncertainty; and by making the markets work more easily, the financial intermediary can reduce uncertainty discounts. Thus for any given market rate, the intermediary will yield a higher 'effective rate' to the saver. Faced by an increase in demand and a higher effective rate for every level of saving, the saver should respond by consuming less and saving more.

Any saver can insure 'out from under' the effects of the change in the price of a single security by holding a balanced portfolio. Since there may be high fixed costs in obtaining small amounts of securities (either the minimum investment size might be large or there may be a high initial search cost), such a 'balanced' portfolio may be available only to savers with substantial accumulations. A financial intermediary, however, by pooling the accumulations of a number of savers, can provide such insurance to any individual no matter how small his own contribution. If we assume that small savers are risk averters this reduction in the variance of returns should increase the net returns and therefore increase the volume of savings. Moreover, in very underdeveloped societies, there may be substantial risks attached to holding cash. In such an economy, where the alternatives to consumption may involve holding liquid assets in a sock or mattress susceptible to loss from theft or fire, an intermediary, simply by providing a safe depository, may increase returns enough to cause a substitution of savings for consumption.

The usefulness of intermediation, however, does not stop with the reduction of the price of the initial investments since, in the absence of intermediation, there are additional costs incurred over the entire life of the investment. Unless one is prepared to make a 'once and for all' commitment and to assume that risk of holding that investment through the life of the assets that it represents, it may be difficult to realize any capital return before the end of that life span. Most homeowners know how difficult it is

106

to sell a house in an area with no formal housing market, but in the absence of a capital market, it is equally difficult to liquidate any paper investment.

In such case, the savers could realize some additional profits if some form of capital market arrangement could be innovated. In addition, it is likely that such a rearrangement would also be profitable from the point of view of firms seeking new finance. Like the saver in the absence of formal capital market arrangement, the firm must undertake substantial search costs if it wants to attract additional capital. Since the costs of negotiating a one-hundred dollar loan are not substantially less than those needed to close a loan for a million dollars, the administrative costs of seeking out small pools of savings are high. Information-gathering activities tend to be characterized by increasing returns to scale. Both search and administrative costs must be deducted from the expected return on the new investment, and, other things being equal, the absence of intermediation ought to reduce investment demand. When financial intermediaries and/or formal direct markets exist, search and negotiation costs decline, and the marginal efficiency of capital increases.

These are the potential gains from the innovation of financial intermediaries even if all capital were accumulated and utilized at the same point of space. These gains are, however, compounded if the transfer process involves mobilization across spatial or industrial boundaries. Once capital has been accumulated, it can add to the productive stream only if it is transferred to someone who wants to use it; and, of course, the contribution is greatest if it is transferred to the firm with the highest marginal efficiency of capital. In very unspecialized economies (and the Robinson Crusoe example is the extreme case), savings and investment decisions tend to be made by the same person. When this is the case, there is no mobilization problem. In the case of an agricultural economy, for example, the farmer takes time out of his production of consumption goods or from his afternoon nap (i.e. his leisure) and clears a part of the wilderness holdings. Here the acts of accumulation and mobilization are identical. As an economy becomes specialized, it becomes increasingly unlikely that the savings and investment decisions will be made by the same person. Specialization, by its very nature, tends to separate economic functions, and in point of fact, development has in the context of American history also involved a spatial and/or industrial relocation of economic activity.

As specialization increases, self employment declines, and this implies that the proportion of persons capable of utilizing their own savings for more than housing investment will also diminish. Moreover, development in the United States involved a shift away from agriculture towards manu-facturing and service sectors along with a shift in the geographic focus of the economy from the Northeast towards the Southwest. Accumulations tended to be generated by established industries and in developed regions (after all, that's where the economic activity was), but the demand for new investment moved to the spatial and industrial frontier. As a result, there was a continual widening of the 'gap' between saving and investing units.

At no time in our history was the United States without some capital market arrangements; however, those that existed in the early years were not only primitive, but were inclined to be tied to particular places and particular types of economic activity. The farther apart were savers and investors, the greater the potential profits that could be realized from the movement of finance across the regional and industrial boundaries. Not everyone would gain since firms in the surplus savings areas were benefiting from the cheap capital. Still, gains were to be realized from arrangemental innovation.

In the absence of such institutional arrangements, transfers are likely to be small. Savers tend to know directly only what is within their normal experience, and the less they know about some 'distant' area or industry, the higher the uncertainty discounts they are apt to attach to their information. It takes some positive differential between 'home' and 'foreign' investment to compensate for the risks of the unknown. In the vernacular of nineteenth century finance, there was a 'disinclination for capital to migrate'. Financial intermediaries effectively substitute something that is known (the specific organization) for something that is less known and, therefore, reduce uncertainty discounts and cause capital to move from surplus areas to deficit areas (assuming other things remain equal).

The innovation of new institutional arrangements, both those designated to aid accumulation and those aimed at mobilization, is not without some costs. In addition to the costs of institutional organization, we have already seen that 'home' industries that had been enjoying cheap capital find themselves in competition with 'foreign' firms. There is another possible cost – difficult to ascertain – that is generated by a sort of 'chain reaction' to the financial intermediaries' ability to alter the velocity of money and in some cases determine its supply. Increases in M (money) or V (velocity) can, of course, have an impact on the level of prices and employment. Insofar as these effects are important and unwanted, they give rise to yet additional external profits that can be recaptured by still further innovation. The existence of these 'secondary' profits is, in fact, the usual justification for attempts by action groups to regulate capital market arrangements by the establishment of secondary action groups. The attempts to recapture these secondary profits, however, frequently inhibit the ability of the institutions to capture the primary profits, and this is a prime area of conflict in the economy today.

(II) Market failure (1): partial arbitrage – the role of the individual

As the discussion in Chapter 1 has indicated, the first attempts at capturing profits arising from market imperfections are frequently made by individuals who stand in a position that allows them to assess intermarket price differentials differently from the community at large. If there are enough of these individuals with sufficient resources, they may arbitrage the market, and there is no need for new institutional arrangements. Even, as was most frequently the case in the American capital markets, where individual effort was insufficient to effect total arbitrage, these individuals, by demonstrating the existence of the potential profits, made it easier to innovate some new voluntary cooperative form to effect the desired accumulation and transfers. The source of these profits lies in the market failure category, and institutional innovation took the form of improved information and, as a result, better markets.

What gives these individuals their unique position? A reading of American financial history in the context of the theory spelled out in Chapter 1 suggests that it can probably be attributed to three different characteristics:

(1) A person in a nearby region or a related industry may assess the uncertainty discount at substantially less than those located at a greater distance. In the early 1870s, an entrepreneur attempted to attract capital to a new Kelly process steel mill in Wyandotte, Michigan. The process was new and the industry far removed from the experience of savers and those in decision-making roles in the formal capital market arrangement that then existed. The enterprise was saved because capital was borrowed from iron makers in both the United States and Great Britain. The iron manufacturers, because of their knowledge of the problems and markets of a closely related industry, placed a lower value on the uncertainty discount than did the typical saver.

(2) Certain savers may be in a position to realize greater profits from some particular investment than can the average person. Although their risk discounts are not less than those of the average saver, their potential profits (the sum of the interest offered to the market at large and the profits accruing to them alone) are higher. The result, as in the first case, is an increase in the 'after discount profit'; however, the mechanism is different. The examples are many, but one from steel and one from transport should suffice. The first Bessemer plant in Harrisburg, Pennsylvania almost failed because of the inability of its management to attract funds through the

formal markets or from the community at large. The necessary capital was finally borrowed from the Pennsylvania Railroad. The road's management, unlike the typical investor who saw little potential profit once expected earnings had been discounted for uncertainty, included in their expected profits not only the interest on the loan, but also the savings that the railroad would realize from having a domestic supplier of steel rails.

Similarly, the Erie Canal (like many early transport projects) was partly financed by farmers and merchants who lived along the right of way. They looked for their profits not only to the interest on the loan, but also to the increase in the value of their land as the transport link tied them into a national market.

These farmers and their counterparts who invested their time and effort in many of the early railroads and canals, while viewing the returns differently than the typical saver, also, because of the unstructured labor market in the frontier region, took a different view on the cost of their investments. Thus, it appears likely that a farmer who would prefer employment in the off season could not find it in the local area. In this case he was forced to buy more leisure than he really wanted and the value of the marginal increment or leisure was very low. If his investment could take the form of a labor contribution (as it often did), it need be valued only at the price of leisure. The result on his profit calculation would have been an increase in the 'after discount value' of the investment – not because of an increase in the return, but because of a reduction in the real cost of that investment.

(3) There were a few people who, because of their personal connections, were able to act like financial intermediaries. Carnegie, for example, is known as a great steelmaker, but a careful reading of his life's story suggests that his fortune was earned not on the plant floor in Pittsburgh, but in the East and Europe where he could acquire the savings of friends who discounted 'foreign' investments (but not Carnegie's investment) and transfer them to business firms who could not otherwise raise needed finance. Years before Carnegie had ever heard of the Bessemer process, he had laid the basis for his fortune by bringing together savers and investors in a series of enterprises ranging from railroads to iron bridges. His real contribution to the steel industry was the funds he managed to acquire. Even late in the nineteenth century, when new firms had begun to compete in steel, all agreed that Carnegie maintained his advantage because of his ability to acquire capital more cheaply than anyone else.

Rockefeller, too, although known as the organizer of the Standard Oil Trust, was able to build that company into the dominant position because of his ability to acquire sufficient capital to innovate the new refining technology when his competitors could not. As we have seen in Chapter 1,

Savings and investment

the new technology was marked by substantial economies of scale, and the firms which could utilize it had substantial advantage over those tied to the old techniques. It was not his knowledge of oil refining, but his ability to present his firm as 'less uncertain' to the Cleveland (and later New York) financial communities that was the basis of his success. In fact, in the late 1880s, as the growth of the kerosene industry began to slacken with increasing domestic competition from gas and electric lights and increasing foreign pressure from the new oil fields in Baku and Grozny, Standard Oil, with its access to the formal capital markets unimpaired, began to look more and more like a bank and less and less like a producing company. While many of its lending ventures were within the oil industry, some were not. For example, among Standard's acquisitions during this period was much of the Mesabi iron range. The size of Rockefeller's fortune attests to the monopoly rents he was able to collect because of his position as a primitive financial intermediary.[1]

The list of these individuals who from their peculiar positions could evaluate the potential profits inherent in an ability to accumulate and mobilize capital is too long to enumerate here. Certainly, however, the most important name both in terms of the extent of his operations and in terms of his role in the process of institutional innovation (an innovation that was to yield a market structure able to accomplish formally what these individuals – no matter how important – could only do informally) was J. P. Morgan. His earliest ventures showed his ability to accumulate and mobilize finance when even the government could not, and from these he expanded his operations to include railroads, manufacturing firms like General Electric and International Harvester, and finally that immense complex, the United States Steel Company. Each of these ventures earned Morgan substantial monopoly profits (he was personally able to overcome the failure of the formal markets). Moreover, those few instances that failed to yield a profit were marked by earlier arrangemental innovation in the formal markets that had dried up the potential profits. Thus, by the end of the nineteenth and the beginning of the present century, arrangemental innovation had already captured the profits available from mobilizing capital for eastern railroads and from Atlantic shipping lines. Before Morgan died, the process of arrangemental innovation had proceeded much farther, but no one can deny that it was Morgan who paved the way for these institutional arrangements that could formally accomplish what he and the others could do informally.

---

[1] Rent is a term economists use to refer to any income earned in excess of that which would be received in the next best alternative.

111

The theory applied

(III) Market failure (2): governmental solution

Buchanan and Tullock have suggested that side markets capable of capturing the external profit can be organized through individual action, through voluntary cooperative arrangements, or through the use of the coercive powers of government. In the case of the capital markets, individuals played a role, but they were not capable of effecting permanent institutional rearrangement. At a higher than individual level, Buchanan and Tullock have argued that voluntary cooperative associations are apt to dominate when rearrangement is imposed on some relatively new type of economic activity, but that government organization is apt to be most important when the vested property rights in more well-established markets make unanimity difficult to achieve. We have argued that the conclusions are probably correct in a static world that assumes the existence of prototype arrangements, but that when interest rates are high and the institutional technology is also a variable, it is likely that organization through government may appear at an early stage of development and only gradually be replaced as new forms of voluntary cooperation are invented and innovated. This was the case in the capital market; in fact, in terms of chronology, governmental arrangements appeared even earlier than many of the persons to whom we have alluded.

The demand for capital to underwrite the development of an East–West transport network in the half century before 1865 required such large blocks of finance that no individual could mobilize the resources personally, and there were no prototypes of voluntary cooperative arrangements that could be readily innovated. On the other hand, the profits (both private and social) from such mobilization were immense. By 1900, a number of alternative private arrangements could have been employed, but in 1820 only the government could effect the necessary transfers. The inducement to innovate a governmental institutional form was not the need to bypass a unanimity rule, but the absence of alternative organizational forms in the private sector. To a lesser extent the same problem had arisen in financing very early manufacturing enterprises in Massachusetts (the Beverly textile mill), Pennsylvania, and Virginia. In these instances the government (federal in the first; state in the latter two) had stepped in to provide the alternative institutional arrangement.

In the case of the transport sector, the pattern (a pattern that was to last until the 1840s) was set by the Erie Canal in the middle of the second decade of the nineteenth century. Transportation projects into regions that lack both population and economic activity are subject to high uncertainty discounts under the best of conditions; and in a world without a well-developed private securities market, the discounts attached to the paper

Savings and investment

securities issues of such enterprises are very high indeed. By 1815, however, there was a market both here and abroad for the bonds of federal and state governments. The market was still thin (as Civil War finance was to prove), but a market it was. Moreover, the United States government had demonstrated a certain fiscal responsibility in its assumption of the war debts of the states. As a result, British savers who appeared unable to distinguish between federal and state governments were willing to absorb state government issues or issues guaranteed by state governments. The state of New York guaranteed the bonds of the Erie, and while at first most bonds were sold to persons with a personal stake in the enterprise, the canal's success rapidly increased the size of the market. The number of savers both here and abroad who appeared ready to invest in government supported transport issues, brought other states into the capital mobilization process. Over the next twenty years, the state of Pennsylvania underwrote the Main Line Canal, the government in Maryland provided the capital support for the Baltimore and Ohio Railroad, Ohio mobilized capital for two major North–South canals, Indiana underwrote the finance for the Wabash and Erie Canal, and Michigan supported railroad development. In fact, there was hardly a state in either the South or West and few in the East that did not utilize some arm of government to mobilize finance for manufacturing, transport or banking developments. Even the federal government got into the act as it agreed to underwrite a part of the construction costs of the Chesapeake and Ohio Canal.

Government supported institutional arrangements did not, however, continue indefinitely. The chief strength of market organization through government fiat (and, of course, its chief cost) is the ability of that agency to use its coercive powers to effect its decisions. In the 1840s, however, when many of the transport and banking projects got into difficulties, the governments for various political reasons proved unwilling to coerce their citizens into honoring the government guarantees. As a result, savers discovered that state obligations were not much safer than private securities. At the same time, the effective organization of a market for private transport securities (an arrangemental innovation of the voluntary cooperative variety) made it possible to accomplish within the private sector what previously only the government could do. This shift did not mean the end of government support to the transport sector (the large-scale government land grants were still in the future), but it did mean an end to the mobilization of transport capital through the agency of the government as opposed to the private sector.[1]

[1] The government involvement in transport in the period 1850–72 did not involve extensive capital mobilization. On the surface it may appear that land grants and financial

The theory applied

Since the 1840s, the government has been involved in a number of attempts to transfer capital from region to region or from industry to industry. It is, however, difficult to separate those arrangements designed to capture the external profits inherent in immovable capital from those designed to subsidize some particular industry. It is possible, for example, that the movement of the federal government into agricultural finance in the years since the 1900s represents an arrangemental innovation designed to capture external profits that both individual and voluntary cooperative groups had failed to internalize. It could be argued that the private mortgage banks of the 1880s and '90s and the mortgage credit offered by commercial banks after the turn of the century failed to mobilize capital for agriculture because certain legal limitations made it impossible for those voluntary cooperative arrangements to insure out from under agricultural failures. Thus, one could argue, because the institutional environment imposed legal limits on the activities of private arrangements, only the federal government was large and pervasive enough to provide insurance against regional and temporal fluctuations in agricultural output and price.[1]

(IV) Market failure (3): voluntary cooperative solutions – commercial banks and related developments

Both the government and the large personal mobilizers ultimately passed from the scene because the innovation of voluntary cooperative arrangements made it possible to internalize more cheaply most of the profits that could come from larger and more mobile accumulations. The private innovations have been of two types:

(1) The widespread innovation of a myriad of financial intermediaries.

---

support are alternatives, but in fact they are quite different things. The government guarantees of transport finance can be viewed as the innovation of an institutional arrangement that permitted society to take advantage of certain external profits by making capital more mobile. Land grants, on the other hand, were institutions designed to provide subsidies to make it attractive for transport companies to extend their networks ahead of demand. By the 1860s, there were well-organized markets for transport securities and there were little additional profits to be gained from reorganization. Yet there may have been substantial external profits available from new arrangemental forms that could underwrite investment in social overhead capital. See Chapter 7.

[1] On the other hand, the innovation of cheap agricultural credit may represent only the use of the political mechanism to transfer resources from the economy at large to some specific political group (the farmers). Such an innovation would certainly be classed as an arrangemental reorganization induced by potential profits, but its connection with the financial sector would be entirely coincidental. While the jury may still be out in the case of agricultural credit, there can be little doubt that the latter explanation accounts for government involvement in home mortgage (FHA and GI) loans and in small business (SBA) loans.

Savings and investment

(2) The organization and development of a set of financial markets that help smooth the flows of finance between savers and/or intermediaries and investors. It would take several volumes to report on the development of each market and each intermediary, and such a task would be well beyond the scope of this work. Instead, it appears useful to touch on a few of the most important and to use their histories as illustrations of the process of arrangemental innovation.

Commercial banks were the first type of intermediary to appear in the United States, and by almost any measure they still continue to be the most important. It is certainly possible that had the commercial banks continued to develop along the lines they began, there would have been little reason to innovate many of the other types of arrangements that since have risen to importance. However, between legal restrictions inherent in the economic environment and the psychological makeup of the banking community, commercial banks have come to concentrate their activities in the 'short end' of the capital market and to leave long-term financing to other groups. While commercial banks did make long-term loans in the 1830s, it has only been in the past two decades that they have again begun to compete in the market for long-term finance.

While legal strictures and economic events were tending to limit the scope of commercial bank loans, changes in the law during the 1830s and '40s appeared to make entry into commercial banking easier, although they also limited the geographic market in which a bank could operate. However, subsequent events suggest the changes were more apparent than real. In 1800 banks organized as corporations and given the protection of limited liability could only be chartered by special act of a legislature. Free banking – the right of any group to charter a bank without special appeal to legislative authority – was innovated in Michigan and New York in 1838 and over the next decade-and-a-half spread gradually across the rest of the North and West. However, despite these changes, states, under pressure from existing banks, have tended to make entry more difficult than a literal reading of the free banking laws act would suggest. More recently the federal government also has acted to restrict entry. The need for deposit insurance has given the Federal Deposit Insurance Corporation an almost monopolistic voice in the question of new bank chartering; and the Comptroller of the Currency, charged with chartering national banks, has usually tended to deny a charter if he felt the new bank would provide 'excessive' competition.

The laws under which banks were chartered, unlike those governing other corporations, tended to preclude branches outside the state (in fact, in many states the charters precluded branching even within the state). The First and Second Banks of the United States, however, were

115

federally chartered, and with the Supreme Court's ruling in *McCulloch* v. *Maryland*, were entitled to open branches in any state. A continuation of the charter of either of these institutions might have resulted in a national system of branch banks much like the English or Canadian systems, but with Jackson's veto, the nation was committed to a system of (at most) state-wide commercial bank operations.

The widespread innovation of commercial banks has helped society to capture some of the profits from greater and more mobile accumulations, but because of the lack of competition and the legal restrictions under which they have been forced to operate, they have been much less successful than they might have been. Let us examine briefly the results of these tendencies.

Regulation and the lack of competition have made the commercial banks very slow to adjust to the changing demands of a developing economy. The 1820s and '30s were marked by commercial bank penetration of the long-term and the industrial loan markets. At the end of that period a rash of failures prompted some states to establish regulations prohibiting such loans; and, even where no legal barriers were raised, the lack of competition permitted bankers to adopt practices similar to those in the regulated states. It is barely possible that in a world where there is little manufacturing, where agriculture needs little credit, and where most of the non-agricultural activity was devoted to commercial enterprises, that a policy of making only short-term commercial loans might have something to recommend it. Even if it could be determined that there ever was such an era in the United States, it had certainly passed long before the 1840s. Despite the growing demands for longer term credits and loans to manufacturing and transportation enterprises, the commercial banks have steadily resisted these pressures. It was the 1930s before home mortgages became important in commercial bank portfolios, it was the 1940s before consumer credit became respectable, and it was the 1950s before long-term credits to manufacturing firms became a legitimate asset for a 'respectable' banker. This change is a result of further arrangemental innovation, but the question of the long delay still remains open. On the one hand it was the product of some reduction of regulation (it became legal for national banks to make mortgage loans in 1914) and on the other some increase in competition. The increase in competition has not come from local commercial banks but from new forms of financial intermediaries (savings and loan associations, for example).

At the same time, state charters and the willingness of the federal government to go along with state law has prevented the commercial banks from serving wide geographic areas and, therefore, from capturing all the potential profits inherent in a mobile capital stock. Even today, only California and North Carolina permit unlimited state-wide branch banking, and some states (Illinois, for example) permit none at all. While it is not illegal for a bank in one state to make loans to firms in another, it is costly, since some administrative organization must be set up in the receiving state. In theory, of course, interbank lending could achieve economy-wide mobility at relatively low cost, but throughout most of the late nineteenth and early twentieth centuries, the Comptroller of the Currency frowned on banks in high interest areas soliciting funds from institutions in savings surplus regions. Until recently, therefore, while the commercial banks were able to mobilize funds locally, they were unable to act effectively across wider areas. Still further arrangemental innovation was necessary to overcome problems of regional capital mobilization.

In the last few decades, the growth of national firms capable of borrowing in one market and using the funds in another has provided interregional competition by the back door. Today, there are probably enough 'national' firms to provide competitive capital mobilization in a manner that only Rockefeller and Standard Oil could do eighty years ago, but today is 1971 and these firms did not exist a century ago.

Given the potential profits inherent in mobilization, an arrangement was innovated in the late nineteenth century, and it was this innovation that was to underwrite the emergence of a national market for short-term finance. The potential profits were there and the commercial bankers were unable or unwilling to capture them. The technology was available – in England if not in the United States. Into this gap stepped the 'festive note broker' or, in the stilted phrases of the economic historian, the commercial paper house (i.e. a firm specializing in purchasing commercial paper – the IOUs of borrowing firms – from banks in high interest regions and selling it to banks in low interest regions). The first firms date back into the 1840s, but with the exception of some slight penetration into the Old Northwest, these activities were largely restricted to the eastern United States until after the Civil War. The delay probably reflects the state of commercial banking in the frontier region coupled with the period of gestation that marks the innovation of any new institutional arrangement. It takes time for a new arrangement to prove itself profitable and more time to spread across a wide geographic area.

The East–North–Central region was integrated into the market in which the houses bought and sold in the 1870s. From there progress was steady across the West, and the Pacific coast was brought into the market by the first decade of the present century. The impact of the commercial paper house can be clearly seen in the movement of interest differentials between the newly integrated areas and the east coast. Within two years of the opening of a branch of a house in an area, interest rates in its cities converged on the eastern rates, and within five years (as the firms pushed out into the country-side), country rates too came into line. Without question, a successful side market engendered by the potential profits from mobile capital had effected a transfer of funds despite the legal and psychological barriers that prevented the commercial banks from underwriting these transfers directly. The process was obviously a slow one, and while the Second Bank of the United States had been able to effect such transfers in the 1830s, it was sixty years later before the new arrangement had successfully replaced it.

Some problems of historical explanation still remain, and these problems reflect how little we do know about the theory of arrangemental innovation. As we explained in Chapter 3, the theory that we have utilized is essentially a lagged supply model with the potential of external profits inducing after some lapse of time an arrangemental change that permits those profits to be captured. In general terms, this theory is quite appealing, but it fails to explain the period of arrangemental gestation and, in addition, it fails to explain areas that reject the innovation. In the case of the United States, the South was such a region. In 1860, it was among the low interest areas, but by 1914, when a national market tied most of the rest of the country together, rates in the South stood substantially above those prevailing elsewhere. Moreover, the commercial paper market had failed to penetrate any but a few of its largest cities. The potential profits were almost certainly there, and an arrangement had been tested elsewhere and had proved efficient at capturing these profits. Why then was it not innovated in the South? Our theory is not well enough specified to provide a certain answer to this question, but it does suggest some possible explanations. First, the market cannot operate if local banks are not making loans and receiving commercial paper in return. In the South, free banking came very late and the region was discriminated against in the initial distribution of National Bank Charters. Second, the Civil War had disrupted normal financial relations, and, as a result, the base for further innovation may have been less firm.

(V) Market failure (4): voluntary cooperative solutions – the rise of non-bank intermediaries and related developments

Although history may belie its truth, there is a widespread belief among savers that long-term finance is more risky than short. As a result, the problems of accumulation and mobilization were less easily solved in the long-term market. The range of institutional arrangements needed was greater; and their period of gestation and growth longer. Because of these delays, it was in the long end of the capital market that the financial capitalists (Carnegie, Rockefeller, Morgan, *et al.*) had their greatest impact.

As in the short-term market, arrangemental innovation in the private sector took two forms:

(1) A series of financial intermediaries that stood between saver and investor.

(2) A market for paper securities that aided direct transfers and increased the liquidity of these pieces of symbolic capital.

The period of gestation was longer than in the short-term market, in part because of the greater number of arrangements that were necessary, and in part because of the legal restrictions that had to be overcome. It is true, however, that in the long run it has been largely possible to change these legal restrictions and it has not been necessary to innovate around them. Once again it should be clear that our knowledge of arrangemental change is not complete, but the model does suggest some explanation of these lags.

Chronologically the first of the non-bank intermediaries were the mutual savings banks. They date from around 1815, and their early innovation probably reflects the known menu of arrangemental alternatives. The mutual savings bank was not an American invention, since the original idea was patterned after similar organizations in Great Britain. The United States mutuals were, however, a much more important force in the capital markets than were their British antecedents. In addition to their direct contribution to finance, they also played an indirect role in the process of arrangemental innovation. They were the first firms in the capital market organized on the mutual principle, and their success led to the innovation of that form of organization in many of the new nineteenth century intermediaries.

The savings banks were well designed to agglomerate the small accumulations of low income savers and to make these accumulations available to the investment market. Begun as benevolent organizations and chartered to teach the poor the benefits of thrift, they actively solicited the business of the small saver. Since their directors wanted to prove that savings was its own reward, they tended to invest their assets in high yield activities. In this respect, they were quite different from their British counterparts. In Britain the law had restricted their investments to government bonds and, thus restricted, the banks were never able to earn profits comparable to those of their American counterparts. In the United States, for example, the Provident Institution for Savings in the Town of Boston poured long-term finance into the New England textile industry, the New York Bank for Savings helped transfer capital into the Erie Canal, and the Savings Bank of Baltimore helped that port remain one of the nation's great commercial centers.

From 1815 until well after the Civil War, the savings banks remained the most important non-bank intermediary, even though their activities were

The theory applied

limited both by their geographic concentration in the Northeast and by their relatively narrow investment horizon. In the Northeast, the poor were able to save something (as against the slaves in the South) and were much more concentrated in urban areas (and therefore unable to invest in farm improvements as their western counterparts could do). As a result, they were the natural target for wealthy philanthropists who, perhaps through concern engendered by the French Revolution, distrusted a propertyless urban proletariat. At the same time, this upper income group believed in their *noblesse oblige* to those less well off, but thought for both social and religious reasons that self-help was God's road to charity. While savings banks were common in almost every town in the Northeast, there were none south of Maryland and few west of the Appalachians. At a later date, when the burgeoning cities of the Midwest might have presented similar opportunities, the social elite had other interests and the profits to be accrued from mobilizing small savings had declined.

Because these banks were semi-charitable organizations, state governments early attempted to provide some protection for the depositors. This 'protection' in many states took the form of regulations on the banks' investment portfolios. At the same time, the managers, even in unregulated states, did take their jobs seriously. Either because they believed that charity begins by making loans at home or because they actually were risk averse, their self-imposed limits were often as stringent in unregulated banks as they were in regulated ones. In the case of Massachusetts, for example, the law prohibited loans to persons or corporations not domiciled within the state. In Maryland, however, where there was no legal regulation, the banks' management produced similar results. Thus, in 1849 (after more than thirty years of operation), the directors of the Savings Bank of Baltimore denied a loan to an Elicott City textile mill operator (Elicott City is thirteen miles from Baltimore) because of 'their lack of knowledge about business conditions in the county'. This compounding of legal and managerial restrictions, while permitting the banks to become an important force in accumulation and in inter-industry mobilization, severely limited their contribution to interregional capital movements.

In fact, in the long run, the greatest impact of the savings banks may have come from their innovation of the mutual principle. While private banks may have been an alternative, it appears that the mutuals, by providing the illusion of depositor ownership, probably induced many to join who would not have trusted a 'for profit' institution. Certainly, the growth of both life insurance companies and savings and loan associations after the 1840s was rooted in their innovation of that same mutual principle.

By the 1900s, life insurance companies had replaced the savings bank as the dominant non-bank intermediary, and they have continued to improve their position in the present century. Given the temporal distribution of premium payments and benefit disbursements, even ordinary life insurance policies can produce substantial accumulations. Add to straight life insurance any savings scheme, and the accumulations that are available for investment become even larger. As an economic institution, however, insurance companies had to wait for an adequate mortality table. By the 1840s, an adequate table was available and the innovation of the mutual principle initiated the first growth of the industry. It was not, however, until the post-bellum decades that these innovations coupled with the 'hard sell' and the new innovations of tontine and industrial insurance produced a surge of growth that saw the life insurance companies pass the savings banks both in size and in their importance in the capital markets.

Initially, the investment policies of the life insurance companies were as handicapped by legal and managerial restrictions as those of the savings banks; however, within a few decades, the insurance companies were largely able to free themselves of the worst effects of these restrictions. Benevolence and philanthropy had never been important motives in the organization of insurance companies, and it is clear that the mutual form of organization was adopted only because of its proven sales value. As a result, the life insurance companies never placed safety and high returns above all else in the determination of company policy. Early laws tended to restrict investment to home states, and this policy was frequently reinforced by a management with a relatively narrow outlook; however, the continual broadening of the sales market tended to force a concomitant broadening of the investment market. By the last decades of the nineteenth century, the insurance companies were effectively accumulating savings and mobilizing these across broad industrial and regional barriers. In fact, a comparison of the differential in mortgage interest rates between the East and West with the differential rates earned by companies located in the West versus the East suggests that the life insurance companies were moving capital from low to high interest areas well before the market in general. Even when they were too small to arbitrage the market by themselves, they did aid that movement.

Not all of the institutional reorganization that affected the insurance industry produced more savings and better distribution of savings. In the four decades before 1905, the companies found themselves under continuous attack by their policyholders because of their high cancellation rates and the failure of their tontine policies to reap the expected benefits. At the same time, new policies required new laws (for example, in order to legalize the sale of tontine insurance the law prohibiting postponed dividends had to be repealed). Faced by these problems (both had political manifestations) the large companies banded together in an informal cartel aimed at neutralizing any policyholder attack and in supporting lobbying activities for the 'benefits of the industry'. In the words of one student, 'In New York state they [the Equitable, New York Life, and New York Mutual] dominated the state Insurance Department and the necessary parts of the state legislature during most of the decade that preceded the 1905 investigation.' Their success is attested to in many ways, but probably nowhere better than by the experience of policyholder James W. McCullough. In 1870 McCullough complained to the Insurance Department about the behavior of the Mutual. An investigation was launched, but quickly suspended. Later, when attempting to ascertain the results of that investigation, McCullough was informed by the Mutual's attorneys that the department's transcript of the hearings had been copyrighted by the company.

The cartel in this instance was stable. The big three dominated the industry, and the costs of allowing the small firms a free ride was not great. At the same time, since the cartel was not aimed at price maintenance and each firm could quickly tell if the others were meeting their obligations, there were no gains from cheating.

It is impossible to enumerate all the organizations that developed to aid accumulation and mobilization, but one fact should be noted. In the case of both the savings banks and the insurance companies, the primary motive for their organization was not financial (in the one case, it was charity; in the other, the sale of insurance), but these organizations had more impact on the financial market than almost any institutional arrangements that were launched primarily to accumulate and mobilize capital. Thus, one can conclude it is the effect of the arrangemental change rather than the stated purpose of the innovated arrangements that is important to the process of capturing external gains.

Before we leave the long-term market, and to prevent the reader from assuming that the process of arrangemental innovation is always successful, it appears useful to mention at least one innovation that failed to capture permanently the potential external profits.

Throughout most of the nineteenth century, there was an excess demand for finance in western agriculture as new lands were opened and as that activity became more finance intensive. Since commercial banks tended to shy away from mortgage loans (in fact, it was illegal for national banks to make such loans until 1914) and since, under any conditions, there was no mechanism to allow eastern banks to buy western mortgages (the commercial paper market was limited to short-term paper), there were potential profits that could be realized if some new arrangements were to be innovated.

Like Carnegie and Rockefeller, there were a few people who assessed the risks differently from the typical investor and these few eastern capitalists began to search out western mortgages. For the first few, the search costs (since they involved sending an agent west) were very high, so the inference is that the returns must have been quite substantial.[1] Once an agent was in the field and had acquired some knowledge of potential investments, it was possible for him to sell this knowledge to any number of potential investors. Given these economies of scale, it is not surprising that the information function quickly became formalized and with that formalization, the costs of search dropped markedly. Moreover, once that type of organization had been established, it was an easy step from a 'broker on order' to a broker who maintained an inventory of mortgages, and another simple step from there to a mortgage bank whose assets were a portfolio of mortgages and who issued stocks and bonds against that portfolio. In this instance, the arrangemental form was not borrowed from abroad (as the savings banks and life insurance companies had been). The period of development began with the agent in the late '60s and early '70s and culminated with the first formal mortgage bank twenty years later. Like most unsuccessful innovations, the banks left few records behind, and it is still unclear how big or even how many of them there were. By 1892, however, almost two hundred such banks (located in almost every western state) had registered to do business in New York.

In the early years, the firms were profitable, there were certainly profits to be realized from their arbitrage activities, and they were not faced by any competing organizational form. In short, there was nothing to suggest that they were not to be as permanent a part of the American financial scene as the savings banks or the insurance companies. Unfortunately, there were some differences. Farm profits tend to be highly volatile, and the mortgage banks had no compensating assets to provide insurance in their portfolios. Drought hit the western states in the late '80s, and the weather, coupled with a generally falling price level that increased the real burden of the mortgage debt, pushed many farms into bankruptcy in the early '90s. As the farms failed, so did the mortgage banks, and by the middle of that decade, the mortgage banking firms had all but disappeared from the economy. The few firms who avoided bankruptcy (Wells–Dickey, for example) turned to other activities, and once again there were potential profits available to anyone who could mobilize capital for western agriculture.

Those profits induced further arrangemental innovations, but these new forms were no more successful. In the years from 1900 to 1921, a number of life insurance companies moved into the farm mortgage market; however,

[1] Swieringa's study of central Iowa suggests that this was, in fact, the case. R. P. Swieringa, *Pioneers & Profits: Land Speculation on the Iowa Frontier* (Ames, Iowa, 1968).

when depression and drought hit in the 1920s and '30s, they fared little better than the earlier mortgage banks. The life insurance companies were saved from bankruptcy by the rest of their portfolios. While they could provide 'industrial balance', they were not large enough to provide 'temporal balance' and, as a result, they too failed to provide the basis for a viable interregional market for agricultural finance. It was not, as we have seen, until the United States government moved into agricultural credit that funds flowed regularly into western agriculture.

These three examples conform (more or less) to our model of arrangemental adaptation. The profit potential after a lapse of time induced some form of institutional innovation that allowed the profits to be captured. The explanations are not as perfect as one would like. Certainly it is clear that the initial purpose of the institutional arrangements need not be the recapture of the external profits, and in many cases, organization may come easier if it is something else. Still, there are the yet unanswerable questions of the length of the lapse of time, of the predictability of success, and finally, of the failure of the long-term institutional arrangements to penetrate the South any more effectively than the commercial paper market did.

There were no savings banks in that region, there were almost no domestic life insurance companies, and 'foreign' (i.e. non-southern) mortgage companies tended to avoid southern investments, and there were fewer mortgage banks in the entire South than in the state of Colorado alone. Profit potential was almost certainly present, since interest rates (even after allowance for risk) stood among the highest in the nation. Capital transfers, when they did occur, tended to take the form of direct investment by northern firms – investment that bypassed the formal markets completely. Although it is not possible to provide a certain explanation to the question of retarded arrangemental development in the South, some observations do appear relevant and they may (in the long run) be able to help us better understand the nature of arrangemental innovation.

It appears likely that some organizational structures are more amenable to innovation than others, and this is as true in the financial market as elsewhere. In the case of the capital markets, it is the financial community that is first affected, and it appears that the southern financial community was more rigid and less able to change than its counterparts in other parts of the country. In the first place, the southern banking community was probably less competitive and more monopolistic than its northern and western counterparts. The evidence is, of course, the long delay in bringing free banking to the region, and the close connection between the established elite and the political structure that permitted the southern bankers to maintain their monopolistic position. In the second place, the Civil War destroyed the existing financial structure, and by its end, many of the cotton factors – the men who were most intimately connected with southern finance – had left the industry and/or the region. By the time the market was again in order, the telegraph and railroads had made the factors' non-financial services obsolete. This absence of trained personnel may also have contributed to the industry's inability to accept new innovation. While these circumstances are suggestive of possible modifications that will be necessary to make the theory usable, the reader should bear in mind the fact that no theory is of any value if in every instance special provision must be adduced to provide adequate prediction.

As in the short-term market, organization comes not only through the innovation of intermediaries, but also through the organization of more efficient markets for long-term finance. The process has, of course, two sides. The markets must be organized and the potential savers and investors must be educated to use them. In the case of the commercial paper market, the users were the banks and their search for profits speeded the educational process. In the stock and bond markets, the savers frequently were individuals who heavily discounted the unknown. The typical saver had to be shown that a piece of paper was as adequate a way of holding savings as farm improvements, housing, or liquid reserves. In this case, the educational process took longer.

The processes of education and arrangemental innovation went hand in hand. While it is possible to learn about paper claims on assets by reading Sylvia Porter or talking with a publicity man from Merrill, Lynch, the best form of education is a profitable investment. Many of the first purchasers of direct issues were persons connected with the enterprise or who intended to utilize its services. Once such a project had proved successful, these investors were often willing to buy securities farther removed from their personal activities, and their friends and relations also revised their uncertainty discounts downward. While state bonds had not proved overly secure in the 1840s, the increase in holdings of federal bonds during the Civil War (Jay Cooke's 5–20 campaign made such bonds a household word) introduced many savers to paper securities. By the 1890s, the eastern savers had proved they represented a fine market for bonds, and the Midwest was considered a potential market of equal quality. The 'Borrow and Buy' campaign to sell the World War I Victory Loan continued the educational process as people learned not only about paper issues but also about margins and the possibility of speculative profits. By the 1920s, the entire country outside the south seemed ready to snap up almost any type of paper issue.

It is interesting to speculate how the course of arrangemental innovation might have differed, if confederate bonds had not gone into default and the

125

The theory applied

northern issues had. The southern default must have set back the educational process just as the South Sea Bubble had delayed developments in Great Britain two centuries earlier. Successful investment tends to reduce uncertainty discounts, but unsuccessful investment has the opposite effect.

While the northern and western saver was gradually learning to hold paper securities, market innovations were reducing the cost of search for profitable paper and making such scraps liquid, if not safe. While 15 million shares of stock were sold on Black Thursday in 1929, 15 million shares were also purchased on that day. The original holders of those shares may have lost money as prices collapsed, but they were able to achieve liquidity. By 1929, the paper securities market was well developed indeed. As one might expect, the evolution of that market was from local to national and from those securities with the lowest uncertainty discounts to those with the highest.

The first markets were local and concentrated on the exchange of local issues. As late as the 1830s, the markets in both Boston and Philadelphia were as large as New York, and within a few years, cities as far apart as St Louis, Chicago, and Detroit all had their own securities markets. If capital is to be mobile, however, there must be a single exchange serving all parts of the country, and the capture of the external profits rests on the linking together of the local into a single national market. For a number of economic and political reasons (they include the demise of the Second Bank of the United States and the development of an effective money market in New York City), the paper securities market began to concentrate in New York City. With the development of the telegraph, exchanges in other cities became satellites of the New York market. Thus, by the time of the Civil War, the term 'Wall Street' had become synonymous with the stock market, although the dominance was less then than it is now.

While Wall Street was achieving national stature in the geographic dimension, it was even more slowly approaching the same position in the industrial dimension. The first securities to be listed were government issues. These, after all, were the ones to which savers attached the lowest uncertainty discounts and they were, therefore, the most easily traded. Following the government issues on to the market came the flotations of the transportation companies: first turnpikes, then canals, and finally the railroads. Savers seemed more willing to hold these issues at an early stage of their educational process, but, of course, mere listing does not imply that capital was being effectively mobilized. In the case of the railroads, for example, both the activities of men like Jay Cooke and J. P. Morgan and the histories of railroads like the Union Pacific and the Burlington show that personal connections functioned better than the formal markets until well into the last quarter of the nineteenth century.

126

Savings and investment

Finally, it was the twentieth century before manufacturing capital was effectively mobilized through the formal markets. Only a handful of manufacturing enterprises were listed on the 'Big Board' before the Civil War.[1] At the end of the '80s, the Department of New Securities of the New York Exchange began to handle a few manufacturing stocks, but it was a decade later before the imprimatur of the great Morgan on enterprises like International Harvester and United States Steel made industrials look safe to the majority of the saving public. Moreover, it was 1914 before manufacturing securities were given equal treatment with government and transport issues as security for stock market loans.

By the 1920s, the formal securities market was operating efficiently enough to squeeze most of the potential external profits out of the mobilization of long-term finance. Thus, while in 1902 no one but Morgan could have managed a flotation like United States Steel, thirty years later (when the law required that investment houses divorce their commercial banking subsidiaries) all but one of the Morgan partners stayed with the bank rather than with the investment house. The external profits had been internalized by the organization of an efficient side market, and monopoly profits accruing from an ability to mobilize capital had disappeared.

(VI) Second order externalities: the government and legislation

Thus far this chapter has focused on the arrangemental developments in the capital market that permitted the capture of certain potential profits inherent in any reorganization that would increase the rate of accumulation and/or the mobility of capital. The process, however, did not end there. The potential profits led to the eventual innovation of new institutional arrangements, and the actions of the new arrangements engendered additional costs. These costs were external to the financial institutions, and were not considered in their profit calculations. Instead they were borne by the general public. Any time such costs exist, it is possible to increase total welfare by some further institutional rearrangement that forces the firms to consider not only the internal costs but the external costs as well, and thus bring together private and social costs and revenues.

As any first-year student of economics knows, the same commercial bank that can increase the rate of accumulation and the mobility of capital is also quite able to manipulate its loan policies in order to alter the money supply and in so doing engender fluctuations in prices and output. Moreover,

[1] Even on the Boston Exchange (the home of New England textile securities), the official price quotations are marked by a warning against the reader putting any great reliance on the reported prices since the shares were tightly held and seldom traded.

127

other intermediaries, by altering the velocity at which money is spent, can produce similar effects on the level of output and prices.

Since no single bank or non-bank intermediary can have a noticeable effect on the supply of money or its velocity, these costs do not enter into the firm's decisions. Moreover, since the costs are economy-wide, rather than pertaining to only one sector, even some form of voluntary cooperative organization that spanned the entire sector could not internalize these costs. In addition to the cyclical impact of their actions, the same Goldsmith principle that underlies the commercial banks' ability to 'expand the money supply' implies that the system cannot last in the face of any general attempt to substitute specie or government issued legal tender for bank money. Unrestrained bank expansion, by undermining confidence, did lead to attempts to substitute against bank money, and whether these 'runs' were met by general bank suspensions or by banking collapse, they tended to cause a breakdown in normal economic relations and therefore implied yet another real cost to the public.

These then were the external costs that a system of private commercial banks placed on the public. In addition, however, banks that were faced with close competition found their loan activities limited by the threat of internal drain, and these bankers often felt that they were placed at an unfair disadvantage in competition with banks that faced less competition. As one might expect, the problems of costs external to the banking community could not be recaptured by any reorganization of the banks themselves, and only the government could provide a solution. The problem of 'unfair' competition could, however, be solved either by a voluntary cooperative association of banking (if the injured banks could find some way of coercing the rest of the banking community to join) or, failing that, they too could increase their profits if they could get the government to alter the institutional arrangements in their favor.

Thus far, we have with one exception limited our discussion to financial reorganizations that permitted the capture of profits that without reorganization would not accrue to anyone else (as those that result from more accumulation) or to those that resulted in a greater total profit even if they did involve some losses to one sector. In the case of mobilization, for example, firms in surplus savings areas that had benefited from lower interest rates were forced to surrender their cheap capital, but since the productivity of the new loans was higher (otherwise the transfer could not have been made), the possibility of compensation existed even if the bribes were not paid. Now, however, we are talking about the possibility of transfers from one sector to another without any clear proof that the net result is an increase in income. Thus, the gains in terms of price and output stability that bank regulation can provide can come only at the cost to the banks and their customers of fewer loans. Again, the reduction in competition from banks less subject to internal drain results in greater profits to some, but certainly lower profits to those banks that previously had not faced the threat of over-expansion. These facts suggest something about the nature of institutional reorganizations. As long as no one is hurt, there is a chance that reorganization can come through some form of voluntary cooperation. If, however, some members of the group are injured, it is likely that private reorganization can be effective only if the units in the private sector desiring reorganization have some coercive power or are willing to bribe the firms that are injured. If neither occurs, reorganization can come only through government action.

Among the first and most successful institutional innovations of this type in the capital market was the 'Suffolk' system, a plan launched by the Boston banks in 1819 to stop the expansion of country banks less threatened by internal drain. While no single city bank was in a position to limit the note expansion of their country competitors, all together could. By collecting country bank notes and threatening to present them in block for payment, the city banks could bring substantial pressure to bear. So great, in fact, was the pressure, that the threat of joint action was sufficient to force the country banks to reduce their loans and to hold 'reserves' in the vaults of the Suffolk banks to insure their future good behavior. The results (at least within New England) were greater bank stability, less discounting of out of town bank notes, and greater profits for the Boston banks. At the same time, the country bank profits were less, and certainly there were borrowers who would have received loans under the old system that were denied credit under the new.

Because of unit banking, the Suffolk plan did not extend beyond New England, and, if national regulation were to come, it probably could not be accomplished within the private sector. If the law had permitted national banking, it is possible that regulation could be achieved through some similar consortium of national banks. In Great Britain regulation, after all, was effected by the Bank of England (a private institution until it was national-ized by the Labor party after World War II). As a result, despite the regional success of the Suffolk system and at a later date, the more limited successes of the private clearing houses in providing liquidity in time of crisis, most regulation was undertaken by government innovation.

In the early period, when there were at most state-wide economies, the regulatory body was most frequently the state. Later, when banks were part of a national market, the federal government assumed the leading role in regulation. However, in Chapters 1 and 2 it was suggested that government organization is partly politically determined, and that a passionate minority can have political influence far greater than the number of votes they command. The reader should not, therefore, be left with the impression that the bankers were left without influence in the regulatory mechanism. In fact, it has been suggested that regulating agencies were frequently more interested in the bankers' problems of unfair competition than in the social costs of an unregulated banking system.

Although state bank regulation dates back into the 1820s (the New York Safety Fund – an early form of deposit insurance – was established in 1828, for example), Louisiana's Forestall System (in 1842) set the pattern for state control. That law, enacted in response to the public outcry at the bank suspension of 1839–42, required that banks hold reserves, that they largely limit their lending activities to short-term loans, and that the state have the right to inspect the banks and maintain a strong voice in their charter. Like the Suffolk system, the product of these new regulations was certainly greater stability (the Louisiana banks were almost alone among American banks in not suspending during the crisis of 1854), but at the same time, they led to less competitive banking and fewer loans to Louisiana businessmen. The regulations were certainly an attempt to equate the private and social costs of banking with the private revenues of banking activities; however, there was no guarantee that that equality was achieved or that the system represented any improvement over the initial situation. In fact, it can be shown that the prohibition on long-term lending places additional costs on the system while providing no significant benefits to anyone.

The expansion of the capital markets from local to state to federal ultimately implied that the regulatory body had to be a political unit whose sovereignty was the entire market – the federal government. As early as the 1830s, it was not unheard of for banks in one region (Ohio, for example) to exchange notes with banks in another (Georgia, perhaps). Since interregional transport was slow and costly, such an exchange largely removed the participating banks from the limitations of lending inherent in our usual notions of internal drain. The Second Bank, with its powers to branch in any state, was, however, in a position to limit these interregional note exchanges, although it was not specifically charged with this duty. Since the Second Bank was both a public and a private organization, it is possible that its interest in regulation was derived not only from a desire to promote financial stability, but also from a desire to increase its own profits at the expense of the other banks. Under its third president, Nicholas Biddle, the bank did, in fact, begin to act like a central bank, but it was never free of the possibility of this conflict of interest. The bankers whose activities were regulated certainly did not believe that the Second Bank was operating in the national interest. In fact, so passionate was the minority of banks and businessmen who wanted easier credit, that the election of 1832 was fought on precisely that issue. Jackson's veto of the recharter act removed the federal government from bank regulation for thirty years and from effective central banking for almost one hundred. Insofar as the Second Bank was an arrangemental innovation aimed at reducing the public costs of banking, it was a failure; although in terms of its structure, it was probably a better designed central bank than anything the country was to see again before the Banking Act of 1935. A governmental arrangement, no matter how well designed, can act to capture or transfer profits only as long as it is able to maintain the political support it needs to exercise its coercive powers.

While the federal government again became involved in banking regulation with the passage of the National Banking Act (1863), the first serious attempt to innovate an institutional arrangement charged with minimizing the economic costs of commercial bank lending came with passage of the Federal Reserve Act in 1914. The previous half century had been marked by a series of financial crises, bank suspensions, and bank induced or supported changes in the level of prices and output. Dissatisfaction with the system came to a head after the panic of 1907, and resulted seven years later in the establishment of the Federal Reserve System. Governmental arrangements tend to be the product of political compromises since the selection of the government as the optimum level of organization (as opposed to private or voluntary cooperation) suggests that all parties do not agree about the need for or the type of institution required. If we assume that the Federal Reserve was designed to minimize the costs of instability engendered by the banking system, it is hard to conclude that it was not designed to fail. There was not one central bank, but twelve, and the only explicit weapon even these central banks had was the power to set the discount rate. Institutional arrangements (or their secondary action groups), however, can invent and innovate new arrangemental forms, and changes in public attitude can induce politicians to rewrite bank charters like any other law. Thus, the 1920s saw the extra-legal innovation of the systems accounts and open market operations, and the debacle of the '30s – the total reorganization along the lines of greater and more powerful central bank operations.

The Federal Reserve System by the mid-1930s had been given the powers to effect a redistribution of costs and revenues in the area where banking and public policy merged. Despite the century of experimentation and all the false starts, the system was (and is) still not without its problems. First, the move toward greater centralization was coupled with the reduction of the influence of politicians on the actions of the system. This reduction, in turn, altered the power structure within the system in favor of the banking community, and it is clear that their goals may be quite different from those of the public. Second, while the system is pervasive enough to influence the action of the commercial banks, it is not large enough to influence the treasury and, as the experiences of both post-war periods have indicated, some of the problems of instability flow from the government rather than the banking community. Finally, the system has no way to induce banks to increase the money supply during depression nor does it have any way to protect the public from the Federal Reserve Bank's own stupidity – a stupidity that was reflected by the concern over the inflationary threat during the depression of the 1930s. In fact, the history of the Federal Reserve Bank in the past three decades seems to support the argument that when there is disagreement about the function of any organization and when each party to that disagreement has the power to modify the actions of the organization, the organization will probably be unable to achieve any goal efficiently.

(VII) Conclusions

As one might expect, the most important sources of profits leading towards arrangemental innovation in the financial sector were those flowing from the need for insurance in the investment portfolio of an individual who was risk averse and those that could be realized from improvements designed to overcome market failure in interregional and inter-industrial capital markets. At the same time, groups within the financial sector displayed a willingness to innovate still other arrangemental forms if those innovations could under-write a redistribution of income away from someone else and toward them. In addition, the evidence suggests that in the financial sector, as elsewhere, the production of information was subject to substantial economies of scale. As a result, the organizations innovated to improve intermarket information flows (and thus reduce uncertainty) tended to be highly specialized firms and markets each large enough to capture those economies. Moreover, the history of the financial sector suggests certain other more general conclusions about the nature of arrangemental change.

In particular, the period of arrangemental gestation and diffusion appears to depend (among other things) on: the adaptability of the innovating group coupled with the extent that that group is insulated from the threat of external competition; the existence of somewhat similar arrangements that can provide ideas and personnel; and the possibility of tying the arrangement to some other generally desired goal. As to the first, in the case of the South, for example, an intellectual environment that had displayed a low tolerance for ambiguity in other dimensions and whose members were protected from external competition by legal barriers, was very slow to innovate the financial forms that had proved so valuable elsewhere. In fact, it was outside competition routed through direct finance rather than through any arrangemental form that finally gave the region some modicum of capital mobility. As to the second, the mutual principle once innovated for savings banks was quickly adopted in life insurance companies and savings and loan associations. Again, Morgan-trained financiers spread quickly throughout the New York financial community and, as they became the agents for the diffusion of his technology, undercut his monopoly position. Finally, where organization could offer a desirable collateral service (for example, philanthropy in the case of savings banks and life insurance in the case of insurance companies), the rate of arrangemental diffusion was much higher than in those instances where innovation depended upon education.

The history of American finance also offers some support for the contentions we made in Chapter 2 about the basis for choosing between voluntary cooperative and governmental arrangemental forms. First, if private innovation involves very high organizational expenses, the arrangement of choice will likely be one that depends upon the government. Thus, while there certainly was sufficient private capital to underwrite the early transport network, the costs of private mobilization were very high. The requirements were so large that no syndicate of a few rich men could bring together sufficient finance. What was needed was the mobilization of the savings of a very large number of persons, and in the absence of private institutional arrangements designed to accomplish that mobilization, the private organizational costs were prohibitive. The continued existence of potential profits from private mobilization, however, did induce arrangemental innovation, and within a few years the total costs of private mobilization (even for projects as large as a railroad) fell below those associated with government mobilization. In a similar vein, schemes designed to redistribute income away from a small group towards a larger group can usually only be effected through the interposition of some government institutional arrangement. There is, for example, no logical reason why banks could not be forced to conform to the community's desires for price and output stability by the threat of a boycott by their depositors. The organizational costs, however, would be exorbitant. In this instance it is once again likely that the necessary coercion can be obtained more cheaply through the development of some government agency. As an aside, it should be noted that when private organizational costs are subsidized by the government (for example, the costs of some ghetto organizations are currently borne by the Office of Economic Opportunity), the costs of innovation of voluntary cooperative arrangements fall. The Negro boycotts of banks pursuing policies of discrimination provide a ready and relevant example. Finally, small groups

133

with a large vested interest are frequently able to divert governmental arrangements for their own purposes no matter what reasons underlay the establishment of those institutions. Thus, the office of the Comptroller of the Currency and the Federal Deposit Insurance Corporation, both arrangements innovated to provide depositors with better and more stable banking facilities, have become agents of the banking community and bulwarks against competitive threats to that industry.

Lastly, the history of the development of financial intermediaries offers some insights into the question of cartel stability. The success of cartel arrangements among insurance companies in the 1890s suggests that the stability of a cartel will be greater the fewer the number of firms. Further, if a number is small enough, and the potential profits great enough, the cartel can be effective despite the existence of a few free riders. Moreover, the history suggests joint policy decisions are easier to effect if they are designed to affect the economic environment rather than if they are aimed at price and output decisions. In this instance it is hard for any member to duck his financial assessment (an unpaid bribe boomerangs very quickly), and once that assessment is paid, it is very difficult for any member to get a competitive edge over his cohorts by breaking the agreement. The result is stability.

CHAPTER 7

TRANSPORTATION DEVELOPMENTS AND ECONOMIC GROWTH

(I) Introduction

One of the chief sources of the growth of output in the American economy has been the continent-wide domestic market within which the process of specialization has been allowed to proceed without the development of any significant barriers to the flow of commodities across regional boundaries. The constitutional prohibition against interstate tariffs was a necessary condition for this development, but it was not sufficient. In addition, to realize the benefits of specialization the economy required a transport system capable of moving bulk commodities across regional boundaries at relatively low cost. In 1800 only the Atlantic Ocean provided such a transport route, and the history of American economic development is closely tied to the development of such a transport system. The successful innovation of new transport techniques, however, required substantial institutional change. Within the transport sector the technical innovations were the canals and railroads.[1] The arrangemental innovations are not so easily described.

This chapter makes no pretense of being a complete history of transport in the United States. Instead it focuses only on the organizational developments within that or some related sector that permitted someone or some group to capture the profits that could accrue from the movements of commodities in interregional trade at prices that would support a fairly high degree of specialization. Both the transport industry itself, and the economy within which it operated, were subject to continual change over the nineteenth and early twentieth centuries. As a result, the process of arrangemental innovation was not a once-and-for-all adjustment, but a process of almost continual adaptation. Like the other sectors that we have discussed, the form of institution that was innovated was a function of the profits

[1] Recent work suggests that most of the benefits of specialization accrued by the American economy might have been captured had technology not developed beyond the canal boat, but in fact, it did. It is, indeed, the railroads that underwrote most of the growth of the continental market.

135

that were to be captured, the current state of arrangemental technology, and the costs and revenues attached to each alternative organizational form.

Although the process of innovation was almost continuous, in this chapter we will focus our attention on those reorganizations that stemmed from attempts to capture (or recapture) profits arising from five sources:

(1) those rooted in the need for large blocks of finance to underwrite construction during a time when the capital markets were not well developed;

(2) those accruing to transport firms capable of achieving certain economies of scale;

(3) those flowing from the divergence between private and social costs and revenues and from differences in private and social rates of discount;

(4) those inherent in attempts to capture the rising land values that accompanied transportation developments;

(5) those arising from competition between railroads and between railroads and other forms of transport in the interregional shipment of commodities.

(II) The capital markets and the development of a finance intensive industry

Compared to most other industries, domestic transport tends to require a substantial amount of capital investment per unit of output. What are the implications of a high capital–output ratio for economic development and what is the relation between a high capital–output ratio, the existence of certain externalities, and the possibility of arrangemental reorganization? The total capital demands for any industry depend not only on the capital–output ratio, but on the level of output as well. Thus it is possible that industries with very low ratios may absorb most of the capital in any economy, and in many underdeveloped countries they do. There is, however, one important difference between industries with high and low capital–output ratios. It is an empirical fact that industries with high ratios are more often characterized by economies of scale in their capital inputs than are those with low ratios. Thus, firms with low ratios frequently are able to start with small amounts of capital and gradually finance additions to their capital stock from savings generated by the enterprise itself. Firms at the other end of the spectrum, however, tend to require large blocks of initial capital and this requirement implies that growth cannot be self financed.[1]

---

[1] A farmer in western New York in the early nineteenth century, for example, could begin by clearing a very small plot of land and then over a time, by reducing his consumption or leisure, gradually clear additional acres and put up fences and buildings. Thus, by the end of a decade, he might own a farm that represented many thousands of dollars in investment. The nature of the investment, however, did not require him to go to outside sources of finance. The same cannot be said about investment in canals and

Transport is an industry characterized by a high capital–output ratio and substantial economies of scale. Thus, large blocks of capital are needed to underwrite initial construction. Moreover, while there were certainly some individual fortunes large enough to underwrite some of the projects, it is likely that the demands for most were so large that they could be met only by pooling the savings of a great number of people. In terms of American development in the early nineteenth century, the demand for these large blocks of external finance had two consequences: it made it impossible to organize the ventures as either sole proprietorships or partnerships (the typical organizational forms of the period); it required that the promoters appeal to the government to aid in mobilizing the necessary finance. Let us examine each in turn.

Since the American legal system has its origins in British common law, it is hardly surprising that, in 1800, the position of legal persons (corporations) in the former country was very similar to that in the latter. In Great Britain the grant of legal life could come only from the King, and in the United States the government had this same monopoly. Thus, until well into the nineteenth century all corporate charters were granted by special act of some legislative body and, given the American Constitution, that body was most often one of the state legislatures. In the eighteenth century, corporate charters had been largely limited to towns, universities, or other similar enterprises whose activities were closely connected with the public interest. The early nineteenth century, however, witnessed a growing realization that the transport sector, if it were ever to develop, needed to be organized on a 'super personal' level, and the corporate form was widely innovated. In the states of New York and Ohio, for example, transport accounted for about one-half of all corporate charters in the early nineteenth century.[1]

The corporation had two characteristics that made it particularly attractive as a form of transport organization. First, unlike other business forms, its owners were granted the protection of limited liability. No matter what happened to the company itself (and many of the early ventures were very risky), its owners could lose no more than their initial investment.[2] Second,

---

railroads. If one wants to build a canal designed to haul western farm produce from Buffalo to Albany, it is not possible to begin with a canal from Buffalo to Syracuse and then gradually lengthen it, nor is it possible to begin with a canal one foot wide and then gradually widen it.

[1] For the best analysis of the composition of early corporations as well as a history of change in corporate law see G. H. Evans, *Business Incorporations in the United States 1800–1943* (New York, 1948).

[2] This statement is not strictly true, but liability was always limited.

The theory applied

unlike a sole proprietorship or a partnership whose life expires on the death of the proprietor or partner, the corporation had an unlimited (or at least a long and predetermined) life. Since most of the assets held by a transport firm are long-lived, it was not therefore necessary to dispose of them at a sacrifice sale should one of the owners die. Moreover, as the capital markets began to develop, the ability of the corporation to issue transferable equity and debt claims (an ability that was founded in its long life and limited liability) permitted large blocks of finance to be mobilized. Limited liability and unlimited life reduced the uncertainties attached to transport investment. The reduction in uncertainty, in turn, made it less expensive to mobilize finance. In the United States the potential profits in transport made it feasible to innovate the corporate form despite the relatively high costs in an era of special corporations.[1]

Although the government alone can grant legal life, the corporation is a form of voluntary cooperative organization. Individual investors are permitted to join in the venture; any one of them, however, can remove himself by selling or otherwise disposing of his shares. No matter what he chooses to do, however, his commitment is limited to the amount of his

---

[1] The search for lower cost alternatives, however, induced the innovations of general incorporative laws as early as 1811, and by the 1870s almost every state in the East and Midwest had some provision for general incorporation. Special incorporation and passage of the general incorporation acts are good examples of the use of the government to change the legal structure to permit the innovation of new forms of voluntary cooperative organization. Similar examples are found in banking and agriculture, and they point up the intimate relation between private and government forms of organization. Despite the fact that Great Britain's transformation from an agricultural to a commercialized manufacturing economy antedated America's, the movement towards easy corporate charter came first to the United States. Thus general incorporation in Great Britain was delayed until the 1860s and '70s, but a similar movement had begun in the United States almost a half century earlier and by the '70s almost every state in the East and Midwest had some provision for general incorporation. Moreover, incorporation by special charter was much easier in the United States. Our model of institutional innovation suggests an explanation for the difference in timing. While the British transport network had been developed without limited liability, the corporate form had been the dominant form of organization in American transportation as far back as the early turnpike companies. Although the costs of special charter may have been high (in terms of the costs of lobbying such bills through the legislature), it was apparent that, given the underdeveloped state of the capital markets in the United States, the revenue from this form of voluntary cooperative organization far exceeded its costs. Costs would certainly have been lower with general incorporation laws, but in the early nineteenth century it was politically difficult to make that innovation. In the United States, however, the pressures were there to innovate some type of corporate form as quickly as possible. In Great Britain, on the other hand, given the better developed capital markets, the potential revenues from corporate organization in transport was much less and institutional innovation awaited changes in the structure of manufacture. For a more detailed discussion of the emergence of general incorporation laws see Chapter 8.

138

actual investment.[1] In manufacture, trade, and agriculture other forms of organization continued to dominate the economy until the late nineteenth and sometimes the present century. In these cases, the benefits of the long life and limited liability were not worth the costs until general incorporation acts reduced the costs of the corporate form. In the case of transport, there was practically no development before the innovation of the corporation. The need for large blocks of initial finance made any other organizational form economically unfeasible.

Given the state of the private capital markets and the size of the blocks of finance required by transport demand, even the innovation of the corporation was frequently not sufficient to effect the necessary capital mobilization. In these instances, additional institutional arrangements were necessary, and frequently these involved reliance on some level of government. Since large portions of the projects, although interregional in their intent, were often located within the boundaries of a single state, the federal government was seldom involved. Instead, it was most often states and cities anxious to enhance their positions as entrepôts to the continental hinterland that became the direct participants. The particular form of organization – private, government, or some combination – varied from time to time and place to place. At times government ownership was the innovation of choice, at times it was some form of private–government partnership, and at times totally private organizations succeeded in mobilizing the requisite capital. The choice of arrangemental technology – since all were on the menu – depended in large part on the state of the private capital markets, the size of the particular project, and the uncertainties attaching themselves to that project.[2]

The first major transport development was the Erie Canal. Its critics were legion, its major proponent lost his office because of his support, and hardly anyone imagined that it could possibly be an economic success. The canal was one of the largest single projects that any group in the United States had ever taken on, and when it was launched in 1817, the private capital markets had hardly begun to develop. It was designed to connect the East with the Midwest, but in that latter region there were few people and even less economic activity. Thus there was no economic base that might produce agricultural products to be transported to or generate income that

---

[1] This statement is not strictly accurate, but for all intent and purposes it is. At times corporations have been granted charters specifying that stockholder's liability while limited is limited at two or three times their initial investment. California bank charters had this characteristic until quite recently.

[2] The following history of transport in the pre-Civil War era draws heavily from C. Goodrich, *Government Promotion of American Canals and Railroads* (New York, 1960).

could be used to finance imports from the East. From the point of view of finance, the Erie was an enormous project. No issue even vaguely approaching $7 million had ever been floated through the New York (or any other American) stock exchange.[1] It is not surprising that in this case government ownership was the most economical form of arrangemental innovation, for even the government of the state of New York had trouble raising the requisite finance. Until the canal had proved itself profitable, most of the capital was raised by persons residing along the right-of-way who saw a portion of their return coming from a reduction in their own transportation costs.

Despite everything the Erie was successful.[2] The guarantee of the state government coupled with the early evidence of success was sufficient to make canal bonds attractive investments not only in New York but in London and Amsterdam as well. Moreover, the success of the Erie also did much to make bonds issued by other government units in support of transport developments highly saleable.

Because of their size, their uncertainty (the Erie reduced but did not eliminate uncertainty), and the underdeveloped state of the capital markets, most of the canal projects launched between 1817 and 1840 were state owned and operated. Government ownership was a characteristic not only of the remainder of the New York state system, but of the large canal projects in Ohio, Pennsylvania, and Indiana as well. There were, however, some noteworthy exceptions. The Pennsylvania and New Jersey coal canals, for example, connecting known mineral deposits with existing markets and involving investments of considerably smaller magnitudes than the interregional canals, were able to mobilize their capital privately. Most of the capital was raised through informal arrangements, but there were occasional appeals to the formal markets. Moreover, even when the appeal had initially been made to the informal markets, the formal markets provided some potential liquidity for the investors. The shares of the Blackstone Canal and the Morris Canal and Banking Company, for example, were both quoted on the New York stock exchange as early as 1825.

As we have seen in Chapter 6, over time the capital markets improved, and the success of the first of the interregional schemes reduced the uncertainty discounts on the remainder. As a result, the need for full government participation became less, although some support was still required.

---

[1] It cost over $7 million, was 363 miles long, 20 feet wide, and 4 feet deep. In addition, to overcome the rise of 630 feet and the drop of 62 feet from the Hudson to Lake Erie, 84 locks were required.

[2] Within a few months of the start of construction, tolls from completed portions were able to cover interest charges; over a million dollars in tolls were received before the canal was completed; and all debts had been paid off by 1829, just four years after 'Clinton's Ditch' was officially opened.

In the case of the Baltimore and Ohio Railroad, for example, initial commitments called for about $3 million in private funds and about one-half that amount from the state of Maryland and the city of Baltimore.[1] This fraction, although large, was far smaller than complete government subsidization. The change in organizational structure, although sometimes criticized by contemporaries and certainly not without its costs, had some benefits from the point of view of both the government and the private promoters. For the promoters, private ownership meant that they, rather than the state, could reap the profits from the enterprise. From the point of view of government, it reduced the amount of finance that had to be raised, and it permitted a part of the financial burden to be passed along to the private sector. This latter aspect proved to be particularly important in the late 1830s and early '40s when many transportation companies failed to produce the profits expected of them and the states and cities were forced to turn to the taxpayers to make up the deficits.

Public support of transport development suffered a substantial setback during the depression of the 1840s.[2] At the same time, however, improvements in the private capital markets and the reduction of uncertainty discounts that resulted from the integration of the old Northwest Territory into the national economy made it increasingly possible for transport finance to be raised without government support or guarantees. The histories of both the Pennsylvania and the New York Central railroad systems bear witness to these changes in the relative costs of alternative organizational forms.

The Pennsylvania, like the Baltimore and Ohio, was originally a product of a government–private partnership – a partnership that required that the state and the cities of Philadelphia and Pittsburgh make a substantial contribution (about 50 percent) to building the road. By the mid-1850s, however, the road's management appeared confident that they could raise funds for further expansion from earnings and from private investment. The New York Central system attested to changes in relative organizational costs at an even earlier date. Unlike the other East–West roads, government finance never played an important role in the growth of the NYC. It was not built as an integrated line (its charter originally prohibited it from competing with the Erie Canal in interregional trade), and so the large blocks of finance so necessary elsewhere were not required. Moreover, since it paralleled the

[1] Because of construction delays and economic conditions, by the time the road reached the Ohio River, government contributions had reached almost one-half of the total.
[2] As far as the canals were concerned, this trend was reinforced by the growing competition between railroads and canals – a competition that the state owned canals were losing on almost every front (the Erie was again an exception).

The theory applied

Erie it passed through country that the canal had already opened. As a result, there were fewer uncertainties about the size and temporal distribution of revenues. When the integrated system did emerge, it represented nothing but an amalgamation of already existing privately financed lines, and it required very little additional capital.[1]

The history of institutional innovation in the early transport network is reasonably well explained by our model of arrangemental change. As long as the project was large relative to the economy and its outcome marked by a high degree of uncertainty, and as long as the capital markets were not well organized, there were substantial profits to be earned by using the credit of the government to raise initial finance.[2] As the road's revenue potential became known with greater certainty, as the growth of the economy reduced the relative size of the blocks of finance required, and as the capital markets became better organized, the revenues from governmental arrangements, as compared to some form of voluntary cooperation, declined. At the same time, the costs of such arrangements (in terms of both government control and the inherent political instability so well demonstrated during the crisis of the early '40s) probably increased. On the one hand, as people began to object to certain practices of the transport companies' managements (their rates and their service offered were two most often cited), the 'stuck costs' of governmental arrangements rose – governments are sometimes more sensitive to the feelings of their voting citizens than they are to the needs of an economic enterprise. On the other hand, the refusal of the voters to underwrite the economic commitments that had been made by their political representatives certainly made such arrangements appear less attractive to both investors and the users of transport services. This restructure of costs and revenues tended to induce reorganization along

---

[1] The Pennsylvania and the New York Central are just two examples, but there were many more in the East and old Northwest Territory. As Johnson and Supple have shown, by the Civil War decade private finance (although more frequently channeled through personal connections or the 'old boy' network than through the formal markets) had proved adequate to meet the needs of transport demand, given the reduced uncertainties that marked further penetration of the railroads into the already settled regions of the Midwest. The costs of organization through government had risen while those associated with voluntary cooperative organizations had declined. See A. Johnson and B. Supple, *Boston Capitalists and Western Railroads – A Study in the Nineteenth Century Railroad Investment Process* (Cambridge, Mass., 1967).

[2] As an aside, unless the transport enterprise could practice perfect price discrimination (which it could not), some potential profits would always be external to the firm. Thus the involvement of the government even for financial motives can, in fact, be viewed as a redistribution of a part of this consumer surplus from the consumer of transport services to the transport company. This same conclusion would hold for any government involvement regardless of the reason.

142

private rather than government lines. While there was little that could be done with existing canal investment, states and cities did tend to sell off their railroad securities, and transport management ceased to lobby for new blocks of government capital. By the 1870s, most eastern roads were in private hands and organized as voluntary cooperative associations. There, after all, was where the profits lay.

(III) Intra-firm reorganization: the search for scale economies

Most of this book deals with interfirm organizations; however, some institutional changes can occur within a firm. We have already seen how the innovation of the corporate form made large firms financially viable. Where economies of scale exist, large firms can capture these gains. The corporate form, while a necessary condition for this capture, is not a sufficient one. With unlimited life and limited liability the firm can be large enough to realize the scale efficiencies, but without further arrangemental innovation the growing complexities of management may more than offset these gains. Further innovation then becomes profitable if that innovation can reduce the costs of managerial control.

The railroads, as the nation's first large businesses, were faced with a number of these organizational problems that had to be overcome if they were to capture the profits inherent in the technical economies of scale.[1] While all firms have organizational problems, their sheer size and the need for rapid and diverse decision making set the railroads apart from other firms in the middle of the nineteenth century. Railroads like the Erie and the Pennsylvania were, by the 1850s, almost ten times as large as the largest manufacturing enterprises (the Pepperell textile mills, for example). At the same time, business was anything but routine, and thousands of very diverse decisions had to be made every day. Not too surprisingly, economic pressures forced these firms to invent and innovate a series of managerial control devices, and these innovations are still widely used today not only in the transport industry but in almost every other sector as well. Without these innovations it would have been impossible to capture the potential profits that existed in large integrated transport networks.

A generation earlier the 'Massachusetts type' textile mills had been faced with similar organizational problems, and they had made the first hesitant steps toward an arrangemental solution. However, their problems were substantially less complex, and it was possible to solve at least some of them by vertical disintegration. Thus, the mills spun off their sales functions

[1] The historical description of the organizational problems of the railroads is drawn from A. Chandler, *The Railroads: The Nation's First Big Business* (New York, 1965).

143

(i.e. separated their sales from their production operations) at a very early date. Their major intra-firm innovation was the separation of manufacturing under a superintendent and finance under a treasurer. It was on this latter innovation that the railroads' arrangemental changes were based. The changes were manifold, but of the total, two were particularly important not only because of their impact on rail transport but also because of their widespread innovation in the manufacturing and service sectors, once their worth had been proven.

This first involved the vertical disintegration of decision-making functions within the firm. In this regard, the railroads' innovations reflect merely a further extension of the production–finance division of the textile mills. Like the mills, the large railroads separated the finance and accounting functions from those relating to traffic and movement. Later, going one step further, they separated traffic from movement (operations). Moreover, J. Edgar Thompson of the Pennsylvania Railroad further subdivided the operating sections into regional divisions, each with its own officers. The resulting organizational structure was much more complex than anything the United States had seen before, but it did manage to provide for rapid decentralized decision making while at the same time permitting central control of corporate strategy.

Such a complex organizational structure had to be formalized, and under Daniell C. McCallum of the Erie, that railroad innovated the first formal Table of Organization. Not only did the table spell out the relationship of staff and line functions, but it provided the formal network necessary to underwrite inter-divisional information flows. Finally, Albert Fink of the Baltimore and Ohio (and later the Louisville and Nashville) developed a system of cost analysis that made it possible for management to make use of the information flowing through the network.

One need only look at the universal dependence on managerial accounting in every firm with more than a handful of employees, and at the widespread acceptance of divisional structures in large firms (General Motors provides an excellent example), to see how important these arrangemental innovations have been. More narrowly, it appears highly unlikely that in their absence the railroads would have been able to capture the profits inherent in a large integrated transport system.

(IV) The investment decision: a theoretical digression

In its simplest form, the theory of investment decision making involves a comparison of a discounted stream of future expected net revenues from a potential investment with the current costs of that investment: the rule is often written in a form almost identical to that used in the specification of our model of arrangemental choice:

$$PV = \frac{R_1}{(1 + r)} + \frac{R_2}{(1 + r)^2} + \cdots \frac{R_n}{(1 + r)^n} \tag{1}$$

where PV equals the present value of the investment, R_n, the net return to year n to be received by the firm making the decision, and r the rate of discount applied by that firm. If the present value of that stream exceeds the cost of the investment, it is assumed that the firm will undertake the investment, and if it doesn't it will not. Before we attempt to use this model to explain American railroad investment in the late nineteenth century, two comments should be made. In the first place, the Rs are not actual but expected returns; and, moreover, they are only the returns that will accrue to the firm making the investment. In the second place, the discount rate (r) is the opportunity cost of capital to the firm, and in a region marked by imperfections in the capital markets, it may be quite high indeed.

Developmental investments (i.e. social overhead capital or infra-structural expenditures in the jargon of the developmental economist) have at least one characteristic that distinguishes them from other types of investment – the returns are a function not of historical but of investment time. For example, a steel firm may decide not to invest this year in a new oxygen process because the technical details have not been fully worked out (the returns when discounted for future uncertainties are insufficient to yield a value greater than cost). Next year, however, if the problems are solved, the investment may appear profitable. Such is not the case for social overhead investment. In 1860 the management of a railroad may have decided that since there are no people in western Iowa it would not pay them this year to bridge the Mississippi and extend their line across that state. Without the investment, however, there is no way for any potential farmer to ship his products to the eastern markets. As a result, the next time the railroad examines the investment decision, since there are no more people in the area than there were previously, it will again decide against the investment. On the other hand, if the investment had been made in the first year, the transport link itself might have drawn people into the unsettled regions, and at some later date there might be positive returns from the investment. In short, the future returns are a function of present investment, but that investment is a function of the existing returns. In this instance, only some arrangemental reorganization that changes the temporal distribution of returns, increases those returns, or reduces the rate of discount would permit the profits inherent in opening the area ever to be captured by any part of society.

The theory applied

Let us then reformulate our model to take account of this problem. Two alterations have to be made. First, the investment model should be altered to allow for the possibility that the returns to the railroad (Rp) may not reflect all the returns that society could accrue from that investment. For example, if the value of land rises because of the railroad and the railroad can not practice perfect price discrimination, this increase may not be reflected in the expected private returns to the road (in this case total returns (R) are the sum of private (those accruing to the firm – Rp) and non-private (those accruing to the rest of society) returns (Rs)). Second, the model should admit the possibility that the social rate of discount may be below the private rate. The higher the rate of discount, the lower will be the value of future returns, and in particular the lower will appear those that are long delayed. Thus, the private sector viewing returns some decades away may find that these have almost zero present value. If, however, society has a lower rate of discount, these same returns may make a substantial contribution to present value. Since neither social returns nor the long-delayed private returns will ever be realized unless the investment is made, the divergence between private and social calculations may spell doom for a socially profitable investment if the investment decision is left in private hands. In short, the model should be reformulated in the following fashion:

(1) If the present value as calculated by the private sector (PVp) is less than current cost (C)

$$PVp < C$$

there can still be potential profits that can be captured by arrangemental reorganization if in addition

(2) the present value as calculated to include true social valuation ($PV = PVp + PVs$) is greater than current cost

$$PV > C$$

where

$$PV = \frac{(Rp_1 + Rs_1)}{(1 + s)} + \frac{(Rp_2 + Rs_2)}{(1 + s)^2} + \cdots + \frac{(Rp_n + Rs_n)}{(1 + s)^n}$$

and s is the social as opposed to the private rate of discount.

Since the increase in present value rests in both non-private and private revenues and in the divergence between private and social rates of discount, the reorganization is most likely to be effected through the government rather

146

than through any form of voluntary private arrangement.[1] The mere existence of a governmental innovation cannot be taken as proof that in fact total present value exceeds cost while private present value is less than that cost, although it is probably sufficient evidence to assert that the re-arrangement was profitable to someone (it is possible that $PV > PVp > C$). In Chapter 2 we argued that government actions do not always reflect the views of 'society at large'. Thus, the residents of some particular area or the transport companies themselves can benefit from a subsidy if they did not have to pay the full costs, even if they would have been willing to under-take the investment without the subsidy. In these instances, if the sub-groups acting as a passionate minority could effect a reorganization they might be able to transfer some profits from someone else to themselves. Of course, even an innovation that increases total income can have a redistributive effect.

(V) Divergence between private and social valuation and the possible need for a transport subsidy

While the Erie Canal did connect a developed market (the East) with an undeveloped one (the old Northwest Territory) and therefore in theory might have required a transport (as opposed to a finance) subsidy, the development of the trans-Appalachian West was so swift that these con-ditions did not prevail for long.[2] In fact, they had largely disappeared before construction of the other East–West links (the Main Line Canal and the Pennsylvania and Baltimore and Ohio railroads) had begun. Western New York state developed apace with canal construction, and settlement of the upper Northwest Territory proceeded more rapidly than almost anyone had thought possible. Practically non-existent in 1828, land sales in northern Ohio, Indiana, and Illinois peaked in 1836, a decade after the completion of the canal. Fifteen years later sales in the first two states, at least, had perma-nently fallen to less than one-tenth their peak level. The development that followed the opening of these new territories and the rapid expansion of

---

[1] It is possible that a large enough private organization might own both the transport system and the land through which it passes. In this case the direct private (as previously defined) and a large part of what has heretofore been deemed social revenues will accrue to the voluntary private cooperative organization. On the other hand, the social rate of discount, by its very definition, is held only by the government. To the extent that the rearrangement is profitable because $r > s$ the institution must be a government one.

[2] We have used the words finance subsidy to refer to the arrangement innovated to provide access to government finance, and transport subsidy to refer to an arrangement innovated to overcome the problems of development investment.

agriculture in the Genessee Valley meant quick profits for the Erie and its competitors in the trans-Appalachian trade.

Such rapid development had not been expected when the plans for the Erie were first drawn, and it was *certainly* not a necessary implication of developmental investment (or what economists have now come to term investment in social overhead capital or the 'infra-structure'). In fact, the opposite view (that is, long-delayed returns) is probably the most reasonable – certainly for the level of expected profits and likely for the level of actual profits as well. In the case of the trans-Mississippi West, settlement and development were slower and the task of building an adequate transport network was larger. As a result, that sector offered large profits to arrangemental reorganization despite the substantial improvements in the capital markets that had occurred between 1820 and 1860.

It is clear that there was reorganization in the transport sector as that network began to push into the unsettled West. In addition, it is certainly possible to argue that such reorganization (in a general sense) *could* be justified on the basis of a divergence between private and social revenues or rates of discount; but we still do not have sufficient evidence to assert that total present value exceeded costs while private present value did not. The work that has been done by Fogel and Mercer seems to suggest that in the case of the Union Pacific and the Southern Pacific, at least, the former was true; but neither says much about the latter.[1] In fact, some of Fogel's conclusions appear to suggest that the latter condition did not hold. From the qualitative evidence it appears likely that at least some of the transport subsidy that went to western railroads was justifiable on the grounds of a 'divergence', but that conclusion can certainly be disputed. Despite this absence of evidence on this point, it is clear that there were profits to be made from arrangemental reorganization. The only question is whether they represented new income or merely redistribution of existing income.

Until 1850, as we have seen, it was state and local government that bore the major share of transport reorganization. After that date, the pressure for arrangemental innovation came not from the financial needs of the roads but from the potential social revenues and from the long delays that the private sector expected to find between investment and profits. The trans-Mississippi roads were built into areas where there was little local wealth and less government organization to support them. Moreover, insofar as the returns accrued to all of society, political expediency dictated that the

---

[1] R. Fogel, *The Union Pacific Railroad: A Study in Premature Enterprise* (Baltimore, Md., 1960); L. Mercer, 'The Central Pacific System: An Estimate of Social and Private Rates of Return for a Land-Grant Aided Railroad System', Ph.D. dissertation, University of Washington, 1967.

costs should be shared by all. Although much of the history of the government land grants has been written in terms of the divergence between social and private revenues, it appears that while this divergence may have contributed to the reorganization, it was probably less important than the difference between private and social rates of discount.[1]

Although the nature of the subsidy was subject to some variation, most federal aid to the trans-Mississippi railroads took the form of substantial land grants coupled at times with some post-construction loans. The contrast between these types of subsidy and the financial support given in the previous era reflects the difference between the needs of 'finance' and 'transport' subsidies. In a period when the potential external profits arose from imperfections in the capital markets, the need was for large blocks of finance to underwrite construction. To this end neither land grants nor post-construction loans would have been particularly useful. In the later period, however, the need was to bring into the near future the profits of the distant future, and this goal could be achieved by land grants coupled with loans. In terms of the investment model, the private present value was raised by increasing returns in the early years and reducing (because of the loan payback provisions) the returns in the distant years.

$$PVp = \frac{(Rp_1 + S_1 + L_1)}{(\text{I} + r)} + \frac{(Rp_2 + S_2 + L_2)}{(\text{I} + r)^2} + \cdots + \frac{(Rp_n - L_n)}{(\text{I} + r)^n}$$

where S refers to revenues from the sale of land-grant land, L to post-construction loans, and negative values of L to loan repayments. It is clear that with appropriate land grants and/or loans, this scheme can overcome any divergence between social and private revenues or between private and social rates of discount, even if the private revenues from the sale of rail services are zero in the early years.

From the point of view of the railroad management, land grants and loans were ideal solutions to the subsidy problem. Since governments have usually attempted to exercise some control over subsidized operations (in the earlier period, for example, the state of Pennsylvania had appointed its

[1] Professor Fogel's landmark study of the Union Pacific Railroad has made us aware of two characteristics of transport investment in the largely unsettled trans-Mississippi region. He has shown that private profits were not as long deferred as many had expected, and that the private sector placed a very high probability of failure (over 70 percent) on the enterprise. Fogel goes on to indicate that actual total (social plus private) returns averaged almost 30 percent over the decade of the '70s, and on those grounds concludes that the reorganization was very profitable. However, he also suggests that private returns alone averaged over 11 percent, and therefore he concludes that the need of government subsidy lay not in the size or temporal distribution of the private returns but in the failure of the private sector to realize how large those returns were going to be.

own directors to the Pennsylvania Railroad), the subsidy could have involved the loss of considerable operational control. There were government appointed directors on the Union Pacific, but not on any of the other roads that received subsidies under the land grant acts. In place of government ownership or even a strong voice in management, Congress required only that the railroad be built.

Although federal land grants in support of the Mobile and Ohio and the Illinois Central Railroad were made in the 1850s, most of the grants were concentrated in the decade 1862–72. By that latter date, federal grants had totaled 131 million acres, and to this states had added an additional 49 million acres (of 180 million total acres the options on some 35 million acres were not exercised before the legislation expired in 1890). The grants varied in size from ten to twenty square miles for each mile completed within the borders of the same state and from twenty to forty square miles for each mile finished in the territories. There were federal grants in almost every state west of the Mississippi River and in six states farther east as well. In North Dakota and Washington the grants constituted more than 20 percent of the state's land area and they totaled over 15 percent in Minnesota, Kansas, and Montana.

After 1864 federal subsidies were limited to land grants, but before that date railroads received both grants and post-construction loans. In the case of the Union Pacific, that road received $16,000 for every mile of track in the eastern and western portions, $48,000 per mile for the stretches through the Rocky and Sierra Nevada mountains, and $32,000 per mile for the section passing through the Great Basin.

Whatever the political ramifications of the transport subsidy may have been, the land grant acts certainly underwrote railroad construction in the trans-Mississippi regions. In 1860 there were less than 500 miles of road in that area, but the three decades from the outbreak of the Civil War to 1890 saw the construction of some 56,000 miles of track between the Mississippi and the Pacific. Thus, during the period of most rapid growth of the American railroad network, the previously unsettled regions accounted for almost 60 percent of the total additions. While not all of this mileage was built by land grant railroads, it was the settlement induced by the subsidized roads that made the others appear profitable.

The period of subsidy through federal land grants was, despite its permanent effects on the American economy, relatively short. The end of the land grant era was brought about by two distinct developments. One related to change in the costs and revenue of alternative arrangemental technologies, and the other to the nature of the arrangemental innovation itself. The very success of the land grant acts in fostering rapid railroad expansion undercut the basis of their existence. Once people had migrated into the western regions, economic activity followed quickly. By the mid-1870s Minnesota, Iowa, Kansas, and Nebraska had all become major agricultural producers and even states like Colorado and Wyoming had been integrated into the national market. As a result, profits that in 1869 appeared to be deferred far into the future were, by the mid-'70s, a reality. Given a railroad connecting Chicago with Omaha and those cities with Cheyenne, the private sector needed no further subsidy to build a feeder line north from Omaha toward Sioux City. In short, the need for land grants declined as the temporal redistribution of potential revenues made railroad investment appear profitable at even the private rate of discount.

At nearly the same time, the institutional arrangement began to break apart under political attack. When the government is utilized to effect an arrangemental innovation, at least some decision-making authority passes out of the control of the individual firms and into the political arena.[1] It is certainly true that, given the nature of American politics, a passionate minority has more 'influence' than the doctrine of one man one vote would suggest; they have, however, less voice than a passionate majority. This fact of political life explains, as we have seen in Chapter 2, the preference of private groups seeking reorganizational profits for institutional arrangements well-insulated from the electoral process.

The federal land grants were the products of special acts of the legislature. Moreover, at no time had the railroads been able to convince all legislators that government involvement in the development of a transport network was a desirable goal. The Union Pacific land grant bills of 1862 and 1864, for example, were passed only after long, hard, and quite acrimonious debate. There had always been a group in Congress (albeit a minority in the 1860s) who believed that the land grant acts, particularly if made without firm government controls, were nothing but 'give away' programs.

In the early 1870s the Credit Mobilier scandal hit the newspapers, the public, and Congress. Recent work has indicated that the profits from the Union Pacific were not substantially greater than the level necessary to induce the private sector to carry out so risky a project. To contemporaries, however, they appeared incredibly high. These 'excessive profits', compounded by the evidence of bribery and corruption, turned the minority into a majority. As a result, no new land grants were made after 1872, and in 1890 new legislation repealed those grants that had not been exercised.

[1] In a voluntary cooperative arrangement each participant retains his veto power if he is able to withdraw at low cost; ultimate control remains with him unless the association is able to effect some coercive control – either through legal powers or through their ability to make his withdrawal economically costly.

The theory applied

From the point of view of society, by 1872 (and certainly by 1890) the need for a transport subsidy had largely disappeared, but the railroads would clearly have preferred that the arrangement survive.

The legislative response to the scandal represented an interesting exercise in political dynamics. From the point of view of our attempt to understand the process of arrangemental change, it is interesting to speculate about what would have happened in 1872 had there still been substantial social revenues from government subsidization of the transport system. The fact that the existing land grant options were not withdrawn suggests that the government was still unwilling to drop the subsidy. It is, however, much less clear what arrangemental alternatives would have been innovated had some profits still remained. Would it have been 'business as usual' or some change in the form of the organization to provide society with additional controls?

(VI) The competition for economic rent[1]

The end of the 'era of national subsidy' did not bring an end to potential profits in transport or to attempts at arrangemental reorganization aimed at corraling them. It did, however, largely mark the end of reorganizations that brought increases in total income. Thereafter, with but few exceptions, arrangemental innovation was aimed at the redistribution of existing income from one group to another. Since an increase in the income of one group frequently meant the reduction of the income of another, it should not be surprising that voluntary associations proved themselves of relatively little value. With increasing frequency the new institutional arrangement involved not only government participation but also more government participation for a longer period than before. Let us first examine arrangemental innovations designed to transfer the economic rents inherent in good access to transport from landowner to railroad, from one landowner to another, and from the public to some landowner.

By the end of the 1870s, private capital markets had developed sufficiently to finance new railroad construction, and the existence of a skeleton railroad network east of the Missouri had made unsubsidized railroad development in that region an economic possibility. Further construction was aimed at filling in the gaps in already developed market areas. The gaps were large and there were important questions about where (within these gaps) new lines should be located. These questions, since they involved potential

---

[1] To refresh the reader's memory, economists use the term rent to refer to any payment to a factor of production that is in excess of the income that that factor could receive in its next best alternative occupation.

profits for someone, induced further arrangemental change in the transport sector.

If above normal profits persist, in the long run there must be some barrier that prevents the entry of new competitive firms.[1] The barriers can, of course, be artificial but they can also be natural.[2] For example, indivisibilities in distribution yield natural monopolies in the public utilities industries. Railroads at times are characterized by a similar, but not quite identical, indivisibility, and that indivisibility lies rooted in the spatial distribution of the market for railroad services. To understand this point better, let us examine the market for railroad services in more detail.

Assume that a firm's production function is subject to increasing returns over some range of output. In the railroad case, once a right-of-way has been cleared and rails laid there are falling long-run average costs up to the capacity level of the road bed – i.e. the road bed is indivisible in the economist's terms. In addition, assume that a railroad will draw trade from an area thirty-five to forty miles on each side of its tracks.[3] Finally, assume that the population density of the seventy to eighty mile band generates enough traffic to support one railroad operating at the low point on its cost curve but not two operating at that level.[4] If these conditions hold, a region may appear an attractive area for railroad investment, and if there is only one railroad that firm could earn monopoly (above normal) profits. However, as soon as one line is built, the existence of even monopoly profits will not induce further entry since a second line cannot expect to earn even normal profits.[5] It is also possible that the spatial distribution of economic activity will yield a mixed solution. Consider the case of railroads connecting two important economic centers (New York and Chicago, for example) but passing en route through relatively sparsely populated areas. In this case, several railroads may find it profitable to compete for the trade in the heavy traffic generating area, but they then find it uneconomic (for the reasons cited above) to compete for trade in other areas. They therefore choose

[1] A normal profit is defined as the return a businessman can earn in his next best alternative. An above normal profit is a level of profits in excess of these earnings.
[2] A patent is an example of an artificial barrier.
[3] Studies in the pre-truck era suggest these figures are approximately correct for farm produce.
[4] One railroad can achieve the economies of scale, but the second would have to operate at much higher costs and could not survive.
[5] More specifically, there will be a tendency for above normal profits to exist in the long run any time there is an indivisibility such that total sectorial revenue when divided among the existing firms yields for each firm an average revenue that is greater than average cost, but the same total revenue when divided among the existing firms plus one yields to each an average revenue less than average cost. In the case of railroads (or for that matter canals) the number of 'existing' firms is likely to be one.

different routes between the centers. This mixed case is, in fact, the basis for the long- and short-haul controversy that was so important to the Grangers and Populists in the last quarter of the nineteenth century.[1]

In addition, assume that railroads represented the least expensive transport alternative and that agriculture must move its products if it is to survive, but that the railroads find it impossible to charge different prices to different shippers for sending the same commodities over the same routes. It follows then, that land values will reflect the distance from the particular farm to the nearest railroad station. The land nearest the railroad will accrue a locational rent on each unit of output equal to the cost of wagon transport for that unit from the most distant point in that transportation market to the railroad. The prices received by the most distant farms must, in the long run, be sufficient to cover their costs of production plus the cost of transport to the market. Since the price at which the product is sold must be the same for all farmers, the farms nearest the railroad receive a price that is above their costs of production plus their railroad and handling charges by the amount of the wagon transport cost.[2] As one moves away from the railroad, locational rents will gradually decline until they reach zero at the farthest point served by the railroad. The capitalized value of these rents will, of course, constitute a part of the price of the land, if the landowners are able to capture them.[3]

A similar analysis can be applied to urban land insofar as that land utilizes the services of transport, and it becomes particularly relevant if the urban center is a commercial entrepôt for an agricultural region. In this latter case, the price of land will reflect the demand for certain activities which are tied to the railroads by elements of joint cost. It is cheaper, for example, to locate a grain elevator near a railhead, since any other location would involve a double handling of the grain. Thus, both farm and urban land values are tied to the proximity of that land to a railroad. Potential transport-engendered increments to the value of land are a source of profits. To capture them a

---

[1] The railroads faced highly elastic demand curves for long-haul transport – that is, any small price change would cause customers to shift from one railroad to another and produce very large changes in revenue to the railroad that changed its prices – that is, where the competition was – but much less elastic demand for short-haul since there were no alternative transport methods to which the customers could shift. Profit maximization, since discrimination was possible, then dictated higher prices in the less elastic and lower prices in the more elastic market. Or in the former terms, higher prices for short hauls and lower prices for long.

[2] That difference is said to be the locational rent – it is an extra profit that accrues to the farm merely because it is located near the railroad.

[3] The rents are a stream of income, but their present value (and it is the present value that should be reflected in the price of the land with the desirable location) is equal to the discounted stream of that future income. The process of discounting (computing present value) is called capitalization.

landowner need only induce a railroad to build its right-of-way near his land, or the railroad need only await the landowner's bribes. For either to happen, however, required arrangemental innovation.

Given these potential profits and the natural barrier that prohibits the entry of a second railroad into a band some seventy to eighty miles wide, it follows that any landowner would like to see the railroad located near his (as opposed to someone else's) holdings. At the same time, while landholders tended to be unorganized (and in fact the nature of the profits made organization extremely difficult), the railroad management was in a strong monopoly position. Despite their great bargaining strength, however, without some reorganization the railroads also found it difficult to capture the profits inherent in the increase in land values. Landowners were numerous and the administrative costs of negotiating with each was high. Moreover, since land values were tied to land ownership, it would pay any owner to let his neighbor bribe the railroad and for him therefore to accrue to the locational rents without cost. Some form of reorganization was profitable, and since it was often necessary to coerce each landowner to participate, primary reliance was most often placed on the government.

Typically, the government of a city or county raised tax revenues and used these funds to entice the management of a railroad to build their line through that political unit. Because funds were raised through taxes, there were no free rides; administratively the railroad had to deal with only one organization, so organizational costs must have been reduced; and, perhaps, since the landowners presented a common front to the railroad, their bargaining strength may have been enhanced.[1]

That these reorganizations were profitable can be readily deduced from the history of midwestern railroads in the 1870s and '80s. A town like Galina, Illinois, for example, an important entrepôt in the pre-railway age, lost its position because it refused to subsidize railroad construction and the road was built some distance away. Again, an attempt to explain the location of railroads in Jay Gould's western empire would turn any economist's hair grey if his only analytical tool were distance minimization, traffic generative abilities, or any other twentieth century criterion. Instead, the location of those roads, twisting and turning across the plains like a terrified snake, can only be explained in terms of the bribes certain towns and counties were willing to pay. Reorganization brought a redistribution of incomes, and

---

[1] We know little about bargaining theory; however, what little we do know suggests that this third alternative is unlikely. The railroad would likely be bargaining with three or four political units, and since there was little payoff from collusion between competing cities, the road would probably receive something close to the bribe that they would have managed had they dealt with a very large number of bidders.

the arrangemental form of that reorganization was a resurgence of local 'aid' to railroads.

A second and related source of potential profits lay in an arrangemental reorganization that could (by redistributing profits from landholders to the railways) induce new railroads to enter a given market despite the barrier of an indivisible roadbed. Thus, a city that had been bypassed by the existing transport network could (if conditions were right) underwrite a portion of the costs of a new road and expect that expenditure would be recaptured in terms of increased land values. While it would not pay a railroad to build a competitive line if their profits were limited to freight and passenger earnings, it might become profitable if they were allowed to accrue a share of the social profits that otherwise would have gone to landowners.[1]

Among the best examples of such an arrangemental innovation was the contract negotiated between the city of Cincinnati and the Cincinnati Southern Railroad in the late 1860s. The Queen city found itself suffering economically from the absence of a railroad link to the South. The Mobile and Ohio had passed through Louisville, and the city was reaping the benefits of the southern trade. To induce another road to build from the Ohio to the Gulf, Cincinnati agreed to underwrite a share of the construction costs with an $18.3 million loan. The money itself was raised from city taxes, and although a portion of it was repaid from railroad profits, a part of it was not. However, the road (343 miles long) provided a viable link to the South, and the resulting increase in land prices certainly more than offset the subsidy. In this case too, an arrangemental reorganization allowed one city to take some profits that without the innovation would have accrued to another. In this instance, however, it is possible that there may have been some increase in total income as well as a redistribution of that income.

Finally, the possibility of transport induced increases in land values was discovered by the residents of some areas where traffic was insufficient to support even a single road. Without a railroad, residents found themselves cut off from the rapidly growing national market, and despite the unpromising economics, they often agitated for some kind of transport link.[2] Local subsidies were useless since the costs far exceeded any potential revenues, and in these circumstances the residents ofttime turned to the state legislature, since it is always possible that an organized and passionate minority can accomplish by political means what they could not effect through the market place.

[1] Redistribution through some new institution can substitute in part for the inability of the railroad to practice perfect price discrimination.
[2] As one student of twentieth century transport problems has argued, 'Every American thinks it is his God given right to be served by a railroad.'

Although there were numerous examples of these political subsidies in the last quarter of the nineteenth century, the general experience is probably typified by the state of Massachusetts' support for the Troy and Greenfield Railroad. Over the years from 1860 to 1873 the state advanced some $18.5 millions to the project, and of this some $9.5 million constituted pure political subsidy. As an economic activity, the railroad was never profitable, but it did generate some additional income for the residents of northwestern Massachusetts. Thus, arrangemental reorganization through the intervention of government induced a redistribution of income from the average Massachusetts taxpayer to the residents of the state's northwest corner. In some sense, one might view these transfers as early precursors of the current distressed areas programs.

(VII) From warring oligopolies, to pools, to federal cartels[1]

As we have seen, the post-bellum decades saw not only the penetration of the railroads into the trans-Mississippi West, but also a fleshing out of the skeletal network in the East and in the old Northwest Territory. In 1860 only two rail links connected Chicago with the East, but by the 1880s the number had risen to six. In addition, there were a number of other less direct routes which, if not integrated, would still allow a steer to travel by boxcar from the Great Lakes to an eastern port city. Between the East and Chicago, however, the routes were widely separate. The direct routes, for example, ranged from the Grand Trunk Western in Canada to the Baltimore and Ohio in the South, and each had a monopoly position in many of the local areas through which it passed. They were, however, directly competitive in the Atlantic–Chicago traffic. Moreover, except during the winter months, they competed not only with each other, but with the Great Lakes–Erie Canal water route as well.

Faced with a highly elastic demand (because of the existence of close substitutes) in the long-distance market and much less elastic demands in the local markets, the railroads pursued an active policy of price discrimination. The results were high charges for local and low charges for through traffic (i.e. the long- and short-haul problem). At the same time, the problem was further exasperated by the bulky nature of most West to East freight and the high value low bulk character of East to West shipments. Since more capacity was required for the former, empty boxcars tended to pile up in the

---

[1] The theory in this section as well as the historical descriptions for the period 1870–96 are drawn from P. MacAvoy, *The Economic Effects of Regulation* (Cambridge, Mass., 1965). Historical descriptions of the impact of regulation in the later period are from G. Kolko, *Railroads and Regulation* (Princeton, N.J., 1965); D. P. Locklin, *Economics of Transportation* (Homewood, Ill., 1954); and J. Meyer, *et al.*, *Competition in the Transportation Industry* (Cambridge, Mass., 1959).

The theory applied

East. This excess capacity acted to force the price of through East to West service down even further. Although the example may be extreme, freight charges for through haulage from Boston to Detroit via Vermont were lower than the rates charged for local traffic from Boston to Vermont.

Given the fact that the first East–West lines had exercised a monopoly position in both local and through service, it is not surprising that as competition increased their management began to search for some institutional rearrangement that would allow them to recapture the profits of the 'good old days'. Once again, here was an opportunity to increase railroad profits by transferring income from shippers and consumers to the railroad if some new institutional arrangement could be innovated. These potential profits, of course, did not represent any net gain to society but merely a redistribution from one sector to another.

The 1870s were marked by a number of attempts by the railroads to arrive at some collusive agreement (a *voluntary* cooperative solution) to set prices and divide the market. In each case, the agreement was designed to maximize the total profits earned by all the railroads. A price–quantity decision that maximizes industry profits, however, may not maximize profits for each firm. A single firm can increase its share of the market by cutting price as long as the rest of the firms in the cartel do not retaliate. Again, an individual firm might find that a price cut (real or threatened) would improve its bargaining position within the cartel and force the others to give it a larger share of the traffic. When either situation existed, there was intense economic pressure on every firm in the cartel to break the agreement, and firms frequently gave in to that pressure. As Professor MacAvoy has shown, throughout the 1870s price cutters were able to make substantial profits at the expense of firms that remained loyal to the cartel.

As a result, the collusive agreements, although numerous, were short-lived and frequently unhonored even while supposedly alive. The initial agreement was made in 1871 when only three routes connected Chicago with the coast. Because of the small number of firms, this agreement worked fairly satisfactorily until 1874. In that year, however, a fourth East–West link (the Baltimore and Ohio) was completed, and the new road's management did little to stabilize the cartel. Initially, they refused to participate, and when finally they did agree, they accepted membership only because the information gained through membership made it possible for them to undercut the agreement more easily. The result was a breakdown of the voluntary cooperative organization and a return to independent rate setting. The railroads lost and the consumers and shippers gained.[1]

[1] It is interesting to note that the breakdown of the agreement as the number of competitors rose from three to four duplicates exactly the findings of Professor Vernon Smith

158

The failure of the voluntary cooperative arrangement touched off a series of rate wars, and these were costly enough to encourage a new attempt at voluntary organization in 1880. The experiment of 1871 had been highly informal, and its failure convinced the railroads that the cartel arrangement must be formalized and the organization given some weapons to use against disloyal firms. In line with these observations, the new cartel was designed to include a formal executive committee with powers to adjust rates and a revenue pooling arrangement aimed at preventing any single railroad from getting more than its share of traffic. Even with these innovations, however, the organization was far from perfect. There were continual arguments with members over traffic shares and with independents who violated the agreement, but it did manage to maintain some semblance of a cartel rate structure through 1882 and 1883. However, it collapsed the next year when two new railroads reached Chicago and the cartel's executive committee discovered that while it could assess penalties it could not collect them. Again the inherent weakness of a voluntary organization without coercive powers had been demonstrated, and although there were further attempts to reestablish the cartel arrangement, they were uniformly marked by failure.

New institutional arrangements were required if the railroads were to effect the recapture of the income that had been drifting to shippers and consumers. In this instance the innovation came from outside the railroad industry, and the railroad managers were relatively slow to realize its relevance to their problem. The railroad managers were not alone in their concern about rates in the 1870s and '80s. While they felt long-distance rates had fallen too low, the farmers who used the railroads thought the rates were both too high and overly discriminatory. In 1870 there were some 6.8 million farmers, and with any large group organization is a problem. The 1870s saw a new institution (the Grange) innovated for social purposes; however, once organized it began to assume economic as well as social functions.[1] The Grange became a base for political action at the local and state levels, and it was from this base that the drive for government railroad

---

in his experimental studies of oligopoly behavior. These results suggest that if information flows are quite complete and there are no more than three firms it is possible for a voluntary cartel to reach an industry-wide profit maximizing set of price–output decisions. Further, however, they indicate that it is not possible to achieve a stable monopoly solution if the number of firms is increased to four or more. While it is highly likely that the agreement between experiment and history is in part accidental (it is hard to believe that there is anything magic in the numbers three and four), it does tend to confirm the conclusions we have drawn from history.

[1] For a more thorough discussion of the innovation of the Grange, see the discussion in Chapter 5.

The theory applied

regulation was launched. In this activity the farmers were supported by urban shippers who were also concerned about railroad rates. Even after the Grange had lost its vitality, the impetus towards regulation remained strong, and during the late '70s and early '80s regulatory laws were passed by a number of farm states. In the mid-'80s the Supreme Court emasculated state regulation and the political arena shifted from the state to the federal level. The movement culminated in 1887 with the passage of the Interstate Commerce Act, an act that almost all railroad managers bitterly opposed. Expectations aside, experience proved that the law gave the railroads an institutional arrangement capable of effecting cartel decisions. As a result, within ten years the most foresighted of the interregional railroad managers became the most avid spokesmen for strong regulation. The Act (a new institutional arrangement) gave the Interstate Commerce Commission (a secondary action group) legal coercive powers that made it possible for the commission to enforce cartel decisions or at least to punish the disloyal.

As originally organized, the ICC did not have rate-making powers, but it was charged with examining existing rates for 'equity and the absence of discrimination'. The commission's power of subpoena permitted them to investigate the existing rate structures (published or secret) and, in line with their charge, they established legal guidelines for 'just and reasonable' rates. Of these guidelines, two became effective mechanisms for cartel control of long-distance hauling. The commission required that all rates be made public. This action drastically reduced the time that any disloyal member could expect to profit from rate cutting before facing the retribution of the other members of the cartel. In addition, they held that a 'just and reasonable' tariff had to apply to all (not just long-distance) rates, and any change in that tariff had to be permanent. The first of these restrictions made it impossible for a railroad to price its long-distance service (where it was faced by competition) at competitive rates while maintaining monopoly pricing over its local traffic. Moreover, it almost guaranteed that it would be the monopoly rather than the competitive price that the railroad would choose when it had to select a single rate for both local and long-distance movements. The second restriction greatly increased the costs attached to rate cuts aimed at increasing one road's bargaining position within the cartel. Any railroad that initiated such a cut would likely find itself permanently stuck with the lower 'wartime' rates.

With the support of the coercive investigatory and regulatory powers of the commission, voluntary cooperative cartels flourished from 1887 to 1894. Although there were a few deviations from the cartel price and market allocations, they were temporary and were easily controlled. It came, therefore, as something of a shock to the management of the interregional rail-

160

roads when in 1894 the Supreme Court began to attack the ICC's investigatory and rate-making power. The first assaults were not fatal, but they
tended to de-stabilize the cartel. Finally, the courts in 1897 stripped the
commission of most of its powers, and the cartel broke down as it had done
in the 1870s and again in the 1880s. The rate wars resumed, and a segment
of management became convinced that more federal regulation was necessary.

While the number of 'enlightened' railroad managers who in the '90s
recognized the desirability of further regulation probably did not represent
more than a substantial minority of all management, that minority included
some of the industry's most important leaders.[1] Moreover, the size of the
group steadily increased as more and more of the railroads' managers
recognized the costs (to the railroads) of an unregulated industry. Possibly
by 1914, and certainly by 1920, the minority had become a substantial
majority.

It was this 'enlightened' group of railroad managers who guided the
Elkins Act through Congress in 1903. The law itself was in large part
written by the railroad lobby, and its aim was to outlaw discriminatory
tariffs and departures from published rate structures. In short, it was an
attempt to reestablish the government supported cartel that had worked so
well from 1887 to 1894. It was, moreover, the first of a series of legislation
that was ultimately to make the cartel invulnerable to attacks by disloyal
members.

Three years after the Elkins Act, the Hepburn Act, second in this series of
laws, was passed. The latter piece of legislation required that any railroad
contemplating a rate change notify the commission before it effected the
change. This requirement reduced to zero the time a disloyal member could
expect to benefit from a reduction in rates. In addition, the Hepburn Act
further strengthened the prohibitions against rate discrimination, and as a
result it reinforced the movement of long-distance rates toward the monopoly
levels charged on the local portions of the lines.

Not all railroad leaders supported the Hepburn Act, and even those who
did must have realized that entry into the political arena (particularly when
the arena is close to the electoral process) carries with it the potential cost of
unwanted regulation. In this instance, the commission was given the power
to set maximum as well as minimum rates, and the railroads were not happy
with that inclusion. On net, however, the act strengthened the interregional
cartels.

Additional reinforcement was produced by the Mann–Elkins Act, the
last piece of railroad legislation passed during the first decade of the twentieth

---

[1] It included, for example, Edward H. Harriman, at that time probably the most respected
railroad magnate.

century. No longer could the individual roads decide whether or not their long and short hauls were marked by 'substantially similar circumstances and conditions'. Moreover, the law further diminished the ability of an individual railroad to initiate rate changes. It gave the ICC the power to suspend such changes for 120 days while the commission attempted to discover if the change was 'justified'.

The ultimate triumph of reorganization through government sponsored cartelization, however, awaited the end of World War I and the Transportation Act of 1920. Until then, despite the obvious cartel strengthening implications of the laws, the publicly announced goal of all regulation was the maintenance of competition in the railroad sector. In 1920 that myth was officially abandoned, and effective cartelization adopted as the goal of public policy. Not only was the ICC given extensive rate-making power, but the concept of a 'fair' return (to which every road was entitled) became embedded in the regulatory legislation. Pooling of earnings was explicitly permitted, and any railroad whose revenues declined because of competitive pressures was permitted to recapture its lost profits from its 'unfair' competitor. Finally, the commission was empowered to set minimum as well as maximum rates, and any road that attempted to undercut the minimum was subject to legal prosecution.

Only one step remained, and even it was already half taken. The railroads, of course, wanted to set the level of 'justified' rates, and some arrangemental innovation was needed to formalize that procedure. During the period of stability under the original ICC Act, rates had been set by cooperative tariff associations; and the court rulings that curbed the powers of the commission did not break up these rate-making groups. As time passed, the associations' procedures became formalized, and the commission tended to listen more and more to their advice. By the 1920s, these associations provided an excellent example of a voluntary cooperative organization that made decisions and a government supported secondary action group that used its coercive legal powers to effect those decisions. After the give and take of political bargaining within a committee, the association suggested a rate schedule to the ICC. That group then made the suggested rates legal ones. Since the 1920s the procedure has become even more formalized and further insulated from attack. For example, the Reed–Bulwinkle Act of 1948 explicitly legalizes the rate-making bureaus and exempts them from prosecution under the anti-trust laws.

(VIII) Organizational response to external competition

Thus far we have examined the organizational response to intra-technological competition, but increasingly after the 1920s the railroads have been faced with inter-technological competition. Although they have attempted to meet that threat by arrangemental reorganization, their institutional innovations in this area have proved much less effective. The new competition has come from autos and airplanes in the passenger market and from trucks in the freight market; and the relatively ineffectual response of the railroads suggests something about the nature of arrangemental change. Faced by the three challenges, the railroads were least effective in their attempts to deal with autos, only slightly effective in the case of airplanes, and most (but still not very) effective in the case of trucks.

Although it now appears that there may well be externalities associated with the operation of autos (smog, to name one), this conclusion was certainly not clear at an earlier date. Moreover, since to the average individual the private revenues from operations appear far to exceed their cost, the automobile was quickly innovated once its price had fallen from the previously prohibitive level. Registrations rose from fewer than 10,000 at the turn of the century to more than 20 million twenty-five years later. Moreover, at the time of most rapid consumer acceptance, autos provided little competition for intercity passenger service. As a result, while it might have been possible for the railroads to effect some control in the first decades of the century, by the time they recognized the competitive threat, the political pressure of the unorganized but highly vocal auto owners was already too strong. So strong, in fact, that the owners have been able to effect substantial federal subsidization of intercity motor transportation – first, in the form of paved federal roads, and more recently, in the form of limited access super highways. As late as the 1930s it was not possible to drive completely across the United States on a paved highway; it soon will be possible to make that trip without stopping for a traffic control device. Once again, it appears that a passionate majority can almost always effect its decisions through the political process.

In the case of the airlines, the regulatory cartel organization has carried over, but the railroads have been unable to prevent the loss of the lion's share of intercity public passenger service. Not only is cartelization enforced by government fiat typical of airline rate making, but also the airlines were able to lean on federal subsidies to underwrite their development. Despite their initial position of political advantage, the railroads have not been able to halt the competitive inroads of the airlines. This failure suggests that it is very difficult to prevent competition through arrangemental reorganization when the competitive form is technically far superior to the existing mode of production.

The airlines, however, have adopted the arrangements first innovated by the railroads to provide protection against intra-technological competition.

163

The theory applied

While the experience in the railroad regulation certainly reduced the gestation period of the innovation, other conditions have limited its effectiveness. Entry into the air passenger industry is much easier than entry into the rail passenger business and the potential forms of competition are greater (you can charter any of a number of airplanes but there is only the one railroad right-of-way). As a result, cartelization through regulation has been less profitable. Rates are probably above the level that would prevail in the absence of regulation, but continual undercutting in terms of service and competition from unregulated carriers have almost certainly reduced them below the industry profit maximizing level.

Finally, in the case of trucking, the railroads have been able to bring interstate carriers under ICC regulations, and, as a result, they have provided themselves with some protection from this form of competitive pressure. Most of the investment in the trucking industry is governmentally financed (the highways), and the minimum efficient firm size is apparently quite small (one truck and one driver). As a result, the existence of unregulated contract carriers has badly undercut the cartel's ability to maintain prices. Today, despite the government's coercive power, the railroads are able to maintain their monopoly position only on those commodity routes where they still have a substantial technological advantage – very long hauls of high bulk low value products. The history of the railroads' attempts at cartelization underline two important conclusions: competition can come either from inside or outside a given technology; and even with government support it is almost impossible to maintain a cartel position if the government cannot prevent entry.

(IX) Conclusions

The history of the transport sector underscores at least one characteristic of arrangemental change. Although the process of change is by its very nature dynamic, it is easy to slip into the conclusion that once institutional arrangements have adjusted, the process of change comes to a halt. The model we have employed to explain arrangemental adjustment tends to reinforce this conclusion. The model is a long-run comparative static one, where the time period is determined not by the life of the physical capital but by the period of gestation of the new arrangement. Like all comparative static models, the system allows one to trace out the impact of some external change (i.e. in prices, demand, or technology) on the arrangemental structure. One should not, however, forget that there is no reason to assume that over time there is only one disequilibrating external shock. In fact, the opposite is most likely the case, and far better than any other sector, the history of transport underscores the continuous nature of arrangemental change.

A second characteristic of arrangemental adjustment can be drawn from the discussion of the role of government arrangements in the process of income redistribution. The history of the transport system emphasizes the potential instability and costs to the economic units of government dictated solutions when the government arrangement is not insulated from the electoral process. The political reaction against financial subsidies in the 1840s and against the land grants in the 1870s both engendered drastic institutional rearrangements. From the point of view of society, external changes sufficient to minimize the costs of this political action had already occurred, but the political reaction did effect an income redistribution and it is clear that the transport companies suffered. On the other hand, the Inter-state Commerce Commission, because of its insulation from the electoral process, provided a much more 'stable' institutional arrangement from the point of view of the railroads. As a result, the railroads prefer to deal with the ICC, just as the managers of the financial sector are happier with the rules laid down by the Federal Reserve Board or by the Comptroller of the Currency than they are by legislation introduced by Wright Patman. It is, however, less clear that divorce from the electoral process represents a superior form of arrangement from society's point of view.

The final question can still not be answered fully, but it appears to be of primary importance if we wish to understand arrangemental change. Why has transport so frequently turned to the government for its arrangemental innovations? The answer to this question should yield some important clues as to the nature and timing of arrangemental changes; unfortunately, at this time, we can only offer a series of very tentative hypotheses. The first involves the relationship between industry and the economy; the second lies in the nature of property rights and the relative amount of the three factors and production (land, labor, and capital) used by the industry; and the third arises from the structure of costs and the technological developments of the industry itself.

Without adequate transport, no economic specialization is possible. As a result, the transport industry has an impact on the economy far greater than its share of Gross National Product.[1] Not only would few economists in the 1970s fail to recognize this importance, but it was equally clear to farmers 150 years earlier. This realization may make the average citizen far more ready to utilize the government than they otherwise would be, and it may

---

[1] As we have seen, if railroads could practice perfect price discrimination, they could then capture all locational rent as well as the other revenues that are external to them. In this case, their share of the GNP would better represent their contribution.

The theory applied

well explain the differential impact of Upton Sinclair's *The Jungle* and Frank Norris' *The Octopus* on the organization of economic activity.

A second partial explanation of the preponderance of government arrangements in transport history lies in the intimate connection between transportation, right-of-way, and property rights. A typical business uses relatively little land, and questions of property acquisition are usually unimportant. In the case of canals, railroads, or even highways, land is a very important input. For the western railroads built through unoccupied government land, at minimum some agreement between the private firm and the government was necessary. In the case of passage through already settled areas, the problems of acquisition are even more complex and frequently depend on the coercive powers of the government for a solution. Once property rights have been vested, every owner has a potential veto of the transport route, and it is, therefore, unlikely that the land could be acquired by private individuals or by any voluntary cooperative group without paying a monopoly price to each owner or without long delays. The exercise of the government's coercive power of eminent domain is required, but dependence implies a close tie between the transport firm and the wielder of that power.

Finally, the technology of the industry made price stabilization difficult through any form of private cooperative arrangement. Given the industry's high capital–output ratio and the highly specialized and long life of its capital, marginal cost is fairly constant and average variable cost lies well below average total cost.[1] There is, as a result, great pressure to cut prices in order to earn any return over variable costs in periods of less than full utilization. This tendency, as we have seen, is reinforced by the continual stockpiling of transport capacity in the East – the result of the composition of commodities hauled in the two directions. Taken together, private cartels are unstable, but cartels backed by the coercive power of government could yield substantial redistributive profits.[2]

---

[1] The life of a railroad right-of-way, for example, is almost infinite and it has few other uses. In 1900 Andrew Carnegie began to build a railroad from Pittsburgh to Philadelphia in competition with the Pennsylvania. The organization of U.S. Steel brought a halt to the project (in fact stopping the road was one of the prime motives for the organization) and the right of way stood useless and undepreciated until the Pennsylvania turnpike was built some forty years later.

[2] As a final comment, it is interesting to note that, despite the absence of any pressing military or purely political reasons for the development of the transport network, the industry's history has almost been as dominated by government regulation as the history of transportation in any European country where military and political considerations have been paramount.

CHAPTER 8

ECONOMIES OF SCALE, UNSUCCESSFUL CARTELIZATION, AND EXTERNAL COSTS: SOME SIDELIGHTS ON THE GROWTH OF MANUFACTURING IN THE UNITED STATES

(I) Introduction

The years from 1790 to 1930 underwrote not only a vast increase in the absolute level of manufacturing output, but also a six-fold relative increase. Textbooks discuss the growth of the economy in terms of the 'rise of big business', and they mean 'big manufacturing business'. Moreover, while the country has produced many famous men, it is the Rockefellers, the Carnegies, and the Fords – businessmen associated with the manufacturing sector – who are most often chosen to typify the nation in the period 1850–1929. Despite the importance of the growth of the new manufacturing industries to the development of modern America, arrangemental innovation has played a relatively small role.

Over the past two hundred years arrangemental innovation in the manufacturing sector has been largely limited to attempts to capture profits arising from four sources:

(1) those inherent in the technical economies of scale that characterized much of the new manufacturing technology that emerged;

(2) those that could be realized from the innovation of a mechanism that could effectively cartelize the large oligopolistic industries;

(3) those that could be accrued to the manufacturing sector if that sector could be protected from foreign competition;

(4) those that would be realized if the manufacturing sector could be forced to recognize certain external costs of their production decisions.

Even in these relatively limited areas, however, arrangemental innovations have proved far from a universal success – particularly if success is measured

167

The theory applied

by increases in total income. Of the four, in only the first case did innovation lead with certainty to greater total income. In the other three, income may have been increased by innovation in one area, but in the other two it certainly led (when successful) only to redistribution. Moreover, in each of those latter three areas, history has been marked by almost as many unsuccessful as successful arrangemental innovations.

(II) Economies of scale and the corporate form

In the case of the transportation industry, as we have seen, economies of scale, coupled with severe limitations on the amount of capital that could be raised by partnerships and sole proprietorships, generated economic pressure for the innovation of the corporation. In that instance the pressure was so great that it paid to innovate even during a period when corporate charters could be obtained only through special act of the legislature (i.e. the potential revenues were so high that the innovation was profitable even when the legal structure made organizational costs very high). In the case of manufacturing, with a few notable exceptions, the pressures were not so great in the early period, and general innovation awaited a decline in organizational costs (the decline came with the passage of general incorporation laws) and sometimes even longer. The suggestions are two-fold. First, a steady stream of small profits from corporate organization made it economic to lobby for revisions in the corporation laws rather than to achieve immediate incorporation by paying a large initial amount.[1] Second, for many manufacturing activities, the gains from larger size were insufficient to make innovation profitable until late in the nineteenth century.

This latter proposition does not necessarily imply that there were *no* economies of scale in these branches of manufacturing. Oliver Evans, for example, in the late eighteenth century designed a flour mill that was the

---

[1] Going back to our investment model (see Chapter 7), we find that the firm faced by small positive expected revenues in each of n years (where n is very large) finds that it is not worth some lump sum payment K in year o to realize those revenues because their values in years far removed are discounted to near zero present value. It is, however, perhaps profitable to expend small sums (k) in each of the several years to achieve the same end. Given appropriate values of i and R, this result can follow even if $\sum_{i=0}^{i=n} k_i > K$ (as long as $K > k_1$).

$$K - R_1/(1 + i) + R_2/(1 + i)^2 + \cdots + R_n/(1 + i)^n < 0 \qquad (1)$$

but

$$-k_1/(1 + i) - k_2/(1 + i)^2 + \cdots + \frac{R_d - k_d}{(1 + i)^d} + \cdots + \frac{R_n}{(1 + i)^n} > 0 \qquad (2)$$

where $R_1 = R_2 = R_d = R_n$.

168

prototype of modern assembly line technology, and there were certainly economies of scale inherent in his design. Those economies, however, since they could be realized by a mill that was not beyond the resources of a typical miller, were insufficient to induce a reorganization of existing arrangements. Over a hundred years later, with the passage of general incorporation acts, the introduction of Hungarian reduction milling (a technique subject to much greater economies of scale) and substantial improvements in the market for private industrial securities, organizational innovation finally became profitable. Although this case is probably extreme, a somewhat similar situation appears to have characterized much of American manufacturing until the last quarter of the nineteenth century.

The most important exception was the low-count cotton textile industry. There, by 1813, the experience of the Boston Manufacturing Company with integrated operations had shown that there were substantial economies of scale over wide ranges of output. The Waltham mill dwarfed the small unintegrated companies in Rhode Island, and within a very few years it, in turn, was dwarfed by the 'giants' in Lowell, Lawrence, and Nashua. By the middle of the nineteenth century, there were textile mills with total assets exceeding two-and-a-half million dollars and these mills had been underwritten by initial equity issues in excess of one million dollars.[1] Although these sums would be considered small today, they were very large in terms of the usual demands placed on the capital markets by nineteenth century manufacturing firms. Moreover, they were much too large for any individual or small consortium to supply. As a result, exploitation of the scale economies required corporate organization in order to protect investors from the unlimited liability imposed on the owners of firms organized along alternative lines. The revenues from corporate organization were very high despite the fact that the gains from divisibility and liquidity – usually important sources of profits from the innovation of the corporate form since they make financial investment attractive – were almost certainly very low in this instance.[2] It appears, therefore, that the benefits of unlimited liability alone were sufficient to make the innovation profitable even though the

---

[1] In addition, the mills were heavy borrowers of long-term capital, and it appears unlikely that they could have commanded even these loan resources had they not been organized as corporations.

[2] Ownership was very tightly held, individual investments were very high, and the shares were seldom traded through the formal markets. The typical investor put up about $13,000 of the average $650,000 of initial equity capital, and, once purchased, these shares were very seldom sold. An examination of a number of 'New England' mills shows that shares changed hands almost solely through estate distribution, and the chronicler of the Boston stock exchange warns his readers against putting too much reliance on his price quotations because of the extreme thinness of the market.

The theory applied

promoters had to rely on special acts of charter. Generalization is, however, certainly unwarranted. The textile promoters had special characteristics that must have made their cost–revenue calculations differ substantially from those made by any other set of potential entrepreneurs.

The cotton textile industry in Massachusetts was promoted (and its equity underwritten) by a group of persons who were drawn from (or perhaps constituted is a better term) that state's economic, social, *and political* elite. In a period of restricted franchise, the political power of this group was immense, and a special legislative act was to them probably no more expensive than general incorporation half a century later. It is interesting to speculate about what the history of the industry would have been had it been promoted by groups not so fully in command of the political process. The actual history, however, underscores again certain earlier conclusions: the cost of political action is a function (among other things) of the initial political strength of the decision-making group; and organization through the political process is more likely the lower are the costs of such action to the decision makers.

The rest of the manufacturing sector had a much different technical (and, as a result, arrangemental) history. Although there is no exhaustive empirical evidence, what there is suggests that until the 1870s most of the important industries were subject to constant returns to scale. In milling there were large firms (in Richmond, Virginia, and Rochester, New York, for example) but above some relatively small size, a large mill was nothing but several small mills. Thus, while they could produce more flour than the small mills, the costs per barrel were equivalent. In pig iron production there were a few large firms (Brady's Bend is an example), but there were no important cost advantages from such organization. Finally, in petroleum refining, large firms merely duplicated several times the facilities of the small firms. Moreover, certain industries (meat packing, for example) were subject to some substantial returns of scale, but the limitations placed on the size of the market by the high transport costs precluded the realization of these economies regardless of the organizational arrangement. As a result, the United States at the end of the Civil War was still a nation of small manufacturing firms.

The next decade saw substantial changes. Developments in transport turned the region east of the Mississippi into a single market for most commodities and integrated at least a portion of the trans-Mississippi West (Minnesota, Iowa, and eastern Kansas and Nebraska) into this now near-national market. At the same time, major technical breakthroughs were achieved in several important industries, and the new techniques were subject to increasing returns over wide ranges of output. In steel, for example, the Bessemer process was widely innovated, in petroleum, new sophisticated methods of fractional distillation were applied, and in milling, Hungarian reduction techniques were widely used in the new mills of the Upper Midwest.[1] All were subject to substantial scale economies.

The average size of a firm grew substantially as new plants and mills, designed to realize these economies of scale and to serve the 'national market', came into production. The formal capital markets could still not provide the initial capitalization for many of these enterprises, but even the capitalist who invested through some informal market wanted to limit his maximum loss. It was, therefore, not uncommon for a firm to incorporate even if its stock was not traded on the open market. Limited liability was important, and even closely held enterprises could benefit from infinite life. For example, while the McCormick Reaper Company did not 'go public' until the early twentieth century, its managers opted for corporate organization nearly a half century earlier. Given general incorporation laws, it was often profitable to seek incorporation even though the innovation of that arrangement did not yet provide the additional financial benefits of divisibility and liquidity.

Given substantial economies of scale and the high costs of corporate innovation under special corporation laws, there was great economic – translated into political – pressure for legal change. The first general incorporation law for manufacturing firms was passed in New York in 1811, but this act was an exception to the general rule. Typically, general incorporation laws were a product of the years after 1845, and the movement was largely completed by the late 1870s.[2]

Although the relationship is not perfect, there is a significant correlation between the passage of general incorporation laws and the importance of manufacturing in a state's economy. Granted the weakness of the evidence, it appears likely that the potential of scale economies in the new manufacturing technology engendered a potential effort by manufacturers to change the law to make that incorporation less costly. We leave it to the interested political historians to test this tentative hypothesis.

---

[1] The old techniques could not be used to produce usable flour from the soft spring wheats that weather dictated must be planted in the region.

[2] By 1880, outside the South, general incorporation was permitted in all existing states except Delaware and Vermont. In four states (Massachusetts, Connecticut, New Hampshire, and Rhode Island), special incorporation was still possible, but there were provisions for general incorporation as well.

The theory applied

(III) Cartels, trusts, pools, and trade associations: attempts at redistribution through voluntary associations

The experience of the railroads suggested that oligopolistic market structures frequently lead to attempts at cartelization. By such arrangemental innovation the oligopolist tried to recapture income otherwise lost to consumers through price competition. There is certainly some doubt about the structure of American industry in the decades before the Civil War, but the evidence suggests that whatever its character, most industries were not dominated by a few large oligopolies competing for a share of a national market.[1] There does, however, appear to have been a shift towards an oligopolistic market structure in the immediate post-bellum period. Changes in technology increased the average size but reduced the number of firms, while improvements in transportation and communications placed firms as far apart as Boston and Los Angeles in direct competition with each other. By the 1880s, many manufacturing industries were dominated by a number of large firms (seldom less than six or more than two dozen). These industries were subject to continual price wars, and, like the railroad case, prices tended to be forced down to near-competitive levels. As a result, there were substantial profits to be earned by anyone who could successfully cartelize an industry and increase its prices to near-monopoly levels.

As we have seen, collusive decisions reached by some form of voluntary association and not enforced by some coercive power tend to be short-lived. Members may threaten to cut prices to increase their market share – but this is a game that is open to all. Further, an individual firm can increase its profits by secretly cutting prices, if it expects to realize a substantial increase in sales before its actions are exposed and the other members follow suit. The success of a cartel, thus, depends upon the speed with which it discovers and retaliates against price cutters and its ability to utilize what coercive power it has to punish those who violate or threaten to violate the agreement. Speed of action and the existence of coercive power, in turn, depend upon the legal structure and the arrangemental form of the cartel itself.

Under German law, cartel agreements are legally enforceable documents, and any member who violates the agreement can be forced to pay damages. Given this degree of legal protection, voluntary cooperative cartels have

---

[1] Many historians believe that the manufacturing sector was quite competitive, and the evidence on the absence of significant scale economies would tend to confirm that view. On the other hand, some argue that, because of the poor information networks and the lack of an adequate transport network, the economy was characterized by many local monopolies.

172

been effective. In the United States, the legal position of cartel-like arrangements is quite different. In the absence of specific legislation, United States law is based upon English common law, and one strain of common law (a strain dating back to the Middle Ages) makes any agreement in restraint of trade illegal. As a result, collusive agreements could not be enforced in the courts. Without coercion, although there were many attempts at cartelization in the manufacturing sector, most were total failures. The steel rail pools of the 1870s and '8os are good examples of the inherent instability of these cartel arrangements. The pools were institutional attempts to halt competition by informal agreements among producers on prices and quotas. While some signers may have been loyal to the agreement, many saw them only as a device to limit one's competitors' actions. The results were predictable, and the pools short-lived. As Charles Schwab said in commenting on their durability, 'many of them lasted a day, some of them lasted until the gentlemen could go to the telephone from the room in which they were made'.[1] Successful cartelization, at least in manufacturing, demanded more than voluntary agreements.

New institutional arrangements were required. In 1879 John D. Rockefeller, capping his search for an institutional rearrangement that would permit him to control his operating companies more easily, innovated the first industrial trust.[2] It is interesting to note that the Standard Oil Trust, the first, most famous, and the trust whose legal troubles spelled the end for this institutional arrangement, was not a cartel device. The participating companies were controlled by Rockefeller before the innovation. The trust was not a new organizational form, but its application to industrial organization was new. The arrangement had been first employed to help handle the estates of widows and orphans. By placing the trustee between the operating company and the owner, it had allowed the unsophisticated investor to benefit from the gains inherent in equity investment without being burdened by operating decisions. A mutation of this initially philanthropic arrangement had, by the middle of the nineteenth century, gained considerable popularity among railroad operators. The stockholders' voting trust had been widely employed to safeguard corporate control in that industry. It was the stockholders' voting trust that suggested the industrial trust to Rockefeller. The arrangement was simple. The owners of each operating company traded their equity for shares in the trust. Thus, the trust held majority

[1] This quote can be found in B. J. Hendrick, *The Life of Andrew Carnegie* (New York, 1932). It is cited in J. R. T. Hughes, *The Vital Few* (Boston, Mass., 1966), p. 239.
[2] It has been suggested that the industrial trust traces its origins to the 'cost-book' mining company in England, but recent work suggests that while there is some similarity, there is no connection. See D. Dewey, *Monopoly in Economics and Law* (Chicago, 1959).

173

voting rights in the operating companies and the trust's director could determine the policies of those companies. Output and price decisions designed to maximize industry profits could be made, and no one had to fear that some member of the 'cartel' would undercut those decisions. Once innovated, the rate of diffusion was rapid, and the last two decades of the century were marked by the emergence of trust-based cartels in a whole series of industries that had previously been dominated by an intermediate number of large firms. The group included such diverse activities as sugar, whisky, and white lead.

From the point of view of income redistribution, the trust (or one of its mutations) was unquestionably the most effective form of formalized cartelization in the American experience.[1] Moreover, there is little doubt that had the legal 'rules of the game' not been changed, it would still be used today. In 1890, however, Congress passed the Sherman Anti-Trust Act.[2] Although the courts held for a time that manufacturing activities were not subject to federal control, the 1911 decisions in the *Standard Oil* and *American Tobacco* cases outlawed trusts in that sector.[3] Since then, the oligopolistic industries have been forced to turn to other (and largely less efficient) institutional arrangements in their attempts to effect cartel decisions.[4] While the vigor of anti-trust prosecution has varied from administration to administration, it is unlikely that any open trust agreement could long survive.

Adam Smith noted in *The Wealth of Nations* that 'people of the same trade seldom meet together, even for merriment and diversion, but the conversation ends in a conspiracy against the public, or in some contrivance to raise prices'. Probably the most famous and successful of these informal gatherings in American History were the 'Gary' dinners hosted by Elbert

[1] One widely used mutation involved the leasing, on a long-term basis, of the facilities of the operating companies to the central organization. This form was employed in the match and cordage industries. While the legal form is slightly different, the arrangement is essentially the same as the trust.

[2] The trust was an effective income redistributing device, but its very effectiveness induced pressure for counter-innovation. Since the device was a 'legal' one, the attacks were directed along government lines. The pressure from a growing vocal majority who felt they were being 'squeezed' by the device was sufficient to elicit a political response – even though the political mechanism was more sensitive to the pressures of the few than those of the many. The cost of acquiring information about the impact of the trust was much reduced by the widespread sale of books like *The Octopus* and the public reaction to this 'free' information induced both political parties to add 'regulation of the trust' to their platforms.

[3] *Standard Oil Co.* v. *U.S.* (1911); *U.S.* v. *American Tobacco Co.* (1911).

[4] It is interesting to note that the holding company is nothing but a slight mutation of the trust form of organization. Its use, however, has been largely restricted to regulated or non-competing industries and it has had little impact on manufacturing.

Economies of scale, unsuccessful cartelization, external costs

Gary for the executives of the steel industry. Although collusive arrangements were never formally mentioned, by the end of an evening each executive had a good notion of both his market share and the price he should charge. The arrangement lacked a formal structure and it lacked an explicit coercive weapon; however, given the structure of the steel industry, it was a successful cartel device. At that time, United States Steel produced almost two-thirds of the nation's steel output and no other firm was large enough to threaten its position of leadership. Moreover, within the industry information flows were good. As a result, the profits accruing to any small producer from a price cut were not large, and the time period between price cut, discovery, and retribution was short. Under these conditions the cartel worked well. The pools of the '80s and '90s had broken down because the number of firms was larger and their size distribution less skewed. As a result, information flows were more imperfect and firms had more to gain. It is also not clear that such an arrangement would work today. The number of firms is larger and the size distribution more equal. In a more recent case, the collusive bids for electric generators, a similar informal arrangement worked well, but there too the circumstances were special. The number of firms was small, and the winning bids were given wide publicity. The question of efficiency is, however, largely academic. The courts held that the Gary dinners (and other informal arrangements) as well as the more formalized trusts were violations of the Sherman Act, and they passed off the menu of alternative arrangements.

With the court decision in the *Standard Oil* case, new arrangements had to be innovated if cartelization was to continue. The trade association, an organization designed for other purposes, was one of the prototype arrangements that was tried. The association performs many functions – it lobbies for the industry, it promotes the sale of its products, it conducts research, and it increases the flow of relevant information among the association's members. In short, it reduces information costs and sometimes can effect income redistribution – both useful services that are independent of the association's ability to effectively cartelize an industry. In such circumstances – an existing organization whose members find membership profitable for other reasons – the costs of organizing a prototype cartel are small, since the organization costs had already been borne by the association and all that is needed is a redirection of the already established organization's efforts. The innovation, therefore, may appear profitable even if the probability of success is small.

Furthermore, some of the day-to-day activities of the association are necessary preliminary steps in any cartel arrangement – that is, there is an element of joint cost. Recent work in experimental economics has suggested

The theory applied

that good information about competitors' costs, capacity, price, and output may be a necessary (but not sufficient) condition for successful cartelization in industries with more than two firms. Information of this type is an association's 'stock in trade'. In addition, the trade association provides an inexpensive method of distributing 'suggested' price lists, and the organization can be a focus for the application of moral suasion to members who prove reluctant to equate suggested and actual prices. Despite these 'virtues', everything we know about the proclivity of members to cheat unless otherwise strongly coerced and the inability of any cartel to stabilize an industry without some control of entry suggests that trade association would be a relatively inefficient arrangement for effecting cartelization. This conclusion was, however, much less obvious forty years ago, and when the Supreme Court ruled that activities of the sort we have outlined were not anti-trust violations, the associations experienced a period of rapid growth.[1] Since then, however, the inherent weaknesses, coupled with a series of adverse court decisions that limited the ability of the associations to collect and distribute cost, price, and output data, have made the arrangement appear much less viable.[2] As a result, associations, while continuing to operate effectively in other spheres, have been less used as cartel arrangements.

Cartels cannot operate efficiently unless the cartel has some power to coerce its members to abide by the 'voluntary cooperative' arrangements. In the United States, the courts have ruled that attempts to enforce these arrangements are illegal (as are often the arrangements themselves). As a result producers turned to government to provide the requisite weapons of coercion.

Retail price maintenance appeared to be one such weapon, and attempts by manufacturers to foster price maintenance laws date back to 1908. Competitive pressures from other producers, however, made most manufacturers lose interest in these schemes by the 1930s, despite the fact that these agreements were permitted under the then current interpretations of the anti-trust laws. As a result, it has been the *retail* trade associations (the retail traders, not the manufacturers, are the chief beneficiaries) who have been the chief supporters of such legislation. Their activities have been marked by a fair degree of success. Since the '30s, a number of states (beginning with California in 1931) have passed price maintenance laws, and these laws have been further strengthened by federal legislation that has made it possible to apply the laws to out-of-state residents and non-signers.[3]

[1] *Maple Floor Manufacturers Association* v. *United States* (1925).
[2] For example, *Sugar Institute* v. *United States* (1931).
[3] The Miller–Tydings and the McGuire–Keough Acts.

176

As far as the manufacturing sector is concerned, retail price maintenance cannot produce successful cartelization. It can, however, provide a vehicle for passing price information in the same way as the Gary dinners and the educational activities of the trade associations. Moreover, because of the publicity given the 'fixed' price, the laws may increase the speed at which information about price reductions is transmitted through the industry. Such an increase would, in turn, reduce the retaliation time. In this way, price maintenance could reduce the potential profit available to a price cutter who wants to increase his market share before his competitors respond. From the manufacturer's viewpoint, however, a retail price maintenance agreement is not an efficient way to effect cartelization.

Much more efficient (but of shorter life) was the experiment in government-sponsored cartelization under the National Industrial Recovery Act of 1933. As we have seen, periods of generalized market failure raise the potential revenue from alternative institutional arrangements, particularly government ones. The 1930s was a period of generalized failure and turned attention to a broad range of possible government arrangemental innovations, including the NIRA. That act created the National Recovery Administration, charged with establishing and supervising a set of 'industry codes' – codes that, when approved, would govern the operation of every firm in an in-dustry, and codes that would have the coercive power of the government behind them.

During its abbreviated life, the administration approved over 550 such codes, covering a large portion of American manufacturing. Although the individual codes differed markedly, most regulated both price and the terms of sale. Less often, but not infrequently, they allocated markets and controlled production capacity. Moreover, in addition to the criminal sanctions im-posed on violators, they often provided for 'civil' damages to those who suffered from the effects of 'unfair' competition. The iron and steel code, for example, levied a $10 per ton fine on any member selling at prices or terms below those set in the code. Finally, since the NRA was financed by a tax of the participating firms, it was not possible for any firm to get 'free rider' benefits.

The Act became law in 1933, but it lasted only two years. In mid-1935 the Supreme Court declared the law unconstitutional in the *Schechter* (sick chicken) case.[1] During its two-year life, though, the act provided the legal framework for as strict cartelization as the American economy has ever seen, and as an instrument for enforcing cartel decisions it was more efficient than the industrial trust. Industrial trusts could operate efficiently

---

[1] *A. L. A. Schechter Poultry Corporation* v. *United States* (1935).

177

only as long as all existing firms agreed to join initially and scale economies, financial requirements, or some other such economic factor provided a barrier to the entry of new firms into the industry. Effective cartelization under the NIRA did not require these additional strictures. All existing firms were required by law to join the cartel, and while there were no legal barriers to the entry of new firms, any new firm was required to abide by the cartel's decisions.

In the form that the Sherman Act was passed, no agency was specifically charged with its enforcement, but in 1903 the Antitrust Division was established within the Department of Justice. The vigor of enforcement, however, has not been independent of the political administration. Both the size of the division's appropriations and the direction of its enforcement policy are set by the party in power. As a result, it has always been possible for industry groups, operating as well-financed and vocal minorities within the political structure, to blunt the law's enforcement. Again, we see that any political arrangement is a function of the state that creates it.

In summary, it appears that the oligopolistic structure of American industry engenders substantial potential redistributive profits external to the individual firms but internal to the industry. These profits could be captured by an arrangemental innovation that underwrites successful cartelization. In the absence of some legal device that can be used to coerce recalcitrant producers, effective cartelization is difficult. In a few exceptional cases (e.g. where the number of firms is small or where one firm dominates the industry), informal arrangements have yielded stable cartel solutions. These exceptions aside – and they do appear to have been exceptions – attempts at cartelization in manufacturing have not been successful. They have, in fact, been so spectacularly unsuccessful that one might conclude that positive enforcement of the anti-trust laws is not required if the sole goal of public policy is the prevention of income redistribution. In this case, all that may be required is the prohibition of legally enforceable cartel arrangements.

(IV) Voluntary association and successful redistribution: the case of tariff legislation and insulation from foreign competition

In our discussion of institutional change in other sectors, we have observed that cooperative collusive agreements aimed at effecting redistribution through political (as opposed to economic) action have often been quite successful. We have also noted that when a new arrangement can be built on the framework of an already existing one (e.g. the political action arm of the Grange on the extant social organization), the costs of organization are reduced. As a result, arrangemental innovation is both more rapid and triggered by a lower level of potential profit. These two points are underscored again by the history of tariff legislation in the nineteenth and twentieth centuries.

It is generally conceded that the first American 'protective' tariff was passed in 1816.[1] From then until the Civil War, rates varied with the strengths of the alternative political coalitions. From the 1860s through the first decade of the twentieth century, rates were high and generally rising. Some remission from these high levels was attained during the Wilson administration, but the trend was reestablished in the '20s, and the high tariff movement culminated in the Smoot–Hawley Act of 1930. Rates embodied in that act were so high that its passage practically destroyed the network of world trade. The 1930s witnessed some substantial tariff reductions with the innovation of reciprocity, and more recently there have been some further slight reductions associated with the Kennedy administration. This brief summary of United States tariff history is not meant to be complete, but it is meant to provide a basis for an examination of the relationship between tariff changes and the organization of certain voluntary cooperative groups, and the impact of shifts in comparative advantage on the institutional arrangements.

Throughout most of the nineteenth century it appears that the United States had a comparative advantage in the production of certain primary commodities, and a comparative disadvantage in the production of most manufactured products. As a result, the manufacturing groups were reasonably unified in their support of high tariffs. Most vocal of all were the wool and iron manufacturers, who were at a substantial disadvantage. Since there were relatively few manufacturers (even in industries characterized by 'a large number' of small firms), organization for united action was relatively cheap. There were, on the other hand, a much greater number of farmers (who enjoyed a comparative advantage), and the costs of organization were very much higher.

Although evidence of organization is lacking, the New England cotton textile manufacturers actively supported the tariff of 1816, and by 1824 there is evidence of some unified lobbying by iron and wool manufacturers for further upward tariff revisions. Thereafter, the manufacturers' organizations became more formal. In 1826, for example, the producers of woolen cloth met in Boston and voted to petition Congress for higher tariffs on foreign cloths. The next year, the Pennsylvania Society for the Promotion of Manufacturers and the Mechanical Arts sponsored a memorial to Congress

---

[1] The preamble to the tariff of 1789 contains the words 'protection of manufacturers'.

that pointed out the need for higher tariffs. By the middle of the century, industrial trade associations had begun to lobby for higher tariffs. The Wool Manufacturers Association, for example, led the fight for an increase in rates in 1866, and the history of the next seventy years can be written in similar terms. Trade associations from specific industries, and those even more broadly-based (the National Association of Manufacturers, for example), continued to press for higher and higher tariffs. Each upward revision was, of course, designed to further redistribute income from consumer to producer.

Usually there are costs involved in organizing a voluntary cooperative group; however, when these costs can be spread over several activities the amount that must be charged against any one declines. Even more dramatic is the case where only the marginal costs of redirecting the organization must be covered by the activities revenue. Thus, a general organization (the Pennsylvania Society for the Promotion of Manufacturers and the Mechanical Arts, for example) can add lobbying to its functions and incur very little additional costs. Moreover, if its members receive substantial value from the organization's primary function (in the case in point, the Society promoted the exchange of technical information in a period when there was no formal technical press), there is little threat that they will withdraw and become free riders, even if the benefits of the lobbying activity are not readily partitionable. This latter consideration is of particular importance since it is all but impossible to partition the benefits of higher tariffs between those firms that supported lobbying and those that did not. Moreover, when the organization is a trade association, the ties of 'value received' are further strengthened by the moral suasion of the relevant peer group.[1]

Throughout the nineteenth century, the power of the vocal minorities who favored higher tariffs was further magnified by the extant political institutions; and, as a result, the marginal return to funds devoted to lobbying was very high. Because senators were not elected directly, they were particularly responsive to the demands of well-endowed (both financially and in terms of local political power) minority groups. As a result, while tariff legislation originated in the House, the Senate never hesitated to exercise its constitutional powers to '*propose* or concur with Amendments', and the proposed amendments were almost always designed to increase tariffs on manufactured commodities.

Political activity underwritten by voluntary cooperative groups proved itself effective in 'protecting' American manufacturers in the years before

---

[1] This aspect of organizations was noted (probably wrongly) very early by students of the labor movement who saw that unions of ethnically or industrially homogeneous groups were much more cohesive than those with more diverse memberships.

1930. It has been much less successful since that date. That change, too, is amenable to analysis, and, in fact, the experience casts further light on our understanding of the process of arrangemental change. The model suggests an arrangement can become less profitable if its costs of operation rise or if its net revenues fall. In the case in question, both occurred.

On 31 May 1913, the Seventeenth Amendment to the Constitution went into effect. The amendment called for the direct election of Senators, and it made the upper house more responsive to the general will and less responsive to the well-financed manufacturing lobby. Vocal minorities still have more power than numbers alone would account for, but they no longer have in the Senate an institutionalized route to effect that power.

Less obvious but probably more important were the changes in comparative advantage that altered the composition of the pro- and anti-tariff blocks, and, as a result, reduced the profitability of a dollar spent on lobbying activity for heretofore protected manufacturers. By the last decades of the nineteenth century, the simple division of the United States economy into two parts – of a comparative advantage in a wide range of primary products and a disadvantage in most manufacture – no longer was an adequate description of reality. Instead, changes in technology, tastes, and resource endowments had produced for the United States a comparative advantage in a wide spectrum of production from primary to very sophisticated fabricated products. In the earlier period, two factors had combined to prevent producers of the 'advantage' commodities from organizing in support of lower tariffs. First, while the connection between comparative disadvantage and a high tariff is very direct, the connection between low tariffs and a comparative advantage is much more obscure. In the former case, the producer is immediately faced by the competition of 'cheap foreign goods', but in the latter the effects are not direct, and depend upon the response of other countries and on complicated relations working through the balance of payments. Second, agricultural activity (the largest 'advantage' sector) was conducted by the very small units and organizational costs were much higher than they were for the affected manufacturers.

The twentieth century, however, saw a growing sophistication about the costs of high tariffs. In terms of the model, improvements in knowledge (in this case, economic theory) increased the expected returns to institutional rearrangements favoring lower tariffs, and for the first time it became profitable for producers with an interest in foreign sales to counter-lobby. At the same time, the costs of joint action declined. The new group of anti-tariff manufacturers, like their pro-tariff peers, were relatively few in number, and it was much less costly to organize them than the far more numerous primary producers. The farmers, as we have seen, had also become better

181

organized, and, while they were never an important force pushing for downward tariff revision, they were more effective than before. As a result, the high tariff lobbies were forced to compete with equally vocal and well-financed low tariff lobbies whose activities were underwritten by equally strong trade associations, and who were supported by the national farm organizations. To the protectionists, the cost per unit of protection had risen substantially.

The result of the Seventeenth Amendment coupled with the change in organizational strength was a shift in the stance of the national legislature away from the traditional high tariff position. An arrangemental realignment in the political sphere had made it possible for new groups to redistribute income. Moreover, the analysis would suggest that today consumers should fear a revival of protectionism much less than a reading of the popular press would suggest.

(V) Traditional externalities: the social costs of manufacture

Although the subject has seldom been explicitly mentioned in the standard texts, a part of American industrial history concerns costs external to the firm but not to society. Such costs are not included in a firm's profit calculations, and, as a result, a firm whose production decision involves such external costs tends to produce more than it would had it considered all costs.[1] Given the firm's vested property rights, it is difficult for society to convince it to pay these external costs if the arguments are not supported by the governments' coercive power. Moreover, because of the free rider problem and the costs of organizing large groups, it is probably equally difficult to bribe the firm to reduce its production without appealing to government. Turning from theory to history, as urbanization and the locational concentration of industrial firms have increased, the level of external costs has also increased. Although there are numerous examples of such externalities, we shall limit our discussion to three that have been important in the history of American manufacturing and that have led to arrangemental innovation: those arising from erosion and water control, water pollution, and air pollution. In each instance, some form of government arrangement has been innovated in an attempt to make the cost-engendering firms bear some share of these external costs. The model predicts that government would be the arrangemental 'technology of choice'; however, the innovations raise some interesting questions that the unrefined model cannot answer. First, the periods of arrangemental gestation

[1] This argument is strictly true only if the external costs are a function of output. This condition holds for those industries that we are discussing here.

182

have been long. Second, resolution has most often been achieved by forcing the firms to absorb the external costs rather than by socializing these costs through a tax system and then using the revenue to bribe the firms.

In the late nineteenth and early twentieth centuries, people came to realize that clear-cut lumbering techniques, by stripping the land of vegetation covering, permitted unregulated water 'run-off'. In one experimental area, for example, less than one percent of the rainfall on forested land ran off immediately, but that proportion rose to 62 percent in areas that had been clear cut. Such uncontrolled run-off eroded the soil, 'silted up' dams and waterways, and increased the probability of damaging floods.[1] All three are examples of external costs.

Since only a small part of these external costs was borne by the lumbering firm, there was little profit in their adopting the more expensive selective logging techniques or of recovering their logged-over land by substantial reforestation.[2] At the same time, the costs were not concentrated but spread over the population of the whole watershed. Given the organizational costs and the benefits of 'free loading', government was the only viable solution, and by the end of the century, affected groups had begun to press for some government solution. In the words of Representative McRae (Democrat, Arkansas), 'Save our forest reservations, and prevent floods on the mighty Mississippi.'

Although a reading of the history of forest legislation might lead one to conclude that conservation was the important question, it was the question of externalities that dominated the legislative debate in the earlier period.[3] While the act of 1891 that established the first national forest preserve was couched in conservationist terms, the rationale for most of the rest of which is now regarded as conservation legislation rested on the question of externalities. The Weeks Act (1911), for example, permitted the government to purchase additional national forest land, but only when those purchases

---

[1] In clear-cut lumbering the logging firm cuts all the trees in a given area and leaves it clear. The alternative is some selection procedure that leaves some trees still standing.

[2] Given the seemingly almost inexhaustible supplies of timber that appeared to be available in the nineteenth century, the price of trees was very low. As a result, there was no rate of discount at which it paid to plant trees for the future nor to conserve existing trees if that conservation decision involved any increase in costs.

[3] Conservation has nothing logically to do with externalities but turns on a deviation between private and social rates of discount. At private rates of discount, it may pay to cut trees now rather than later, but at some lower social rate it may pay to defer cutting. In terms of the investment model presented in Chapter 7, cutting now yields positive returns at private rates of discount, while the deferred returns from conservation are so heavily discounted that they have a negligible present value. At a lower social rate of discount, those deferred returns loom large and may make the present value of the conservation alternative increase above the value of the 'cut-now' policy.

183

would help protect navigable streams and waterways.[1] The case for enactment was pitched entirely in terms of the need for preservation of the soil in the interests of agriculture and the need for preventing excessive run-off in the interests of river navigation, to minimize flood damage, to increase the commercial usability of land along the waterways, and to minimize silting. Moreover, even the opposition did not challenge the bill on these grounds. Instead they argued that these supposed externalities were but a mask for an unconstitutional attempt to protect the forests. It was not until the Clarke–McNary Act of 1924 that the legislative justification for national forest policy shifted from external costs to conservation.

Despite the shift in emphasis, concern for external costs continued, and it was reflected in further arrangemental innovation. The Soil Erosion Service (established in 1933) has reforested broad areas of already cut-over land, and within the national forests, only selective logging techniques are permitted.

In this instance, the innovations really involve the absorption of the external costs by the citizens of the country. This conclusion is immediately apparent in the case of reforestation, but it is not so obvious in the case of selective logging. Since, however, the timber from the forests must compete with timber cut by less expensive methods, the sale price of national forest trees must be below the price of trees in private woodlands. Thus, the income the government must forego is equivalent to a bribe paid to the logging firm to induce it to use a technology with higher private (but lower social) costs.

The problem of industrial water pollution is not new, but it has only been within the recent past that arrangemental innovations designed to reduce the external costs in a systematic manner have been innovated, and these arrangements have not as yet proved themselves completely effective.[2]

The delay in mobilizing the power of the national government reflects both the size of the gains from innovation and the costs of that innovation. On the benefit side, the costs of water pollution are both cumulative and distributed in a more-or-less rectangular fashion over time. Since the costs were cumulative, even recognition of pollution did not always make its elimination profitable since the costs of a little pollution may be less than the expense of eliminating it.[3] Moreover, these costs were subject to little year-to-year variation and so in no one year did they appear high. In the case of

---

[1] Since there were no public lands in the East, there were no national forests in that area before 1911.

[2] There is a long history of local innovation, but there has been little coordination between localities.

[3] One can observe pollution gradually building up, but it may not pay to get rid of that pollution until it reaches some threshold level.

184

floods, although flooding was rare, when it did occur the costs were high and the sudden recognition of the potential costs frequently led to attempts at prevention. In the pollution case, the delay in innovation suggests an interesting hypothesis: Namely, it pays to seek outside arrangemental protection if there is a probability (even a low one) of great loss, but that it pays to self-insure if a single loss will not be crippling.[1] Further, in terms of organization, those who bore the costs of water pollution were, until recently, mostly consumers of leisure who were not easily organized and, under any conditions, their per capita costs were low. The exceptions were pollution of city water supplies and in these cases arrangemental innovation was rapid. On the other side, those who engendered the costs were few in number, very directly affected, and in positions of great political influence. It was easy and obviously profitable for them to organize against any action aimed at the forcible internalization of the external costs.

Much of water pollution is of industrial origin. It kills the aquatic life, and may in extreme cases make the water unfit even for recreation. The actual cost varies from firm to firm and industry to industry, but serious problems have been caused by the discharge of chemicals, dye-stuffs, and oils. The pollution caused by the grain dumped by distillers and the wastage from paper mills are particularly notorious, but many other industries have also been involved.

Pollution is an example of a classic externality since the firms do not bear the costs of their actions. Moreover, between property rights vested in the polluting firms and the high costs of organization, action against pollution by any voluntary cooperative group is both expensive and slow.[2] Effective solutions have, therefore, tended to rest on the application of the coercive power of government. Attempts to utilize the power of state and local governments to control pollution date back into the nineteenth century, however; because laws are not uniform, because firms face national competition, and because local manufacturing firms possess a great deal of local political power, the locally-based institutions were never very effective.[3]

[1] This proposition is well known in insurance, but it is equally useful in understanding arrangemental change, and it appears likely that the analytical framework we use to explain arrangemental lag should be modified to take account of it.

[2] Recently some firms have found that by-products have a positive value and have ceased dumping their waste because they find they can sell it. There are examples of this change both in the synthetic phenol process and in the recovery of ethyl alcohol from the waste of sulphite paper mills. Except where the organization of some information network makes the firms aware of the potential profitability, there is no gain from institutional reorganization in this instance.

[3] The city of Cleveland, for example, had an ordinance that prohibited the dumping of gasoline (a useless by-product of kerosene production) into the rivers or the lake as early as the 1870s. A reading of John D. Rockefeller's papers suggests that the rule was not

The theory applied

In the more recent past, the geographic scope of regulation has been increased by the shift in political focus from the local to the national level. The Federal Water Pollution Control Act of 1956 permits the federal government (under certain conditions) to initiate prosecution of manufacturing firms that pollute water. Even here, however, the weight of the political influence of the polluting firms has delayed a resolution of the problem. Thus, the political influence wielded by the Lake County, Indiana, steel firms has delayed until the mid-1970s interstate attempts (underwritten by the federal government) to halt pollution of Lake Michigan.

In short, when political action takes the form of requiring that the firms internalize the externality, and when those firms still have political muscle, resolution is apt to be very difficult. Moreover, since the new institutional arrangement, when it does operate, frequently involves the total prohibition of any pollution, there is no reason to believe that it is Pareto optimal.[1] Given these two facts, and assuming that there are external costs in pollution, it appears that some form of bribery rather than forced internalization (since it would reduce the political resistance) might reduce the length of the organizational lag. It certainly did in the case of lumbering. Some form of special tax write-off for waste disposal equipment or a subsidy for by-products produced from waste might prove more effective, and it almost certainly could be implemented more quickly.

Finally, the nation in the past few years has come to recognize the external costs of air pollution. Industrial pollution is not new. There are references to the air pollution caused by steel firms in the late nineteenth century and by meat-packing firms almost half a century earlier. Recently, however, the growing urban concentration of industry and population and the compounding of pollution that has come from the widespread innovation of the automobile have made everyone aware of the external costs. Almost every large city in the country has some kind of smog problem.

While a wide variety of manufacturing activities have contributed to the smog problem, the most important are the pulp and steel mills, the cement plants, the petroleum refineries, and the power and chemical companies. Like the problem of water pollution, the costs are borne by society at large. Unlike the water problem, however, no one firm causes pollution,

---

well enforced. Competition from unregulated refineries made it impossible for the Cleveland firms to internalize the external costs there, if firms located in other areas did not have to follow suit; and the position of the Standard Oil Company in Cleveland blocked any serious attempts at enforcement – at least against them.

[1] A Pareto optimal solution is one that can not be altered without leaving someone worse off. There is no reason to believe that a total ban on pollution is optimal. It might, for example, be possible to the firm to pollute, pay those who bear the costs, and leave everyone better off.

and it would often be impossible for a single firm to effect a smog control program even if it so desired. At very minimum, some form of voluntary cooperation is needed, but, in fact, only the application of the coercive power of government has proved effective. Under the threat of legal punishment the steel industry has spent a quarter of a billion dollars on air pollution control devices over the past decade-and-a-half, and it expends an additional $30 million per year to operate them. The figures for other major industrial polluters show similar trends.[1] No one can say that the results have been Pareto optimal. In fact, the supposition is probably to the contrary. Still, change has occurred.

The success of arrangements designed to control industrial smog, coupled with the relative failure of total smog control programs, emphasizes another aspect of the problems of arrangemental change. The firms themselves are forced to bear a part of the cost of smog (higher absentee rates and difficulty in employment are two manifestations of these costs), and, as a result, they have been fairly willing to support political solutions to the problem. Thus, for example, Pittsburgh business firms paid close to $400 million to suppress that city's smog, and, although there were some complaints, the experience was quite different from the water pollution case. In Pittsburgh, the government provided a solution perhaps not far different than a voluntary cooperative group of business firms might have achieved in time. The anti-smog drive was, in fact, led by the community's business group. In the case of smog in most other areas, however, the major offenders are not manufacturing firms but automobile users, and the democratic political process has not yet been able to force a majority of the people to accept a solution that they do not approve. Thus, while political institutions may force minorities to internalize external costs, it is unlikely that they can force the majority to bear such costs.

While states, and more recently the federal government, have become involved in the enforced internalization of the external costs of air and water pollution, local zoning codes have been the most widely innovated organizational form designed to effect this internalization. Zoning laws not only recognize that the use to which I put my land may affect the value of someone else's property, but also imply that society has some stake in the use of my property. Their innovation, therefore, required a drastic revision of the traditional American concept of private property. External costs have been recognized in common law since the Middle Ages, and there are many examples of statute laws regulating the use of property dating from the same period. For example, it was common to restrict the number of mills

---

[1] The figures for the chemical industry, for example, are $212 million and $24 million.

The theory applied

located on a river because each additional mill reduces the power available to the existing firms.

Even in the United States, there are any number of common law nuisance decisions that tended to restrict particular business operations; however, they were not uniform and had little basis in statute law. In fact, the court's interpretation tended to imply that, while a certain activity might be a nuisance in one location, there was always an appropriate place for it.[1]

In 1885, an ordinance was passed in Modesto, California, that restricted laundries to certain parts of the city. Although the law had definite racial overtones (most laundries were operated by Chinese), the courts upheld this exercise of police power, despite its implications for private property. The Modesto ordinance was a zoning law in the modern sense of the word, but it was the first decade of the twentieth century before there was any significant innovation of this legal device. In 1909, Los Angeles adopted a general zoning law, and seven years later, New York City followed suit.[2] The new laws were frequently challenged in the court, but two landmark decisions set the stage for modern zoning. In a Los Angeles challenge, the courts held that zoning was a legal use of police power and that the only test of an ordinance was that it be reasonable and subserve the interests of *the public at large*.[3] Thirteen years later, the court held that a master zoning plan was legal and that a political unit could exclude all manufacturing activities.[4] Since then, zoning has most often been the 'arrangement of choice' for forcing manufacturing firms to internalize their external costs. The reader should bear in mind that exclusion laws are not necessarily Pareto optimal, and they may yield a solution farther from optimality than the one replaced. As we have seen, there is no guarantee that income is maximized when pollution is eliminated.

Within the past fifty years, there has been an increasing awareness of the external costs associated with certain manufacturing activities. Given the concentration of the cost-generating activity in a few hands, the diffusion of those costs across broad population groups, and the nature of vested

---

[1] In the *Tubner* case, the court held that 'if a business be necessary and useful, it is always presumable that there is a proper place and a proper manner for carrying it on': *Tubner* v. *California State R.R. Co.* (1884).

[2] Los Angeles City Ordinance #19,500 (ns), adopted 12 December 1909.

[3] *Hadacheck* v. *Sebastian* (1913). This case was particularly important since the law was used to force the owner of a kiln out of a residential neighborhood even though his operation antedated both the zoning law and the annexation of the neighborhood to the city.

[4] *Euclid Village* v. *Ambler Realty Co.* (1926). The constitutionality of zoning was upheld in another case of about the same date. See *Miller* v. *Board of Public Works of the City of Los Angeles* (1925).

188

Economies of scale, unsuccessful cartelization, external costs

property rights, it is not surprising that arrangemental innovation, when it occurs, tends to depend on the coercive power of government.

(VI) Conclusions

The history of arrangemental change in the manufacturing sector has underscored several points that must be kept in mind when the theory is finally reformulated. First, the manufacturing sector (made up of industries marked by a substantial degree – i.e. usually more than ten firms – of oligopoly) appears to have benefited much less from voluntary or governmental arrangements than did either competitive industries or those that were more heavily concentrated. In the former case, the size of the producing units was so small that the individual firms were unable to finance their own research and had no significant individual political power. They were, as a result, forced to innovate some superfirm arrangements to accomplish these ends.[1] In the latter case, because of their small numbers, cartelization came relatively easily through some form of voluntary cooperative or governmental arrangement. In the case of the manufacturing oligops, however, larger numbers and the continued threat of still further competition (both from entry and from new technologies) made innovations to effect cartelization appear less profitable. At the same time, the firms were large enough and well enough insulated from direct competition to make investment in research profitable. In addition, their size also gave them substantial individual political power – at least at the local level. When the firms were forced to turn to the national political arena (for protection from foreign competition, for example), arrangemental innovation did appear profitable.

Second, although cooperation leading to cartelization was unprofitable, voluntary cooperation among large groups can be profitable if the goal is political action. While displaying little ability to innovate efficient cartels (given the legal framework), the oligops quickly innovated quite profitable arrangements when the aim was higher tariffs. The potential profits from higher tariffs were immediate and large (particularly to firms who were at a substantial comparative disadvantage), and there was little room for cheating. In addition, costs to individual firms were relatively small, so there was little incentive to become a 'free rider'. Given these conditions, arrangemental innovation at the voluntary level can be rapid and stable.

Third, the history of the sector suggests that when recourse is made to government (either to redistribute income or to internalize some externality),

[1] In the case of agriculture, as we have seen, the farmers turned to the government to finance research and to some voluntary cooperative organizations to focus their political power.

189

if that innovation could result in some redistribution of income from the few to the many, it is apt to be long-delayed. Moreover, when the innovation is finally effected, it is likely to lead to *that* redistribution, even if that outcome is Pareto inferior to some alternative arrangement. Broadly based groups operating in the political arena are not apt to make close profit calculations, and, if they have long been thwarted, they are apt to revenge themselves on their tormentors, even if there are real costs associated with such revenge. In this regard, the experience of the manufacturing sector merely underscores the lesson that should have been learned from the history of the railroads.

CHAPTER 9
INSTITUTIONAL CHANGE IN THE SERVICE INDUSTRIES

(I) Introduction

Today more than half of the labor force in the United States is employed in what are traditionally conceived of as service industries. Ever since statistical measurements of the distribution of the labor force were first undertaken, the percentage in the service industries has been rising. In 1870, little more than 19 percent of the labor force was so employed, but by 1965 it was approximately 55 percent, making the service sector today the dominant source of employment in the economy. This change has received a great deal of attention as a typical characteristic of an affluent society.[1]

In this chapter we shall explore briefly some of the general institutional changes that have accompanied this redistribution of occupational employment. Of necessity, our discussion will be highly selective and incomplete, not only because of the inadequacies of the model, but in this case more particularly because our knowledge of the economic characteristics of the service sector is deficient. Unlike manufacturing, agriculture, and other sectors that have been analyzed and explored at length by economists, the service sector has received comparatively little attention.[2]

We have defined the service industries in the same way as Fuchs to include wholesale and retail trade, finance, insurance, real estate, general government (including military), and activities comprising professional and personal repair services. Perhaps the most evident characteristic of such a listing is its heterogeneity. It embraces industries of rapid productivity

[1] See C. Clark, *The Conditions of Economic Progress*, 3rd ed. (London, 1957).
[2] The most complete modern account is contained in a new study of the National Bureau of Economic Research by V. R. Fuchs, entitled *The Service Economy* (New York, 1968). In addition to Fuchs' research, the report rests on a number of other pioneering National Bureau studies such as G. Stigler, *Trends in Employment in the Service Industries* (Princeton, N.J., 1956); H. Barger, *The Role of Distribution in the American Economy Since 1869* (Princeton, N.J., 1955); S. Kuznets and M. Friedman, *Income from Independent Professional Practice* (New York, 1945).

growth and slow productivity growth, industries which are large and industries which are small. But what they have in common, by and large, is that most of them are manned by white collar workers; most, although not all, are labor intensive; most deal with the consumer; and, perhaps the most pervasive characteristic of all, nearly all of them produce an intangible product.

Fuchs points out that there have been three general explanations for the relative growth of the service sector: the more rapid growth of final demand for services; a relative increase in intermediate demands for services; and a relatively slow increase in output per man in services. In his exploration of the issue, Fuchs emphasizes that in his opinion it is the third explanation – slower growth in output per man – which accounts for the relative rise of the service sector in modern times. This finding certainly is still controversial since the problems of measurement of the output in the service industry have as yet not been resolved, and therefore it is extremely difficult to determine efficient measures of productivity increase in that sector. Whether or not we accept Fuchs' finding as an explanation for the relative growth of the service sector in recent times (since 1929), our examination will try to show the probable truth of the second explanation – the growth in demand for services in terms of a demand for intermediate goods – as an important contributing factor to the growth of the service sector in the nineteenth century. We shall explore this aspect particularly in our case study of wholesale and retail trade, and again in the conclusion.

In terms of our model we should note that important parts of the service sector have grown specifically as a means to reduce transactions costs. Such services encompass the industries concerned with information flows and the spreading of risk. Expansion in the size of markets and the development of actuarial information have been continuous sources of disequilibrium inducing the innovation and very rapid growth of institutions in these industries. We present a case study of the development of institutional arrangements to reduce information cost and risk in the development of the cotton trade in Section II below.

The heterogeneous character of the service sector makes it difficult to provide many initial generalizations about the forces making for the character of its arrangemental structure. Therefore, our conclusions must be much more limited than in other sectors where the basic economic characteristics are far more homogeneous. Fuchs has delineated four basic characteristics of the service industry which distinguish it from other sectors. These are:

(1) that a good deal of the service sector engages in nonprofit-making activities;

(2) the unique nature of its labor force;

Institutional change in the service industries

(3) that the growth of the service sector betokens just the reverse of the subjugation of man to the machine classically attributed by economic textbooks to the Industrial Revolution;

(4) that the size of the firm in much of the service sector is small scale.

While these distinctive characteristics may be an efficient heuristic device in some aspects of economic analysis, they don't turn out to be equally useful in explaining institutional arrangements. Certainly small size was important to the small degree of corporate organization in the sector. It may also be true that the characteristics of the labor force would contribute to low unionization, but beyond that we must turn elsewhere to find the sources of arrangemental innovation in that sector. We believe that the case studies that follow will illuminate some of the forces making for institutional arrangement in this heterogeneous sector.

In subsequent sections of this chapter we shall examine the decline of transactions costs in the cotton trade and then explore institutional arrangements in two service industries: one is the changing institutional structure of wholesale and retail trade and the forces that have made for those changes; the second provides an examination of perhaps the most successful voluntary organization that we have – the American Medical Association – and its ability to influence its environment and to control supply. We shall then conclude with a few generalizations about the sector, while emphasizing that we have little more than touched upon an analysis which would itself have to be more than book length to adequately explore the variety of institutions that evolve in this complex and varied sector.

(II) Declining transactions costs in the cotton trade[1]

The development of the cotton market in the nineteenth century illustrates the way institutions served to lower transactions costs in one of the most important agricultural trades of that century. The organizational forms that evolved were, for the most part, voluntary; the appeal to government was limited to laws for standardization and grading of products (since enforcement by government was more effective and cost less than by voluntary means).

The American cotton trade involved movement of the crop from the southern planter–producer to the Manchester, England or New England

---

[1] The sources for this section are: N. S. Buck, *The Development of the Organization of Anglo–American Trade, 1800–1850* (New Haven, Conn., 1925); T. Ellison, *The Cotton Trade of Great Britain* (London, 1886); M. B. Hammond, *The Cotton Industry* (New York, 1897); L. C. Gray, *History of Southern Agriculture 1706–1860* (Washington, D.C., 1933); J. E. Boyle, *Cotton and the New Orleans Cotton Exchange* (New York, 1934).

193

manufacturer. At its inception in the 1780s and '90s it had meant the transfer of a few bags of cotton as part of a general cargo to England, where it was handled by brokers who primarily dealt in other products. From these simple beginnings it grew in volume until by the end of the nineteenth century it involved the annual movement of approximately 4 billion pounds of cotton from the southern plantations to manufacturing centers. In the course of this evolution transactions costs per pound fell to a very small fraction of what they had been at the beginning of the century. It is evident from the account that follows that new organizational forms emerged in direct response to vertical disintegration which was the result of the increasing size of the market in response to technological changes – of which the railroad, the telegraph, and the Atlantic cable were the most important. These developments enabled new institutions to reduce uncertainty by increasing the speed of information and changing the nature of risks.

At the beginning of the nineteenth century the transaction was typically of the following form: the planter on this side of the Atlantic either shipped his cotton directly to a port on the Gulf or the Atlantic coast and sold it to a factor located there, or, at times, he might sell it to local merchants or factors in interior towns who handled its transfer to ports. A few large planters consigned the cotton directly to importing merchants in Liverpool or New England markets, but for the most part this transaction was handled by the factor as an intermediary. The factor had emerged early (as in the prior tobacco trade) both as supplier of credit to the planter and as importer of his foodstuffs and other needs. On the far side of the Atlantic the importer in the very early years dealt through a broker who was usually unspecialized, and who engaged in cotton brokerage amongst other functions. But as the volume of cotton transactions increased at the beginning of the nineteenth century a number of brokers focused their services on cotton alone. There were both buying brokers and selling brokers, the latter selling the cotton to Manchester manufacturers.

Between the beginning of the nineteenth century and the Civil War, relatively few changes took place in the structure and organization of the trade on the American side of the Atlantic.[1] The primary development was an

---

[1] Perhaps the most interesting attempt at institutional innovation in the cotton trade of pre-Civil War America was a failure. That was the effort by Nicholas Biddle and the Bank of the United States to control the cotton market through purchasing cotton and thereby regulating the supply of cotton in the English market. The purchases were made in 1837, 1838, and 1839, and totalled approximately $9 million. The cotton was to be disposed of in 'orderly' fashion in the English market by the firm of Humphrey and Biddle (Nicholas Biddle's son). However, not even the resources of the bank were capable of controlling the market in 1839, and a loss of over $900,000 in that year ended this effort.

increase in information resulting both from the publication *Prices Current* which quoted prices and volumes continually – and from circulars issued by individual cotton brokers, although these frequently added little to the information in such publications as the *New Orleans Price Current* and the *New York Shipping List*. On the other side of the Atlantic far more dramatic changes were occurring in the organization of the market. Two changes that resulted from the growing size of the market led to two arrangemental innovations. One was the inauguration of a new buying mechanism: instead of buying by auction after actual inspection of the shipment, purchasers now were shown samples from which cotton was ordered. A second change was that manufacturers began to employ their own brokers to buy directly from the importing merchants, thus bypassing one step in the commissions heretofore paid to the complex of intermediaries. The development of the Liverpool and Manchester Railway in the early nineteenth century accelerated the dealing of Manchester merchants directly with Liverpool. The cost of information also fell markedly, another reflection of the growth of the market. The first weekly circular devoted exclusively to cotton was begun in 1805, and a more elaborate one followed in 1811. A general circular for all cotton brokers, issued in 1832, was subscribed to by sixteen firms. And weekly meetings of cotton brokers at the offices of certain firms led gradually to the development of the Liverpool Cotton Brokers Association in 1841.

After the Civil War, we witness further specialization in cotton marketing, arrangements that became profitable because of the growing size of the market. In 1865 the Bureau of Agriculture in Washington, as well as the *Commercial and Financial Chronicle* in New York, began publishing weekly and monthly information on markets and the probable future supply of cotton. Bradstreet also commenced a similar survey in 1873. More specifically, however, came the development of cotton exchanges – the National Cotton Exchange in New York and then, in 1871, the New Orleans Cotton Exchange which became the major center for cotton information and for the cotton futures market. This arrangemental innovation came about when the size of the market made it profitable to engage in the exclusive buying and selling of a single commodity. It was not a new innovation, but rather an adaptation of an existing institutional technology which had its origins in the English coffee houses, was carried over to stock exchanges, and reached its ultimate refinement and specialization in an exchange dealing with a single commodity.

An equally notable development in this period was a basic change in marketing methods, most evident in the decline of the factor and the rise of direct trade between inland brokers and New England manufacturers. In any market where buyers and sellers are spatially separated there are serious problems in providing the requisite information. Even in the modern stock market, it is necessary for the specialist to buy and sell as he attempts to match the desires of buyers to the desires of sellers. The factor provided the specialists information service to the cotton trade.

The change occurred because of technological developments in communication and transportation afforded by the telegraph and the railroad that permitted manufacturers, by dealing directly with inland brokers to bypass the succession of commissions and storage and inventorying costs that had developed through the earlier use of factors. In Europe a similar set of changes occurred for technological reasons. In this case, it was the Atlantic cable which allowed manufacturers to bypass the traditional merchant–importer and to deal directly, purchasing cotton via brokers. In short, the telegraph and the Atlantic cable served to reduce transactions costs by eliminating commissions of a number of middlemen. A second productive aspect of the overall development of communications was the inauguration of the futures market, which began in a small way during the Civil War as an effort to hedge against the uncertainties of delivery of cotton during hostilities. Subsequently, it became an organized part of the cotton market, and provided a shield against the risk of future price changes. The futures market in Liverpool and New Orleans resulted in a reduction of risk, of price fluctuation, and of the transaction costs. In England the Cotton Clearing House was formed specifically for trading in futures, and the highly specialized Cotton Bank permitted settlement of transactions directly and readily.

The fall in transactions costs as a result of this set of institutional developments of the nineteenth century was dramatic. The bill opposite, listing the items involved in transfer just between the dock at Mobile and that at Havre, shows that the average charge for just this part of the total transfer was 2.51 cents per pound in 1836. This had been reduced to approximately 1 cent per pound by the 1880s. Of the difference, two-thirds of 1 cent reflected a decline in ocean freight rates, but the rest was strictly a decline in the commissions, brokerage costs, inventories, wharfage, etc., resulting from the developments described above.

The innovation of institutions in the cotton trade illustrates the way in which the arbitraging of markets was accomplished as individuals and groups perceived profits in the reduction of transactions costs and uncertainties which can be realized by arrangemental innovation. Specifically, innovations in communication and transportation and growth in the size of the market created the potential for profitable arrangemental innovation. In the case of the technological innovations, the reduced costs could be realized by a

196

MARKETING COSTS 1836

	lb.	lb.
Account sales, 100 bales cotton		42,000
Deduct – samples	100	
tare, 4 lb. per cwt.	1,500	1,600
Net weight		40,400

	$
Price 4⅜*d*. (8¾c.)	3,535.00

Charges in U.S.

1. Bagging, twine, mending, marking	14.50
2. Wharfage $4.00, cartage $10.00, storage $8.00	22.00
3. Fire ins. $3.81, postage, etc. $3.50	7.31
4. Marine ins. 1% on $3,578.81	35.79
5. Policy	1.50
	$80.85

Charges in Liverpool

6. Dock dues £4 0*s*. 6*d*.	19.32
7. Town dues 16*s*. 8*d*.	4.00
8. Duty 35*d*. per cwt.	252.50
9. Cartage, porterage, weighing £3 14*s*. 1*d*.	17.78
10. Canvas, twine, mending £2 9*s*. 0*d*.	11.76
11. Warehouse rent, 12 weeks £5 0*s*. 0*d*.	24.00
12. Postage and small charges 10*s*. 6*d*.	2.52
13. Brokerage ¼%, insurance ¼%, interest 10 days discount 1¼%, 1¾ on £736 9*s*. 2*d*.	66.26
14. Freight ½*d*. per lb. on 40,400 lb.	404.00
15. Five percent primage on freight	20.20
16. Commission and guaranty 3%	106.05
17. Three months' interest on cash charges $974.70	14.62
Total charges	$1,023.14

(or 2.51c. per pound)

restructuring of the cotton trade. The growing size of the market made it profitable to devise regular information sources and the market for cotton futures that together narrowed risks and reduced uncertainty. In each case we perceive that the organizational innovation evolved as one or more groups perceived the possibility – through organization – of achieving more efficient transactions in the cotton trade.

(III) Institutional innovation in trade – four major changes

The cotton trade is concerned with the movement of a single commodity from grower to manufacturer. We enlarge the compass in this section to

197

The theory applied

embrace wholesale and retail trade and explore some major institutional innovations in the movement of goods from producer to consumer. We shall concentrate on four major institutional changes which mirror the evolving patterns of trade. In each case we shall see that the sequence of change conforms quite neatly to the theoretical framework which we have advanced. The four institutional changes are (A) the rise and decline of the auction system in the importing trade; (B) the rise and decline of the independent wholesaler; (C) the evolution of large-scale retailing via chain stores, department stores, and mail-order houses; and finally (D) the inception of the low-margin, self-service type of retail outlet.

(A) *The auction system*

The auction system had its greatest influence on trade in America in the period immediately after the second war with England, roughly in the years from 1815 to 1830. Before the War of 1812, British manufacturers typically sent their goods to America via one of two methods. Either they were consigned by the manufacturer directly to an agent or they were assigned to a British merchant who in turn acted through a fellow commission merchant or an agent in the United States. When the war ended, manufacturers and their agents had large stocks of goods available both in Britain and in Halifax for the American market. Immediately after the war, a vast inflow of goods was received and disposed of by traditional methods; but by late 1816 the market clearly was satiated at existing prices. The pressure of unsold inventories induced businessmen to search for a new institutional arrangement. In this case, they turned to an auction system.

The auction system had existed to a degree before the War of 1812, but it had traditionally been confined to damaged goods or occasionally to prize goods. It received substantial impetus during the War of 1812 when American privateers began bringing in prize goods which needed to be disposed of rapidly. This specialized institutional technology was innovated for general distribution of goods and services. During 1816 and 1817 large volumes of goods were disposed of through that means.

Exactly as the name implied, the goods were sold at or near the dock, with professional auctioneers knocking them down to the highest bidder, thereby eliminating all the problems both of developing wholesale and retail outlets and of holding inventories over time. The obvious reason for its success was that it provided goods for the consumer more cheaply than the importing merchant could because, given the poor state of market development, local wholesalers and retailers better understood their markets than would any middleman.

198

It is not surprising that the British merchant recognized the important advantages of the newly evolved system over the more cumbersome development of a whole network of importers and connections in his effort to spread his products throughout the American market. The innovation was so successful that it seriously hurt the traditional American importer. For a number of years, it was the target of a strident outcry by importers who demanded congressional action to limit or abolish the system, but it was profitable to its innovators.

The decline in the auction system in the 1830s and thereafter can be clearly explained by examining the factors that made for the rise of the system. The system's greatest expansion resulted from the necessity for British manufacturers to dump on the American market in the brief period of 1816 and 1817. But the underlying reason for its success at the expense of the American importing merchant was the absence at that time of two essential market ingredients. After the second war with England there simply did not exist adequate information about the structure of prices and markets throughout the United States, nor were there any well-organized patterns of wholesale and retail institutions which could move the goods efficiently throughout the system to the final consumer.

The auction system was best suited to serve individual wholesalers and retailers in the American market who had specific knowledge of their own particular needs. It was they who came to the dock and purchased the amounts that they needed, rather than depending as the importer had on the involved machinery and costly research required to gain information about a wider market. In short, the auction system mirrored a country in which the size of the market was still too small to underwrite the high costs of information essential to the growth of an institutionalized organization designed to carry goods through the importers to the final consumer. In these terms the decline of the auction system was inevitable. As the size of the American market grew, the domestic trade developed a whole series of institutional forms to convey goods from manufacturer to consumer, and the advantages of the auction system disappeared and gradually the importing trade was taken over by specialists in a chain of institutions which evolved between manufacturer and consumer.

(B) *The rise and decline of the wholesaler*

The central task of the wholesaler is the assembly and distribution of goods, therefore in effect he is a specialist in information about distributive channels. It is not surprising that the wholesaler, originally a subsidiary to the importer, gradually evolved into a specialized entity in his own right

199

as the structure of trade in the United States proliferated and developed in size and scale. In effect, wholesaling paralleled the growth of the scale of production, as commodity markets expanded geographically and became more specialized. One major characteristic of the evolution of wholesaling reflected the vertical disintegration of manufacturing firms. The early manufacturing firm in the United States of necessity carried out its entire operation from gathering together the factors of production, through producing, and finally distributing its commodity. As the economy expanded, these functions could more efficiently be separated, allowing the firm to concentrate on manufacturing alone while the distributive processes were handed over to newly established specialists in that field. In this respect the rise of the independent wholesaler was more than anything else a result of specialization and division of labor evolving in the context of a growing market size.[1]

We may detail the factors accounting for the rise of the wholesaler as follows:

(1) As the geographic size of their market grew the manufacturers needed to distribute their goods over greater and greater distances to an ever larger number of retail outlets. To cope with the task they had the alternatives of opening branch warehouses, of organizing a partially autonomous sales division, or of selling to wholesalers. There are economies of scale in wholesaling. Given small population size in many areas, the sales of a single manufacturer were insufficient to realize any of these economies. A wholesaler, however, could realize these economies by serving several manufacturers.

Progressive specialization of function did not stop with the breaking off of production from distribution. In many areas wholesaling and retailing were combined, but as each grew increasingly large there was a tendency for the retail functions to be sloughed off and for wholesaling to become specialized. Indeed, some legal discrimination and trade association sanctions were levied against jobbers who also engaged in retailing.

(2) As the range in variety of products increased, wholesalers tended to restrict their activities rather than handle a broad array of commodities. Again, this trend reflected the growing size of the market that permitted such highly specialized functions and the inherent economies of scale that dictated their profitability.

The decline of the independent wholesaler reflected again the changing pattern of services, primarily as a consequence of the increasing size of markets and concentration of population. Two major forces led to this

---

[1] This, in fact, is a title of a classic article by George Stigler, *Journal of Political Economy*, 59, no. 3 (June 1951), 185–93.

decline. As markets increased in size, the sales of single manufacturing firms were now sufficient to realize the economies of scale inherent in wholesaling. Manufacturers now found it profitable to begin their own regional warehousing and branch wholesaling establishments. The dominance of the independent wholesaler persisted longer in the West, and particularly on the Pacific coast where population was less concentrated than in the more industrialized East, where conditions were less favorable for his function. At the same time, large-scale retail outlets were developing a new institutional innovation – the chain store, the mail-order house, and the department store. These bypassed the wholesaler by dealing directly with manufacturing or in some cases by engaging in manufacturing on their own behalf. We shall now take a closer look at these three large-scale retail outlets.

(c) *Large-scale retailers*

In the mid-nineteenth century, the family-size enterprise was the dominant mode of retailing. The first significant move towards large scale retailing was the rise of the chain store. The pioneer, the Great Atlantic and Pacific Tea Company, founded its first store in 1859. Between that date and 1929, the A and P expanded enormously; in the heyday of its most rapid expansion the company opened fifty new stores a week for the entire year of 1925.

There are economies of scale in retail merchandising and as store size increases, sales per employee rise. Additional economies could be garnered by bypassing the wholesaler and engaging in large-scale buying. Since 1929, chain stores have ceased expanding and in the case of A and P and some others they have contracted substantially. In part this stems from counter-moves by existing retailers who had been badly hurt by their competition. Here, we have an example of an institutional innovation which, while increasing total income, also redistributes income drastically, and there are large losers. Our model would predict that these losers would attempt to prevent redistribution by political and economic means and they have. On the one hand, in many states they have successfully lobbied for heavy taxes on chain stores, and on the other hand, they devised new voluntary institutional arrangements to overcome the disadvantages of their small scale; namely cooperative wholesale buying. As chain stores replaced earlier forms, so the discount stores and supermarkets ultimately tend to replace chain stores. We shall examine this evolution in the next section.

The department store began earlier than the chain store, in the decade before the Civil War to be precise, but its great expansion was at a later date. Stores such as Macy's and Gimbels in New York – prototypes of the department store – offered the advantage over other stores that one could buy all manner of goods in one location and therefore enjoy a new convenience in service. Again, sales per employee were higher and therefore costs lower in such enterprises, but they required large, very dense, urban populations for success.

The third type of large-scale retailing was of completely different origin, reflecting not the growth of large urban aggregations but rather the increase in income of farm populations together with the development of rural free mail delivery, a subsidy paid to farmers by the rest of the population. Given this combination of economic events, the mail-order house became feasible. As noted in the agricultural chapter (Chapter 5), Montgomery Ward was a new institutional innovation devised in response to Grange efforts to bypass existing retail outlets. It opened in 1872 with its catalog consisting of a single sheet. Ward's served many of the goals of the Grange in that it offered a cut-rate price to farmers for a variety of goods which they could not get in local areas. By 1890 the catalog had expanded to 540 pages, and Montgomery Ward's mail-order sales became a major component in farm purchases. The other major mail-order house was Sears Roebuck, whose growth again reflected aggressive and even gaudy advertising during the heyday of its expansion. The rise of the mail-order houses was propitious in a world where farm population was large and decentralized and the cost of transportation from farm to major urban centers very high, and this cost, through mail service, could be passed on from farmers to the rest of the population. Therefore, the relative decline of mail-order houses is obviously a function of increasing farm income, and the rise of the automobile and modern transport. The mail-order houses have had to modify their institutional arrangements to meet these conditions and as a result have evolved into something approaching the modern discount store.

(D) *The self-service store*

The striking feature of modern retailing has been the development of the self-service, low-margin, discount house and supermarket type of store. Such stores are not a new idea in modern times, but their success in replacing more traditional forms is attributable to contemporary attitudes and practices. Partly, the stores reflect the preferences of consumers for self-service as against the higher prices imposed by rapidly rising labor costs in stores engaging in traditional extensive services. Partly, too, the change is due to the increased valuation of consumers' time and their desire to make purchases rapidly and conveniently without long periods of waiting. These factors together have led to the most recent revolution in retailing. Prepackaging by manufacturers is well adapted to self-service stores; so is the extension of manufacturers' guarantees with products, so that a dissatisfied customer may appeal directly to the original manufacturer for any faulty equipment and may return such products to their point of origin. These were institutional arrangements which became profitable for the manufacturer to innovate with the emergence of the self-service store, and which reinforced the trend toward such stores. One striking feature that has accompanied them, and indeed has made the change possible, has been a sharp increase in the size of the average retail transaction. What we witness in modern retailing is a decline in services performed by retailing establishments and a relative rise in consumer self-service, under the pressures just described.

The general evolution of wholesale and retail institutions in the movement of goods from producer to consumer reflects more than anything else the changing size of the market in American economic history. Technological changes such as the automobile have played a part; so, indirectly, have other innovations that have fostered vast urban conglomeration. But primarily it is the growth and concentration in population and the growth of income which has paced and determined the revolutionary changes in the institutional structure of wholesale and retail trade.

(IV) Industry self-regulation – the American Medical Association

The history of medicine in the United States is an illustration of a successful effort by a voluntary organization to achieve control over supply in its own industry and to redistribute income in its own favor. The American Medical Association was founded in 1847, but before that time there had been numerous efforts by doctors to regulate the industry against widespread quackery and unqualified medical practitioners. The long history of patent medicine was just one manifestation of the variety of purveyors of cure-alls which sprang up all over Colonial America and the early United States. As a result, efforts to regulate began early, although in colonial times Massachusetts and some of the colonies lacked any provisional regulatory policy. In the beginning of the nineteenth century a substantial number of regulatory acts were passed. Even before Independence the city of New York had passed an act to regulate the practice of 'physick' and surgery within its bounds. The statutes required that two judges of the Supreme Court with the aid of physicians examine an applicant; a fine of five pounds was assessed for practicing without a license.

The first organization attaining the right to regulate medical practice was the Massachusetts Medical Society. The law detailed the various

The theory applied

official duties of the officers, the society's right to sue and be sued, and kindred legal niceties. The president and fellows were authorized to examine all candidates for the license, and anyone refusing to serve as examiner was subject to a fine of one hundred pounds. When Harvard College opened its medical department the following year, it was decided that since its requirements were satisfactory, Harvard graduates would be admitted to practice without further examination.[1] Other states followed the lead of Massachusetts, and in 1806 New York State decided to place medical regulations in the hands of the state society. Yet this early self-regulation within the industry did not last, though it foreshadowed the action of a century later. By 1835 a wave of repeal of state medical laws began and continued. The regulatory function of the New York State Medical Society was ended by 1844, as were those of other states. In effect, the populace had not been convinced of the qualitative difference between the physician and the many non-licensed doctors who put pressure upon the legislatures to avoid the licensing and regulatory procedures of the medical association.

It was not for another three-quarters of a century that doctors were able to effectively persuade legislative bodies that industry self-regulation was advantageous and that the skills of trained and licensed doctors would improve public well being. Right after its founding, the American Medical Association developed two basic propositions – one, that medical students should have acquired a suitable preliminary education; and two, that a uniform elevated standard of requirements for the degree of M.D. should be adopted by all medical schools in the United States.[2]

The first proposition was achieved in the following half century – that is, doctors were able to convince most state legislatures to license the practice of medicine. Thus, the various states set up boards of medical examiners to administer examinations to test the qualifications of applicants. But the second stage took much longer. Its initial success began with the forming in 1904 of a Council of Medical Education of the American Medical Association. Determined to improve the quality of medical education, the association appealed to the Carnegie Foundation for support in a critical examination of existing medical schools. The subsequent report of Flexner and Caldwell in 1910 was not only a classic but, in terms of its consequences, had probably as far-reaching effects as any document in American economic history. It was Flexner's view that doctors should be fewer but better trained; with this goal in mind he argued in the report that a substantial number

[1] H. Schafer, *The American Medical Profession, 1783–1850* (New York, 1936), pp. 206–7.
[2] A. Flexner, *Medical Education in the United States and Canada*, Bulletin number 4, Carnegie Foundation for the Advancement of Teaching, 1910, p. 10.

Institutional change in the service industries

of medical schools in the United States were substandard and should be shut down.

Persuaded by the report, state legislatures decided that the American Medical Association should be entrusted with the determination of what was, or was not, a first-class medical school, that standards of acceptability for a license to practice medicine should be determined by state medical examining boards, and that these boards should consider only graduates of schools approved by the AMA, or by the American Medical Association of Medical Colleges, whose lists are identical.[1]

The results were certainly dramatic, as the two tables below indicate. Table 9.1 shows how drastically the number of students in medical schools dropped after the report and indicates that the number did not again reach the total of 1904 until 1954, fifty years later. Even more conclusive is the evidence from Table 9.2 which shows that the number of doctors per 100,000 population fell continually from 1900 until the 1950s. The results would be expected to lead to a change in doctors' incomes, and this they do. Consecutive series are lacking for the early part of the century, but between 1939 and 1959, when we have good data, mean incomes of physicians increased by 434 percent.[2] This exceeded the rate of increase for other occupational classes by the following wide margins:

Professional-technical and kindred workers   75%
Managers, officials, and proprietors   105%
Full-time employees all industries   66%

The results also show up in a discontinuity in the distribution of skills and ability as reflected by income. The income distribution of medical earnings is unlike that of any other industry in the United States. Not only is the coefficient of variation higher (a measure of the relative variation of earnings) but the distribution is extremely skewed toward the upper end. What this illustrates is that the medical practitioner with the M.D. attains a high level of income, then a long gap occurs before one reaches the income levels of the various other workers involved in the health field. There is no middle group of semi-professionals having lesser categories of skills. The obvious implication is that the licensing procedure for an M.D. permits no variation for minor levels.[3]

[1] Rueben Kessel, 'Price Discrimination in Medicine', *The Journal of Law and Economics* (October 1858), 27–8.
[2] These and following figures come from Elton Rayack, *Professional Power and American Medicine* (Cleveland, Ohio, 1967).
[3] These findings are continued in a provisional and preliminary study by the National Bureau of Economic Research, *The Manpower Gap in Health and Services*, by V. Fuchs, E. Rand, and J. Garrett.

205

TABLE 9.1 *Medical schools, students, and graduates: selected years, 1904–64*

	Schools		Students		Graduates	
Year	Total	Class A or approved	Total	Class A or approved	Total	Class A or approved
1904	160	a	28,142	a	5,747	a
1905	160	a	26,147	a	4,606	a
1910	131	66	21,526	12,530	4,440	3,165
1915	104	67	14,891	11,314	3,536	2,629
1920	88	70	14,088	12,559	3,047	2,680
1921	86	70	14,873	13,488	3,191	2,811
1922	83	69	16,140	14,625	2,629	2,304
1923	81	70	17,432	16,454	3,120	2,881
1924	80	70	17,728	16,775	3,562	3,343
1925	80	71	18,200	17,462	3,974	3,842
1926	79	71	18,840	17,887	3,962	3,732
1927	80	73	19,662	18,754	4,035	3,798
1928	80	74	20,545	19,794	4,262	4,091
1929	76	75	20,878	20,843	4,446	4,412
1930		76		21,597		4,565
1931		76		21,982		4,735
1932		76		22,135		4,936
1933		77		22,466		4,895
1934		77		22,799		5,035
1935		77		22,888		5,101
1936		77		22,564		5,183
1937		77		22,095		5,377
1938		77		21,587		5,194
1939		77		21,302		5,089
1940		77		21,271		5,097
1941		77		21,379		5,275
1942		77		22,031		5,163
1943		76		22,631		5,223
1944		77		23,529		5,134
1944 (second session)		77		24,666		5,169
1945		77		24,028		5,136
1946		77		23,216		5,826
1947		77		23,900		6,389
1948		77		22,739		5,543
1949		78		23,670[b]		5,094
1950		79		25,103		5,553
1951		79		26,186		6,135
1952		79		27,076		6,080
1953		79		27,688		6,668
1954		80		28,227		6,861
1955		81		28,583		6,977
1956		82		28,639		6,845

Institutional change in the service industries

TABLE 9.1 (continued)

Year	Schools Class A or approved	Students Class A or approved	Graduates Class A or approved
1957	85	29,130	6,796
1958	85	29,473	6,861
1959	85	29,614	6,860
1960	85	30,084	7,081
1961	86	30,288	6,994
1962	87	31,078	7,163
1963	87	31,491	7,264
1964		32,001	7,336

[a] Data not available.
[b] The 167 students at the University of Washington are not included in this total since this school, which opened in 1946, had only three years in operation and was not included in the official statistics for 1948–9.

SOURCES: *The Journal of the American Medical Association*, 3 September 1949, pp. 27–93; 8 September 1951, pp. 131–69; and 13 September 1952, p. 109 for data through 1950; 16 November 1964 for 1962 through 1964. U.S. Department of Health, Education, and Welfare, *Health, Education, and Welfare Trends*, 1961, for data from 1951 through 1961.[1]

The American Medical Association clearly evidences a successful effort by a voluntary organization to control supply. This control and its implications for income redistribution could not have been accomplished without the support of the government's coercive power. The action group was the Association in collaboration with the Carnegie Foundation, and the institutional instruments used were licensing procedures and state laws which effectively stipulated licensing requirements. Medicine is a very skilled profession, and it was and is the control over the training in these skills that provides the basis for the group's ability to restrict supply and therefore keep prices artificially high. But the government's regulatory power depended to some extent on the at least tacit support of the electorate who were convinced that they would prefer to have better quality doctors without perhaps a thorough understanding that the price they paid was higher medical fees and smaller numbers. Licensing exists in other industries, but without effective control over entry, it increases the level of investment required, but does not produce monopoly profits.

[1] E. Rayack, *Professional Power and American Medicine: The Economics of the American Medical Association* (Cleveland, Ohio, 1967), pp. 68–9.

The theory applied

TABLE 9.2   *Number of doctors of medicine and rate per 100,000*
of population, 1900–59

Year	Doctors of medicine	
	Number	Per 100,000 of population
1900	119,749	157
1910	135,000	146
1920	144,977	136
1925	147,010	127
1927	149,521	126
1928	—	—
1929	152,503	125
1930	153,803	125
1931	156,406	126
1934	161,359	128
1936	165,163	129
1938	169,628	131
1940	175,163	133
1942	180,496	134
1947	—	—
1949	201,277	135
1950	203,400[a]	134
1951	205,500[a]	133
1952	207,900[a]	132
1953	210,900[a]	132
1954	214,200[a]	132
1955	218,061	132
1956	—	—
1957	226,225	132
1958	—	—
1959	236,089	133

[a] Estimated.
SOURCE: U.S. Department of Health, Education, and Welfare, *Health, Education, and Welfare Trends*, 1961, p. 24.[1]

(V) Conclusion

How well does our model predict the pattern of institutional change in the service industries? To begin with, it is not as useful as in other sectors of the economy where the characteristics of the industrial structure are more homogeneous. The most fundamental feature of the service industry is that its components show very few common characteristics. This heterogeneity results in widely diverse patterns of institutional change stemming from the varied sources of 'profit' potentials assumed by our model. However, while there are few general sources of institutional change, when we explore in more depth specific parts of the service industry, our model does enable us

[1] *Ibid.* p. 71.

to make some limited and hopefully useful analyses of the evolving arrangemental structures. Quite clearly, for a large part of the service industry where
no significant economies of scale are attainable over a broad range of output,
our model correctly predicts the absence of the corporation and kindred
organizational forms aimed at capturing the gains from scale. Proprietorship
and partnership continue to characterize much of the service sector.

In Chapter 1, we postulated that information had many of the characteristics of a public good; that is, once generated, it could be used by one,
one hundred, one thousand, or one million people at no additional cost of
gathering. From this we infer that there were substantial economies of
scale in the gathering of information and we also saw in the agricultural
chapter that the free rider problem sometimes made it difficult to finance
private information-gathering and disseminating services. In this chapter,
we have seen that the private sector functions efficiently to gather and
disseminate price information. What is the difference? We suggest that the
difference lies in the useful life of the information itself. *Ceteris paribus*, the
longer lived the information, the more nearly a public good it becomes. It
is easier to exclude free riders for a short period of time, but in the long
period, they climb over the wall.

Our model is most appropriate to explain institutional innovations
designed to reduce transactions costs as we have described in Sections II
and III. Here the source of disequilibrium which created the potential for
new profitable opportunities by institutional reorganization was technological
change and size of the market in America. But even here our model has
some significant limitations, especially in those cases where the potential
gains from a new form of institutional organization led to immediate and
rather large losses to groups in the society and thereby engendered political
opposition. Even the early auction system raised a widespread outcry from
traditional importers who sought legislation to outlaw its use. Similarly, the
success of the chain store in the last half of the nineteenth century led to
widespread efforts by small-scale retailers to negate its cost advantages by
taxation of the large corporations.

Similarly, our model would correctly predict the pattern of relationship
between service industries and political organization in those areas where
state regulation developed early. This was particularly true in finance,
insurance, and banking. The history of the large life insurance companies
in New York before the Armstrong investigation of 1905–6 is a story that
has been told elsewhere.[1] In this case we see the regulatory machinery of

[1] See D. C. North, 'Entrepreneurial Policy and Internal Organization in the Large Life
Insurance Companies at the Time of the Armstrong Investigation of Life Insurance',
in *Exportations in Entrepreneurial History*, 5, no. 3 (March 1953); also M. Keller, *The
Life Insurance Enterprise, 1885–1910* (Cambridge, Mass., 1963).

The theory applied

New York State being employed by the major life insurance companies for more than three decades to promote their expansive policies and to thwart the discontent of policyholders. Such a result would predictably stem from our model and can be equally usefully applied to examining the history of state regulation of banking and other types of financial enterprise such as consumer loans, etc. However, the limitations of our model are also evident at this point, since it in no way enables us to tell the outcome. Thus, in the case of the history of the life insurance companies' control over the New York State Insurance Department, our model would certainly predict that the regulatory machinery would be a battleground of the major companies (as it was) but we could not foreshadow the Armstrong investigation. Actually, that investigation resulted from the conflicting interests of dominant financial groups. Moreover, the subsequent history of life insurance shows a significant retreat from such gaudy political activities apt to attract the public eye. This was clearly a consequence of the thoroughness of the investigation and its traumatic results that reverberated through the industry. Since that time the life insurance industry's influence over the regulatory machinery has been far more discreet and basically redirected. These consequences, too, we could not foretell.

Our model is correct in its prediction in another area. In cases where the populace could be convinced of the need for self-regulation by highly professionalized groups, this conviction would lead to a degree of internal control over their environment resulting in limitation of supply and a degree of monopoly power. Our case history of the American Medical Association presented in Section IV above is but one illustration. It is worthwhile to note that many other types of professional groups have attempted such licensing procedures and efforts to regulate supply. The legal profession, like the medical profession, has a skewed distribution of income which suggests that it, of all other professions, has been most successful in emulating the American Medical Association.

Overall, therefore, our analysis of the service sector provides no such general ability to explain and predict the pattern of institutional change as in other industries. It does provide more limited and specific insights into particular segments of the industry and even into the general pattern of institutional evolution. What it lacks, basically, is the capacity to predict the outcome in those frequent cases where certain groups stand to lose substantially in the course of institutional change.

THE LABOR FORCE: ORGANIZATION AND EDUCATION

(I) Introduction

Earlier in this book, we explained that the economy's production capabilities are determined by the supply of the three basic inputs – land, capital, and labor – and the technological relationship that governs their combination. As we have seen, the need for both land and capital has stimulated arrangemental innovation (i.e. underwritten an improvement in the state of institutional technology) that promoted either income redistribution or increases in total income. The need for labor can also inspire the innovation of institutional arrangements. Slavery, indentured servitude, the importation of Oriental labor, European recruitment drives for industrial workers, and the governmental employment centers established during World War II are some examples of arrangemental attempts to increase the supply of labor and make that labor more mobile and efficient. Each of these attempts has generated an array of institutional arrangements. Slavery, for example, inspired the development of formal markets to facilitate the flow of slaves between regions; later, firms emerged whose only function was to make available to potential European immigrants the information and funds necessary to come to the United States.

In addition to those innovations that supplement the existing labor supply, there have been many arrangements devised to educate and train the labor force to meet technological advances in production. Some, such as secretarial and speed reading schools and schools that train computer operators and programmers, are tailored to fit specific but general needs of production and have traditionally been carried out by an arrangemental technology at the individual level. These private ventures are profitable only when the workers themselves perceive an expected return (in terms of higher future earnings) and are willing to assume training costs for a particular job.

In other instances, when the skills are specialized, the firms themselves bear the cost of training their own workers. The perceived value of such an arrangement to any given firm depends on the returns that firm expects to realize from the investment in training. If the firm has a monopoly position in an industry and if it requires workers with a specialized skill peculiar only to that industry, then it pays the firm to train its own workers. (The training programs of the many firms that make up the Bell System provide an example of industry-financed education.)

Finally, if a firm required a large number of skilled workers for plant maintenance (such as electricians, carpenters, pipefitters, bricklayers, etc.) and the market price of these workers is high because of artificial restrictions on entry into these occupations, it may be profitable for a firm or group of firms to underwrite apprenticeship programs. This kind of arrangement can only be profitable if the firm can induce its trained workers to remain in its employ, either by offering something that competing firms do not offer (such as job security), or by joining with other firms in the industry to establish minimum and maximum wage scales for specific jobs (labor unions are most helpful in enforcing this kind of provision).

Throughout most industry, however, there is no way to guarantee that after the costs of training have been borne by one firm, the revenues will not accrue to another. After all, a firm cannot force a worker to remain in its employ. Under such circumstances, as our model would predict, it is likely that firms would attempt to spread training costs through the body politic and that governmental arrangements would be innovated. Section v of this chapter explores this aspect of training in more detail.

Although all three of the factors of production – land, capital, and labor – have stimulated a variety of institutional arrangements designed to acquire and exploit these inputs, the labor factor differs in one important aspect. Labor is, after all, made up of men – each himself a profit maximizer and ever on the watch to capture potential external profits or to redistribute income in his own favor. An examination of the labor sector from this point of view reveals a variety of institutional arrangements that can be analyzed in terms of the model. Nearly all are aimed at income redistribution, and the most well-documented fall under the general heading of 'organized labor'. We will focus on some of these arrangements, and while it can be argued that this chapter reads like a standard labor history text, it is hoped that the application of our model to the traditional and well-known history of organized labor will give the reader a new perspective into why organized labor developed as it did.

(II) Unions and the redistribution of income: some notes on theory[1]

The history of organized labor is a story of attempted income redistribution and the growth of trade unionism is a picture of arrangemental innovation.[2] Before we can explain labor's story in terms of the model, it is necessary to delve into a little theory regarding unions and income redistribution. After all, the predictive powers of our model depend on the determination and comparison of alternative costs, and certainly these costs are influenced by the amount of potential income, who has it, and how difficult it is to capture it.

Theory tells us that there are certain requirements for effective redistribution and that, under certain conditions, the redistribution can be from business firms, consumers, and the owners of certain specialized factors of production.[3]

Not too surprisingly, effective redistribution requires that there exist some income that can be redistributed without causing the death (economically or physically) of the previous recipient or without causing that recipient to withdraw the service that produced the income. In the case of the firm, if there are no excess profits or rents accruing to the firm because of the ownership of some specialized resource, there is no excess income that the unions can accrue no matter how strong that union may be.[4] In the case of the consumers, the condition implies that there must be some income in

---

[1] Some of the theoretical issues in this section have benefited from lengthy discussion with Christopher Archibald.

[2] Since phrases like trade union and labor union are commonly used without clear definition, it appears useful to clarify the terms used in this chapter. Trade union and labor union are used synonymously to identify any group of workers who organize in an attempt to redistribute income toward or resist redistribution away from members of that group. In turn, labor unions are divided into two subsets: The term 'craft union' will be used to denote those unions made up of workers with a similar job skill involving a substantial amount of training. Under certain conditions these unions are able to establish monopoly control of labor supply in particular specialized areas. These groups, in many cases, are able to achieve income redistribution with no more governmental assistance than a 'hands-off' attitude. The term 'industrial union' will refer to those unions whose members (or at least a majority of whose members) do not possess a specialized job skill. These unions, therefore, are not able to effect monopoly power over labor supply. In order for them to achieve income redistribution, they must rely on the direct intervention of government or physical coercion.

[3] To the economist a factor of production is something that goes into the production of a good or service (land, labor, and capital are the classic examples) and a specialized factor is one that can be used only in the production of a particular type of good or service.

[4] As we have previously noted, rent (despite the common usage of the term) is used by economists to denote any income earned by a factor over what can be earned in the best alternative.

excess of subsistence, and in the case of the owners of specialized resources, that their rents are positive even after redistribution.

For firms that are purely competitive in both their product and factor markets and own no specialized resources, unions are powerless to capture any of their income. If, however, the competitive firm does own some specialized resource (one not available to the other firms in the industry) – a particularly good location or easy access to raw materials, to give two common examples – then its profits will be higher than those of its competitors, and these extra profits could be redistributed without threatening the life of the firm. Similarly, if lack of knowledge about alternative employment has kept workers tied to a particular firm (no matter what the market structure), the firm can be thought to be accruing a rent from their lack of knowledge, and a union that provides information about alternatives can allow those rents to be redistributed from employer to employee, or, alternatively, if it suppresses that information it can effect a redistribution from employer to union official.[1] As a matter of fact, as opposed to theory, these exceptions are precisely that and we would not expect the firms in a competitive industry to yield much potential redistributive income.

If the industry is non-competitive in either the product or factor markets, however, frequently there are substantial rents that can be captured if the union is strong enough. A non-competitive position in the product market can result from a barrier (artificial or natural) that acts to prevent the entry of potentially competitive firms and therefore keeps profits above the minimum level necessary to hold the firm in the industry. It makes no difference whether the extra profits are the result of the possession of a patent, a special franchise, or some natural indivisibility, these rents can be expropriated by the union, if the membership can bargain both for wages and the level of employment.

If the firm is non-competitive in the factor market, these rents can also be expropriated by the union if it is strong enough. In this case the unions do not even have to bargain over the level of employment, they can let the firm make those decisions. All that is required is that they be able to establish uniform wages and working conditions, and it may be possible that they will manage to increase both the amount of income accruing to the workers and the level of employment.

Even when there are no excess profits or rents accruing to one or more firms in an industry, it is still possible for a successful union to effect a redistribution from the consumers to the laborers. (And at times the firms themselves may accrue a fraction of the income so redistributed.) Three

---

[1] As we shall see, it is this later condition that makes it possible for racketeer locals to effect 'sweetheart' contracts with certain employees.

cases appear particularly important from the point of view of American development.

First, in a largely competitive industry where labor costs are a high proportion of total costs, a union may provide the coercive power that permits the owners to organize an effective cartel. Once the union has set a floor on wages, the gains that an individual firm can accrue from cheating on the cartel price are small, and this alone may convince them to abide by the group's decision. If that is insufficient, the union itself may assume the policing function and strike any employer who sells for less than the cartel price. If, in addition, some method of prohibiting entry can be found, and here also the union may act as an effective deterrent, long-run prices are maintained at levels that yield extra normal profits, and the added income is divided between employer and the members of the union.[1] We would expect in this instance, and in fact history bears out our expectations, that the employers support the organization activity of the unions.

Second, if the union can bargain across an entire industry, it may be possible to increase wages in even a completely competitive industry. No one firm can afford to accede to union demands since it has no excess profits, and without a price increase it would be forced out of business, and if it attempts to increase its prices its sales will fall to zero. What no single firm can afford to do alone, however, all firms can afford to do together. Thus an industry-wide agreement could raise costs across the board and effect a redistribution of income from consumers to the union membership. Since higher prices would almost certainly lead to lower total industry sales, we would not expect firms to favor such bargains; however, since the costs to any given firm are likely to be small (with a fall in demand, marginal firms would go out of business, but the rest of the industry would in the long run be largely unaffected), their resistance to an industry-wide agreement would almost certainly be less than their resistance to union attempts to bargain individually with each firm.

Third, during periods of full capacity utilization (full employment and probably inflation), the demand curves of individual firms tend to become less elastic. The less elastic is a firm's demand curve, the more of any cost increase the firm can pass on and the less it must absorb in terms of lower output. Similarly, in periods of excess capacity the quantities demanded tend to become more responsive to changes in price and it becomes difficult to pass on all or nearly all of any cost changes to the consumer. Thus we would expect firms to be more tractable to union demands in periods of inflation (since the costs to them are low), and we would expect substantial

---

[1] Even if no way can be found to prevent new entry the cartel can be effective in the short run.

The theory applied

resistance to union demands for higher wages in periods of widespread unemployment, since at those times the firms are likely to be forced to bear the largest portions of the increases.

Finally, in the case of a resource that is specialized from the point of view of the industry but not from the point of view of a particular firm, there are rents accruing to the owners of that resource. It is, however, very difficult for a union to effect that redistribution. Any attempt at negotiating with a particular firm will cause the owners to shift their resources to a competitor, and attempts at industry-wide bargaining will be met by severe resistance from all the firms who do not possess the specialized resource. Only an industry-wide contract that affects only the firm employing the resource represents a theoretical alternative, and the difficulties involved in negotiating such a contract are immense. Moreover, as long as the owners of the resource have some finite reservation price the redistribution is limited to the rents accruing above that price, since any attempt to extort more will cause the owners to withdraw their resource from the market.

These, then, represent a set of necessary conditions for effective redistribution. They are, however, nowhere near sufficient. Not only must there be income available for redistribution, but also the unions must have some effective coercive powers if they are going to force the present recipients to surrender a portion of their purchasing power. The most obvious and widely used weapon of coercion is the strike – the withholding of labor services – but under what conditions are the strike or threatened strike effective? First, the institutional environment must be such that a strike does not carry with it threats of legal punishment whose costs exceed the potential gains. Thus, the threat of deportation to Australia was sufficient in eighteenth-century England to paralyze almost all attempts by worker groups to effect significant income redistribution. Given legal permission to collude to withhold labor services, the effectiveness will be greater the greater is the control exercised by a union of the supply of a skill that is needed in the process of production, and for which there are no ready substitutes. If the skill is the basis for the redistribution, there are no limits on the recipients of that income; however, a union of the skilled workers alone can always, if it chooses, collect the total redistributed income for its members.

In the absence of a monopoly on the supply of a skill, workers can still strike to coerce redistribution, if they can prevent employers from reaching beyond or within the union for replacements. In the United States in the present era a first approximation of this legal monopoly is the law that requires employers to bargain in good faith. This requirement makes attempts at massive 'external' substitution (non-union for union) against

216

The labor force : organization and education

striking workers difficult (but not impossible). The unions attempt to bolster this first approximation with some additional requirement that can be used to force all workers to abide by the majority's decisions and to prevent an internal substitution against union minded members. The threat is always present that if some workers do not strike the management can keep operating and, if 'employment quality' is not controlled, employers will be able to replace redistribution-minded workers with others. Union security provisions are, for example, attempts at legislating these second degree prohibitions against 'internal substitution' at the firm level. Although the coercive powers inherent in these legal monopolies are usually substantially less than those based on supply of a needed skill (it is often easier to get around legal prohibitions than economic ones), they can be an effective weapon for redistribution. Moreover, they will be more effective the more sympathetic are the governmental agencies charged with enforcing the legal barriers to substitution. This suggests why it is that unions whose coercive powers are based on law are more conscious of political problems, while those whose powers are based on skill are usually more concerned with technological ones.

One final comment. If a union has sufficient power to effect redistribution, it still must decide how it intends to divide up the spoils, and very often that decision comes down to a choice between employment and income. In general, the greater the redistribution the smaller will be the number of members who will have jobs, and while appropriate side-payments could solve this problem, such payments are almost impossible to negotiate (it is very difficult to convince employed workers to share their incomes with those who are not). As a result, any particular wage–price bargain ofttimes implies that some members will gain and others will lose, and the decision of more wages or more work will frequently depend upon the relative bargaining strengths of the losers and winners groups within the union.

(III) Exogenous changes in the legal environment and institutional innovation[1]

In Chapter 4, we discussed the environmental factors that help to determine institutional innovation and the influence of a changing institutional environment upon the menu of permissible arrangemental alternatives. We have argued that the institutional environment may be altered by constitutional

[1] Most of the material in this section is drawn from J. R. Commons *et al.*, *History of Labor in the United States* (New York, 1918), H. A. Millis and R. E. Montgomery, *Organized Labor* (New York and London, 1945), and S. Lebergott, 'Labor', in *American Economic Growth: An Economist's History of the United States* (New York, 1971).

The theory applied

amendment, court decisions, and changes in the way the community evaluates public v. private arrangements. All economic institutions function within the framework of political ground rules and are affected by changes in these rules.

Not only does the labor sector give us a particularly good demonstration of the link between an institution and its environment, but it demonstrates the influence of environmental alterations upon the structure of the sector itself. As the political ground rules have been altered over the course of American development, the labor force has been progressively divided into three distinct subgroups. At any given time, each group is offered the same menu of arrangemental alternatives, but the costs vary for each group and, therefore, so do the perceived values.

(1) Trade union as the alternative of choice

For many years, those economists and historians who study labor institutions have felt that three court decisions stand out as being particularly important to the development of organized labor. Yet in the absence of theory, there has been no analytical basis for these feelings. Our model confirms the significance of these decisions and suggests both why and how they had such an impact on organized labor. Let us turn to the three decisions and expand on their implications in terms of our model:

(A) *The* Philadelphia Cordwainers *Case (1806)*

The decision of the court (an exogenous change) held that unions *per se* were an illegal conspiracy and heavy penalties could be imposed upon members. Thus, for all of the labor force, trade union organization was too costly to be of any positive value, and the menu of permissible alternatives was reduced for all.

Three years later, a New York court opened the door to unionism a little by declaring that a union organization itself was not an illegal conspiracy, but if union members took any joint action that injured either workers (through work restrictions) or consumers (through higher prices), their action was an illegal conspiracy. It was left to the courts to decide whether or not a particular union's wage demands did, in fact, injure consumers, and therefore it was no longer a certainty that union members would be prosecuted. As suggested earlier in this chapter, redistribution is more likely to occur during full employment and rising prices when firms are better able to pass along cost increases to the consumer. In nearly all cases,

218

the consumer will absorb such increases rather than institute legal action to prevent it. It is, after all, less costly for any individual consumer to accept a moderate rise in prices than to bear all the expense of an appeal to the courts. In times of depression, however, when cost increases are not so easily passed on and income, therefore, is distributed from the firm to union members, it is quite likely that firms would appeal to the courts. Thus, the costs of trade union organization vary with economic conditions: during prosperity, when court action seems unlikely, the costs decline and the value of such an arrangement appears positive; during depression, the likelihood of prosecution increases the costs and the value falls. In addition, it must be remembered that even in times of prosperity, income redistribution can only be effected by those groups who, because of their skill advantage, are able to exercise some degree of coercion.

History confirms these hypotheses. During the depression of 1820, for example, there were few trade unions that could act to redistribute income without risking criminal prosecution. As a result, the perceived value of such arrangements fell and the trade union as a redistributive arrangement almost passed out of existence. As prosperity returned, unemployment began to decline, the threat of prosecution fell and the value of trade unions as the arrangement of choice again became positive. For example, beginning with 1824 and continuing through 1825, strikes were called in a number of cities by unions representing tailors, carpenters, housepainters, stonecutters, hand loom weavers, stevedores, and cabinetmakers.[1] Without exception, all were trade unions organized by craftsmen along craft lines.

Thus, the political rules of the game decreed that union activity can at the whim of the court be punished. In theory, this decision places a high cost on trade union membership and relegates all workers to a single unorganized category. Concurrent with this aspect of the institutional environment, fluctuating business conditions at times caused the value of trade union arrangements (even though they were illegal) to become positive for those few workers who could exploit a coercive advantage and who could avoid prosecution. For this reason, during times of prosperity, we see the emergence of a bipartite labor force – the organized (open only to skilled workers) and the unorganized.

(B) Commonwealth *v.* Hunt (*1842*)

The court ruled that the actions of unions were not illegal unless their intent or their means were illegal. In short, the court held that unions were

---

[1] J. R. Commons *et al., History of Labour in the United States* (New York, 1918), vol. 1, p. 157.

The theory applied

not illegal, but failed to say that they were legal. For most of the next century, American unions existed in limbo between legality and illegality. This ruling altered the institutional environment by placing trade unions permanently on the menu of legal alternative arrangements, and this made permanent the bipartite division of the sector. The decision forced the government into a general permissive role *vis à vis* the unions and allowed skilled workers to exploit their natural monopoly position for economic gain. For these workers, unionism was placed permanently on the menu of permissible arrangemental alternatives, and with few exceptions, it has continued to be the arrangement of choice.

Just as the *Hunt* decision had an important bearing on the number of trade unions innovated, a second exogenous change of this period affected the organizational structure of many trade unions. Improved transportation facilities (railway mileage increased from 2,800 in 1840 to 30,660 in 1860) contributed to the geographic expansion of the market, and local trade unions soon found themselves unable to redistribute income because 'foreign' labor provided a ready substitute. In order to retain monopoly control of the supply of skilled labor, trade unions discovered that they needed national organizations. At least five national unions were in existence at the time of the *Hunt* decision; after the decision a dozen more were innovated. By the end of the 1860s, there were at least thirty national trade unions, and by 1883, there were fifty.

Not all trades formed national unions, however. In 1883, for example, national organization in fifty trades was matched by purely local organization in fifty others. In fields such as building construction where the market remained local, unions were not forced to deal with national competition. They did, however, continue to form local city-wide trade assemblies for the purpose of helping one another during strikes and to block entry into the local labor force of immigrants from 'foreign' cities.

The significance of the *Hunt* decision upon the innovation of trade unions as the arrangement of choice cannot be measured by determining the ratio of union members to non-union members or even by comparing the ratio of skilled union members to skilled non-union members at any given point in time. Rather, we should look at the times and places where theory suggests that income redistribution can occur and see whether, in fact, it does. Theory suggests that income redistribution would occur among skilled workers. The innovation of national trade unions (made desirable by the growth of national markets, but made permissible by the *Hunt* decision) illustrates an increasing utilization among skilled workers of the trade union arrangement in the decades following 1840.

Still, the trade union arrangement was not an arrangement of choice for most of the labor force, and, we suspect, not even for most of the skilled labor force. It is difficult to determine whether the very slow diffusion of the trade union arrangement among skilled workers is a lag to be explained by the model or by the fluctuation of those economic conditions under which redistribution is likely to occur. Certainly, depressions and the war lowered the value of redistributive arrangements, and because most trade unions tended to disappear during such adverse times, workers were faced with repeating the organizational process each time the economy indicated that redistribution was again possible.[1]

As more and more union members began to perceive the value of holding together during times of depression, we begin to see more unions riding through depression with their organizational structures still intact. Trades that did not have to suffer post-depression organizational pains were able to grow at a much faster rate than others. For example, of the thirty national unions in existence during the decade of the 1870s, only eighteen survived the depression. Even though, in most cases, their membership at the end of the depression was small, the unions that had existing structures grew to a much larger size. For example, the Carpenters and Joiners Union, founded in 1881 with 2,042 members, had 3,293 members in 1883; while the Brick-layers and Masons, founded in 1865, had a total membership in 1880 of 303 and grew to 9,193 by 1883.[2]

The American Federation of Labor played an important role in keeping alive the organizational structure of its affiliates during those periods when income redistribution was not likely to occur. At the first convention in 1886, the enumeration of the duties of the executive council of this new federation of trade unions included: securing the unification of all labor organizations (disseminating information to member unions regarding the wisdom of staying organized and, of course, staying in the federation); assessing the legitimacy of boycotts and appealing to affiliates to honor the sanctioned ones (thus strengthening the coercive advantage of trade unions); and issuing general appeals for voluntary financial assistance to striking member unions. In short, the AFL provided information designed to persuade workers to maintain their union structure even during those periods when they received no direct gains. The reduction of reorganizational lags was a contributing factor to the marked increase in trade union membership during the late 1880s and 1900s, as shown in Table 10.1.

For the non-skilled workers, the *Hunt* decision was of little importance.

---

[1] A very few trade unions managed to keep their organizational structures intact during depression years by functioning as insurance and benefit societies. Thus the organizational costs would not have to be borne again and the organizational lag was not repeated.

[2] Commons, *History of Labour*, vol. 2, p. 313.

The theory applied

TABLE 10.1   *Labor force and union membership, 1897–1920*

	AFL membership (000)	Union membership (000)	U.S. labor force (000)
1897	262		
1900	625	791	29,070
1910	1,587	2,116	37,480
1920	4,093	5,034	41,610

SOURCES: AFL figures: Leo Wolman, *Ebb and Flow in Trade Unionism*, National Bureau of Economic Research, New York, 1936; all other figures from Stanley Lebergott.

These workers had no inherent coercive power, and government's new attitude did not affect them directly. Interestingly enough, however, many unskilled workers entertained hopes of utilizing the coercive advantage of skilled workers to effect income redistribution for both the skilled and non-skilled sectors. It was to achieve this end that many unskilled workers joined the Knights of Labor.

Founded in 1869 by Uriah Stephens, the Knights desired to transfer income from capitalists to producers. Stephens did not recognize the bipartite nature of the work force and believed that the interests of all workers were basically the same. Even though the Knights professed to be opposed to both strikes and craft-based unions, they often attempted to act as a more traditional trade union.

The Knights were an agglomeration of craft unions, industrial unions, and random individuals, some of whom were self-employed. In many instances, craft unions joined the Knights en masse, retaining their former arrangemental structures, and their inherent coercive powers. The members of the true craft assemblies wanted to use their coercive powers to effect economic gains for members of their own groups, while the Knights' membership at large wanted the craft groups to use that power to effect income redistribution for the total membership. Most of the redistribution that did occur was the result of the craft-based assemblies who won economic gains for their members, but seldom for unskilled workers in allied industries. The fundamental conflict between skilled and unskilled workers ultimately led to the Knights' dissolution, and it suggests that no voluntary cooperative group can hold together when some of the members are expected to transfer income to others with no offsetting gains to themselves.

(c) Jones & Laughlin Steel Company *v.* National Labor Relations Board (*1937*)

This suit upheld the provisions of the National Labor Relations Act (Wagner Act) of 1935 and established that union membership was a right of all citizens – a right to be protected by law from attempts at infringement by employers. The law required employers to bargain collectively with employees, and it prohibited the dismissal of employees because of their union affiliation. This governmental action conveyed to a large number of unskilled workers a source of coercive power similar to, but much less strong than, the natural coercive advantage of the skilled worker. In addition, the decision reinforced and strengthened the position of the skilled workers.

With the decision the American labor force was divided into three distinct groups: skilled workers who have a natural coercive advantage; nonskilled workers who derive coercive power by statute; and workers who, for a variety of reasons, are not affected by federal labor legislation and who for the most part continue to be unorganized.[1]

It was the growth of the industrial union that characterized the period following the Wagner Act. In 1929, about 17 percent of organized workers were in industrial unions; in 1933, 33 percent; and in 1940, it is estimated that over 50 percent of all organized workers were affiliated with unions that could be categorized as industrial or a combination of craft and industrial.[2] The model would predict that subsequent to the mid-1930s, because of the alterations in the institutional environment we would see an increase in union membership – an increase that would include the nonskilled sector. The figures bear this out. The AFL can point to substantial trade union growth during the period 1933–42, and while it is true that the skilled sector continued to organize into craft-based unions, the most dramatic membership gains occurred in those unions that either had a tradition of industry-wide organization or expanded their scope to include the unskilled workers in their respective industries (see Table 10.2).

Also, as our model would predict, the most rapid organization of nonskilled workers occurred in those industries where existing unions were willing to accept non skilled workers into their ranks, thus reducing the organizational lag. Approximately 60 percent of the total increase in union membership in the ten-year period 1933–43 was due to the expansion of existing organizations.

With the advent of the Committee for Industrial Organization in 1935 (renamed in 1937 the Congress for Industrial Organization), organization

---

[1] Despite federal legislation that encouraged union membership, many workers remain with no effective coercive powers. These unorganized workers include southern workers (where the local power structure has been successful in preventing the enforcement of the right of union membership), agricultural workers (who are not covered by federal labor legislation), government employees (who in most cases are prohibited by statute from exercising any coercive power), and employees of many small businesses (where the diseconomies of small-scale operations sometimes preclude organization).

[2] Millis and Montgomery, *Organized Labour*, pp. 198–9.

The theory applied

TABLE 10.2 *Growth in membership of selected trade unions, 1933–42*

	1933 (000)	1942 (000)
United Mine Workers[a]	300	600
Amalgamated Clothing Workers[b]	125	275
Brotherhood of Electrical Workers[c]	94	201
Machinists[d]	65	222
Bakery Workers[e]	17	84

[a] Traditionally organized on industry-wide basis.
[b] Most of the membership gain consisted of journeymen tailors, and shirt, neckwear, laundry, cleaning, and dyeing workers who comprised an almost negligible percentage of union membership before 1940s.
[c] This union was composed largely of electricians in railroad and construction industries before 1933. In 1939, its 105,000 members included employees of power houses and electrical manufacturing plants.
[d] This union began to organize workers in the aircraft industry on an industrial basis.
[e] In 1936, this union began to seek bargaining rights in mechanized bread and cracker bakeries.

SOURCE: Millis and Montgomery, *Organized Labour*, pp. 198–9.

along industrial lines occurred where previously there had been no effective means of income redistribution. With the CIO (a voluntary cooperative group of existing unions) willing to underwrite some of the organizational costs by providing leadership and financial assistance, the perceived value of such an arrangement to the unorganized sector became readily apparent and the organizational lag was short.

In steel, for example, the old Amalgamated Association of Iron, Steel and Tin Workers probably had no more than 5,000 members in the early 1930s. Since it was almost totally unable to effect income redistribution, by 1936 it faced extinction. The CIO, through a subsidiary, the Steel Workers Organizing Committee, took over this union in 1936, and with a $500,000 campaign chest supplied by John L. Lewis, organized the United Steel Workers of America. By summer of 1941, its membership was estimated at 350,000 and by 1942, it had grown to more than 500,000 – a figure that represents three-fifths of all workers then employed in American steel plants.

The CIO similarly organized other new unions: the Automobile Workers with an estimated 1941 membership of 600,000; the United Electrical, Radio, and Machine Workers, 300,000; the Rubber Workers, 57,500; the Aluminum Workers, 31,000; the Glass, Ceramic, and Silica Sand Workers, 22,500; the American Newspaper Guild, 19,000; and the Cannery, Agricultural, Packing and Allied Workers, more than 100,000.

Our model has confirmed the hunches of those historians who have attached great significance to the three court decisions. The model has explained how these decisions altered the institutional environment by making substantial changes in the costs and values of trade union arrangements, thus helping to explain further the ups and downs, twists and turns of trade union history.

(2) The political party as a redistributive arrangement

We have seen how changes in the institutional environment affect the innovation of trade union arrangements, but the history of organized labor is not limited to trade union arrangements. It appears useful to examine the institutional environment and its relationship to other redistributive schemes that have been attempted.

As we have seen in Chapter 4, the period between 1820 and 1830 was marked by the extension of the franchise (an exogenous change) to most workingmen in the large cities of the east coast. This extension held out to the labor sector the possibility of political action as an alternative redistribution arrangement. During the early years of the decade, full employment and prosperity insured that trade unions would be innovated to redistribute income. As we have stated earlier, trade unions were formed and they did redistribute income, even though under the law their activities were clearly illegal. In the mid-1820s, however, the country lapsed into industrial depression, and trade unions were no longer able to achieve their demands. As the present value of trade unions declined to zero, labor began to look to the political arena for substitute arrangements.

In 1827, for example, the Philadelphia carpenters, supported by a city-wide coalition of trade unions, lost their strike for the ten-hour day. Having failed to achieve their objective by utilizing the trade union arrangement, they formed America's first labor political party (Workingmen's Party) in 1829, and campaigned for measures that would redistribute income toward labor groups. Workers in Boston and New York pursued similar activities. Even though workers became an important ingredient to political coalitions in many eastern cities (their votes wooed by established parties now more sympathetic to the conditions of the economically submerged, but recently enfranchised, workingman), redistributive gains were positive, but small, and the actual value of political arrangements was substantially less than the workers had anticipated. The explanation is a simple one – workers in that period of time did not represent a majority of the electorate, and, despite labor's apparent assumption to the contrary, it is seldom that a majority will voluntarily redistribute its income to a minority in a democracy.

We do not mean to imply, however, that there were no positive values to

The theory applied

the political solutions. Clearly, if there exists on the menu only one alternative that has a positive value, its innovation is profitable. If, on the other hand, changes within the economy raise the value of some other alternative, the model suggests that a shift to the second arrangement will occur. The prosperity of the 1830s, for example, brought temporary immunity from trade union conspiracy prosecutions and increased the present value of trade union arrangements. The model suggests, and in fact we observe, that workers would redirect their efforts from political activities toward the innovation of collective bargaining backed by threats of economic coercion.

After the *Hunt* decision, most craftsmen elected the trade union as the arrangement of choice. Because non-skilled workers possessed no coercive advantage, trade unionism failed to carry a positive value for them; and as a result, non-skilled workers continued to agitate in the political sector for redistributive gains.

In 1866, for example, the National Labor Union, a loose federation of certain labor and political reform organizations, campaigned for the eight-hour day, government assistance for farmers and producers' cooperatives, reduction of interest rates, restrictions on profit margins, and protection from underbidding by Oriental and female labor. Monetary reform, it was thought, was the key to successful income redistribution, and Greenbackism dominated labor's political goals. As with the earlier attempts to organize a labor party, this effort failed; however, many of the demands were picked up by established parties, and legislation was eventually enacted to satisfy some of labor's desires.[1] Although the tactics changed slightly, for the unskilled workers, there was little arrangemental innovation through the first decades of the twentieth century except in the political arena.

Political activity was focused in two divergent directions: attempts to work within the existing political system either by affiliation with existing political parties (as with the Bryan campaign), or with the establishment of new worker-based parties (for example, the Socialist Labor party); and attempts to overthrow the existing political system by direct action (as proposed by the Industrial Workers of the World). As we have noted, some direct redistributive gains were achieved in attempting to work within the system. Some historians infer a causal relationship between the political activities of the pre-*Hunt* and pre-Wagner Act eras and the subsequent changes in the political ground rules, and conclude that indirect gains were achieved, as well. It is not within the scope of this work to develop such a theory, and until such time as political scientists develop an appropriate model, the subject is open for speculation. For this same reason, it is difficult

[1] The Bland Allison Act of 1878 (aimed at inflating the money supply), the establishment of the eight-hour day for government workers, and the Chinese Exclusion Act.

to assess the true gains accruing to trade union members when the union engages in political activity.

Attempts to redistribute income by overthrowing the system, however, failed in all cases. Such radical schemes, by their very nature, stimulate political responses from the total community that greatly increase the costs of such schemes.

Since the innovation of politically based redistributive arrangements can stimulate political counter-responses, the potential costs of such arrangements can be quite high. In addition, gains are very often indirect and unevenly distributed. As a result, political arrangements tend to be innovated only when the present value to trade union arrangements is negative or when they can complement existing trade union organizations.

(IV) The distribution of arrangemental gains

As we stated in Section II of this chapter, once a union possesses sufficient coercive power to effect income redistribution, it must then decide how it intends to apportion the gains. Sometimes gains in income are traded off for job security, and sometimes gains are secured for the majority of the membership by distributing some income away from the minority, and sometimes the opposite redistribution takes place.

The model suggests that the forms of the arrangement reflect the desires of the primary action group. In a trade union, the primary action group consists of those members who make the decision to accept or reject a collective bargaining agreement. The model assumes that the common goal of profit maximization holds a primary action group together. Therefore, it is assumed that each member of a union's primary action group strives to secure a collective bargaining agreement that is most beneficial to himself. In the case of unions where severance costs would be high enough to make withdrawal unfeasible, it is possible to get a divergence of opinion between that fraction of the membership that constitutes the primary action group and the rest of the membership. Let us look at some of the ways a union may redistribute income from consumers and employers to its own members, how a union may decide to trade off income gains for a few members for job security for many members and, in addition, the relationship of these decisions to the composition of the primary action group.

(A) *The steel industry: a study of shifting goals*[1]

Less than a dozen companies produce 80 percent of America's steel, and the United Steel Workers of America is the union that represents the nearly half million maintenance and production workers in those plants. Since all

[1] The material in this section comes from the *New York Times* and *Business Week*, selected issues 1957–66.

union members vote to accept or reject collective bargaining agreements, the primary action group is very large. Given the sheer size of the group, it appears reasonable to assume at least some diversity and disagreement among its members. However, just as the steel industry has problems peculiar to itself, so do the steelworkers, and this often provides a common thread, although perhaps a fragile one, that ties the membership together. They constitute an aging labor force, characterized by long service and, in many cases, they are trained for jobs found only in the steel industry.

The collective bargaining agreements negotiated in the steel industry between 1957 and 1965 reflect the shifting goals of the steelworkers' union from income redistribution to job security and then to a combination of the two. Exogenous changes during this period of time altered the industry's demand for labor, and a study of the contracts illustrates how the primary action group does indeed shape a union's redistributive policies.

In October 1957, America witnessed an all-time high in the production of domestic steel; the following month demand began to decline, and for six years steelworkers faced the possibility of periodic lay-offs or permanent unemployment. During that time, the United Steel Workers of America negotiated three collective bargaining agreements. If the predictive powers of our model are of any use, the interests of the primary action group (in this case, the membership of the union or to be precise, 51 percent of those voting) should determine the terms of the agreement and the agreement should reflect their interests.

In 1959, after two years of decline in output and employment, the USWA set out to negotiate a contract that was somewhat traditional for almost any American industry: i.e. modest increases in wage and fringe benefits. After a six-month strike, management and labor signed a two-year contract that provided for an increase in fringe benefits as well as an immediate wage raise (with a second scheduled for 1961). In order to secure this unspectacular contract, the union gave up its demand for an extension of the 'escalator clause' that provided for automatic cost-of-living increases that had been part of the previous contract.

Output in the steel industry continued to decline: massive lay-offs occurred and in addition, many workers found themselves reduced to three or four days' work per week. As the time neared for the negotiation of new contracts, workers were concerned about job security and seniority protection. Younger members of the work force felt the older men should be forced to retire in order to open up more jobs, and all men with long service (half of the steelworkers have more than fifteen years' seniority) believed that a system of plant-wide seniority should supplant the existing departmental seniority arrangement.

228

In April 1962, steelworkers ratified a two-year contract that was tailored to fit the needs of workers trapped in a declining industry. It provided for no wage increases; instead, job security, income protection, and the expansion of job opportunities were the only areas of consideration. Benefits included a guaranteed 32-hour work week or equivalent pay, an increase in supplemental unemployment benefits, and an increase in unemployment benefits paid to workers who are no longer eligible for state benefits. A new savings and vacation plan was put into effect. It credited workers with an extra week of vacation pay for each two years of continuous service before that time. In this way, older workers were able to accumulate a fund to draw on in case of disability or lay-off, or they could add all their accumulated extra vacation benefits to the thirteen-week vacation they received at retirement (age sixty-five). If a worker refused to retire at sixty-five, these extra benefits were to be reduced by 10 percent for each three-month period he continued on the job. It was hoped this penalty would encourage retirement and thus expand opportunities for laid-off members.

In addition, the contract denied the worker the option to work through his regular vacation for additional pay. Seniority rights were strengthened; laid-off workers were to be permitted to claim other jobs within the plant on the basis of plant seniority and, in some instances, in other plants owned by the company.

This two-year agreement provided for a reopening of negotiations after a one-year period. Before the contract was six months old, steel buyers had stockpiled a substantial cushion of steel to protect their own production schedules should a reopening of negotiations introduce the possibility of a strike. Despite this stockpiling, total demand continued to fall and 2,000 more basic steel production workers joined their 50,000 idle brethren. The United Steelworkers of America prepared to reopen negotiations and the primary goal was an attempt to redistribute the work force among the existing jobs (and thus redistribute income among competing employees).

Contract talks began in January 1963. In June, the new contract was announced – a two-year agreement (without a reopening clause) and once again no wage increase. Instead, the primary feature of the contract was a once-in-five-years thirteen-week vacation for the senior half of the work force. This mandatory paid vacation was supposed to create somewhere between 10,000 and 20,000 new jobs. In addition, it restricted the company's right to contract out work that would be performed by workers outside the jurisdiction of the USWA and prohibited supervisors from doing work that was ordinarily performed by steelworkers. Also, the company agreed

229

to discuss with the union any decision it made that involved putting employees on overtime rather than recalling laid-off workers.

Four months later, steel demand began to boom. Eight years of technological research (an exogenous change) had begun to pay off; the oxygen converter and better methods of separating impurities enabled steelmakers to use a lower grade of pelletized iron ore and drastically reduce production costs. The installation of new continuous casting plants eliminated many steps in the production process and increased output per man hour. President Kennedy's relaxation of the rules regarding plant depreciation (a transfer from government to the private sector) left steel companies with large savings that, in part, were reinvested in research and plant improvement. The decline in the demand for labor per unit of output was offset by an outward shift of the labor demand curve as steel prices fell and the quantity of steel demanded increased dramatically. Steel could be produced more cheaply, and this price decline encouraged demands in areas previously not served by the steel industry. At the same time the economy moved toward full employment, and the demand in the traditional areas rose as well. In building construction, for example, steel plate became popular for outside wall construction. In addition, many consumer goods now carried the 'Steelmark' label. The market improved, and in 1964 the industry equaled its all-time production record of 117 million tons.

Steel companies continued to operate at almost full capacity to satisfy increasing demand, and as negotiation time again rolled around in the spring of 1965, steelworkers were acutely aware that they had not received a raise in four years and that the customary method of sharing some of the fruits of increased production through overtime opportunities was virtually denied them because of their contract.

The new three-year agreement ratified in September 1965 provided for raises in hourly rates and substantial increases in fringe benefits. Of more importance from our viewpoint, workers were allowed to accept pay in lieu of their regular vacation in excess of two weeks, and they were also given the option of accepting up to three weeks' pay for their extended vacation.

In summary, then, we can see that the primary action group eventually recognized that while total income was declining because of an exogenous change over which it had no control, this decline was accompanied by a redistribution of the residual income because of the unequal distribution of lay-offs, short work weeks, and plant shutdowns. The primary action group appears to have two redistributive goals: no workers were allowed to get too much income when others were out of work; and senior employees were to be guaranteed a minimum income and the full burden of unemployment was to fall on the junior employees. The goals obviously reflect the union's democratic political structure (both employed and unemployed members are allowed to vote) and the absolute majority of senior workers.

In terms of our model, the 1959–60 agreement should have dealt with job security, but it did not. There was a marked perception lag before the primary action group realized the seriousness of the situation, but the lag can be explained. Steel employment is always heavily cyclical, and it is not uncommon for a steelworker to suffer periodic lay-offs when a business cycle turns downward; but the income fall is temporary, and the worker usually has a chance to recoup a good portion of his loss through overtime work when business improves. In 1961, though, with 50,000 basic steel-workers on the street and many more working reduced hours, the member-ship realized that this was no ordinary slump. The group acted to protect its members by trying to redistribute jobs among those with seniority. The following year, faced by still further decline in employment, the primary action group intensified its efforts to prevent income redistribution away from its members and set into motion the thirteen-week vacation, early retirement, restrictions on overtime, and limitations on the work to be performed by non-members. Finally, as prosperity returned, the union no longer felt obligated to protect the incomes of the many from the extra earnings of the few and removed those restrictions which were designed to distribute income evenly; however, there was no attempt to repeal the seniority provisions that guaranteed jobs to the majority.

(B) *A racketeer local: redistribution from the many to the few*[1]

In the case of the United Steel Workers where the primary action group is the membership (or a majority thereof), it appears that the model does have explanative or predictive powers. The same is true in the case of a union whose primary action group is very different from its membership.

The 1957 Senate hearings on improper activities in the labor and manage-ment field provide some illustrations of unions whose primary action group has only a single member: i.e. the leader of the union. These are the 'racket-eer locals' controlled and dominated by one or a few for the purpose of their own financial enrichment. In this type of union, the membership does not have a voice in the nature and scope of the contract agreement; in most cases, they have no voice even about whether or not they wish to be mem-bers of the union. Rather, they are coerced by the collusive power of manage-ment and the union leaders.

[1] The material in this section is based on *Hearings Before the Select Committee on Im-proper Activities in the Labor or Management Field*, 85th Congress (U.S. Government Printing Office, Washington, 1957).

The theory applied

Let us examine the workings of a racketeer local in some detail: the story of Louis Lasky provides a perhaps overdrawn, but still insightful, glimpse at the operations of these one-man locals. At the time of the Mc-Clellan investigations, Lasky was chief administrative officer for Local 136 of the Retail Clerks International Association, Local 136a of the National Independent Union Council, Local 142 of the Aluminum Metal Alloys and Allied Trades, Local 631 of the Amalgamated Textile Workers of America, the National Union of Butchers, Drivers, Helpers and Warehousemen of America, and the Amalgamated Metal Craft, Wood, Plastic, and Wire-workers Union 136a. With the exception of the Retail Clerks, these were all independent unions and while their leadership may have varied, the case of the RCIA Local 136 is probably not atypical. For that union (formerly Local 102 of the United Auto Workers – AFL) the list of officers read as follows: President, Harold Weiss (Lasky's brother-in-law); Secretary-Treasurer, Louis Lasky; Recording Secretary, Louis Lasky; Business Manager, Louis Lasky.

Space precludes discussing each of Lasky's organizing activities, but we can draw the following composite scenario. The owner of the Gilbertsin Company, a Brooklyn mailing house employing about a hundred Spanish-speaking workers, received a telephone call from the business manager of a bona fide chartered union local whose total membership at that point consisted of the manager's wife, brother-in-law, and at most, a few close friends. The manager explained that he was conducting an organizational drive and would like to have the workers in that plant become members. The owner was willing (if not, there would have been picket lines in front of the plant the next day). He desired to cooperate because union affiliation *per se* keeps other unions from trying to organize his firm (the law prohibited a union certification election from being held more often than once every two years).

Negotiations took place immediately. The business manager (the primary action group) made known his demands and an organizational bribe was agreed upon and paid. In addition, the owner agreed to collect weekly dues ($1.00 per person) from each worker and to collect a $15 or $20 initiation fee from each new worker or re-hired worker. These sums were turned over to the business manager, and in return, the owner put to rest his fears of possible labor difficulties. He was assured of the continuance of a cheap labor force with no 'outside agitators'.

The workers knew they were unionized – they had weekly dues deducted from their pay envelopes. Otherwise, things were the same as before. They got raises when the federal minimum wage went up, they got two to four paid holidays per year, no sick leave, little or no vacation

The labor force : organization and education

pay, no welfare benefits, no seniority rights. They were not part of the primary action group and suffered an adverse income redistribution.

Here is an extra-legal arrangement that effected income redistribution by exploiting the lack of information flows and the isolation of a group of workers. What are the conditions that must exist if such an arrangement is to be successful? First, once organized, the workers must be prohibited from withdrawing from the union. This condition requires either physical force or as in the case with Mr Lasky's locals, the collusion of management who stood ready to fire uncooperative employees. Second, information flows between the workers and the rest of the community must be very poor and the costs of disseminating such information very high. The workers cannot know their alternatives nor can they know what protection the law affords. Language can be an effective barrier to information flows. Third, management must be willing to collude. If the industry is competitive, the fear of legitimate labor organizations is strong (any increases in wages not matched by increases in competitor's wages will drive the firm out of business). Moreover, excess profits can only be earned by forcing wages below competitive levels or by resisting wage increases that competitors are forced to pay. Competition, then, would tend to lead the businessman into a collusive arrangement with the union leader. Fourth, since one of the costs may be a jail term, it is necessary that the union leader be willing to assume unusually high risks or that his personal evaluation of the costs of a jail term is less than that of the community at large.

In terms of counter-redistribution, arrangements designed to provide information flows to isolated workers can be very effective. Because of the free rider problem, it is unlikely that any such purely informational arrangement will be innovated at the individual voluntary level. It is interesting to note that as late as 1957, most of the organizations supplying information to workers were altruistic (the Association of Catholic Trade Unions is an example) or had tied benefits or possessed some cohesive power. The National Education Association, for example, disseminates information to school teachers about market conditions of employment. Unlike the CTU, however, it overcomes the free rider problem by utilizing a variety of mechanisms. It operates credit unions for members only, it operates summer resorts for members only, it provides insurance for members only, but perhaps most important, it has agreements with thousands of small school districts across the country that require NEA dues-paying membership as a condition of employment.

As the model suggests, it is the primary action group that determines the way in which gains are apportioned among union members. Before the model can be used to explain the redistributive *modus operandi* of a given

233

trade union, a careful assessment must be made of who, in fact, constitutes that union's primary action group.

(V) Arrangemental innovation and the evolution of public education

Education is a service whose production and consumption can be analyzed within the framework of micro economics and whose institutional structure can be examined usefully within the context of our model of arrangemental change. Education has some of the characteristics of both a consumption (it can increase one's ability to enjoy life) and an investment (it can increase one's income) good, but it is not the investment–consumption dichotomy that interests us here. Instead, from an arrangemental point of view the history of the educational sector is important because of certain inherent externalities, because of some possible divergence between private and social rates of discount, and some questions about the optimal composition and geographic distribution of the relevant primary action group. In addition, there have been attempts to use education to redistribute income and our model has something to say about them as well.

What evidence we have suggests that the production of educational services is subject to some economies of scale. However, while they appear to be sufficient to preclude self-education, with a few notable exceptions, they are not substantial enough to rule out even very small scale units on cost grounds alone.[1] In short, although there are apparent gains from specialization, minimum firm size is small enough not to preclude any level of institutional arrangement. The history of education in the United States suggests that there has been (at least until the past few years) a continual tendency to replace individual and voluntary cooperative arrangements with governmental ones. How can this tendency be explained?

(A) *Externalities in education : investment*

Because of the open character of our society, it is impossible for an individual to accrue all the revenues that are generated by an investment in education when that education is designed to aid the production rather than the dissemination of basic knowledge. This divergence has been particularly marked in the 'pure' sciences. In those areas no patent rights make it

---

[1] The most notable exception is probably modern graduate education where indivisibilities in faculty as well as laboratory and computer facilities imply a substantial minimum size. Even here, however, it appears that the substantial scale economies are a function of the past few decades.

234

possible for the scientist who has financed his own education or for almost any voluntary group that might decide to subsidize the scientist's education to recover those costs through the sale of the scientific principle.[1] In the absence of some form of subsidization, the decision that maximizes private profits produces a less than optimal level of expenditure on educational investment and it may yield no investment at all. If slavery were permitted, it might pay very large firms to underwrite such education (if their share of the social revenues exceeded their costs and the free rider problem did not preclude it). Since slavery is illegal, emigration (from the industry) is possible, and we would expect that the scientist with his general education would move to the most lucrative alternative – almost certainly not the industry that subsidized his education.

In the nineteenth century, the United States was a technological follower and could, therefore, borrow most of its pure science from the rest of the world. In most areas, the gains from internalizing the pure science externality were neither very certain nor, perhaps, very large. In agriculture, however, we were a leader, and in the area of agricultural chemistry there was no pool of international investment on which to draw. Here, where potential profits were both high and fairly certain, arrangemental innovation did occur. It was, in fact, under the steady prodding of the farm sector that the Morrill Act (establishing the system of land grant colleges) was pushed through a reluctant Congress.[2] That bill had as one basic goal the training of students capable of undertaking basic research in the natural sciences (at least as far as it applied to agriculture) and in the long run that research underwrote substantial increases in agricultural productivity. It would not, however, have paid any individual or voluntary group to undertake that level of investment.

By the middle of the twentieth century, however, the United States had become the technological leader of the world and could no longer afford to depend upon the rest of the world for the necessary basic research. Moreover, the entire structure of technology had changed, and where one hundred years before new technology had been largely based on empirical observation, by the 1950s new technological developments had become voracious consumers of basic research. The gains from such research could still, however, not be captured by any single individual or voluntary group. Moreover, World War II had proved the intimate connection between

[1] Nor would any change in the law likely affect this result. Given any known mechanisms of control it appears almost impossible to enforce patent rights on such basic principles.
[2] The agricultural sector was large both in terms of its contribution to national output and its political muscle. The United States Agricultural Society was the leading lobbyist for the bill.

science and military preparedness, and given the political tensions of the post-war decades, the political revenues from basic research also rose markedly. These too, however, could not be captured by individuals or voluntary groups.

Given large and certain profits from arrangemental innovation, an inability to capture these profits by individual or voluntary group action and the prototype arrangement that had proved so successful with agricultural research, the model predicts the emergence of a governmental arrangement after a very short total lag. Nor does reality deviate far from the prediction. By the late 1950s the National Defense Education Act and a number of similar pieces of legislation had underwritten a rapid increase in federal funding for graduate education leading toward the production (rather than dissemination or application) of basic knowledge. The states had begun to move in the same direction in the nineteenth century, but by 1960 the president of the University of Chicago was able to speak of his institution as 'one of the Federal universities'.

(B) *Externalities in education: consumption*

Of more importance to an explanation of the institutional structure of American education are the externalities in consumption. The first four decades of the nineteenth century were marked by a continuing struggle between supporters of private and free public primary education. In traditional educational history the ultimate victory of public education has been associated with the reforms of the Massachusetts public school system instituted by Horace Mann. Recently Albert Fishlow has argued that the period was characterized not by reform in Massachusetts but by the export of that state's educational system to the rest of the country. This later interpretation is consistent with our analysis, but our interest lies in the explanation of the victory of public education rather than in an exposition of the content of that education.

The stability of any democratic political system depends on the behavior of at least a majority of voters. Any individual's welfare in a democratic system depends not only on his political choices but those of the other voters as well. Since at the simplest level, literacy is a minimum requirement for rational political choice, my utility is increased by my neighbor's consumption of education, if that education leads to a better political environment. Admittedly this type of externality is on a slightly different footing than those we have dealt with before, but just because we cannot provide a reasonably precise estimate of the external income does not mean that there is no income, nor does it mean that we will not have innovation

The labor force : organization and education

designed to capture that income. Moreover, it should be equally clear that the free rider problem precludes a voluntary solution.

While the United States has only gradually moved toward true political democracy, it has always had something of a democratic heritage, and in the colonial era that heritage was probably strongest in Massachusetts. Since the welfare sacrifice from illiteracy is highest where democracy is strongest, it is not surprising that it is in Massachusetts that these externalities were first internalized through the innovation of universal free (i.e. tax-supported) primary education. The externality was recognized and legislation effected to internalize it within two decades of the establishment of the Plymouth colony. The School Act of 1642 reads in part: 'The Court taking into consideration the great neglect of many parents and masters in training up their children in learning ... which may be profitable to the common wealth ...'

Two hundred years later, as public debate raged over the extension of that system into other parts of the country, the rhetoric turned on the need for a literate public, if that public were to have a major voice in political decision making. Moreover, the timing of the diffusion of public education conforms (at least loosely) to the predictions of the model. Outside of New England, public education was innovated most quickly in those states with the broadest suffrage and most slowly in those with the narrowest. And, the treatment of enfranchised groups also conforms to our expectations. If certain groups are excluded from the political process, there are few external revenues that can be captured by education, and there is no economic reason to socialize the cost of their education. In the United States, women were only gradually granted the right to vote, and there was substantially less public education available to them in the years before they were granted that vote. Thus, in many Massachusetts towns the word 'children' in the School Act was interpreted to mean male children, and as public education spread across the rest of the country the standards for women almost always lagged behind those for men. In the same vein the total absence of Negro education before the Civil War and the poor state of Negro schools since appears to be yet another reflection of the absence of this consumption externality. If the theory is to be believed, other things being equal, we would expect that the extension of the effective franchise to Negroes in both South and North should lead to a marked improvement in black education not only in Atlanta but also in Chicago. Of course, the model also suggests that the level of education provided any group depends in part on their political voice in the relevant primary action group. Therefore, if blacks have less than proportional representation or can be successfully screened from political effectiveness at the level of government

237

that makes the educational decision, there will be less economic pressure to socialize their education.

There is yet another element in the consumption externality that has tended toward an extension of public education from primary, to secondary, to higher education. In Chapter 2 we argued that if an electorate is single-peaked in regards to some political decision, both parties will move toward that peak,[1] and the ideological differences between the parties will be largely lost. The more issues that are single-peaked the more stable is the political system since both sides realize that the costs of losing an election are low (the other party's policies after all do not differ much from those of your own) and neither is tempted to move outside the system. If, however, the distribution of the electorate on one or more very important issues is multi-peaked, the parties may center on a position far removed from that held by one group of voters, and that group is less likely to accept the democratic solution. If, for example, the distribution is as we have illustrated in Figure 10.1, the parties will choose position $\bar{x}$ (the position that divides the number of votes equally) and those voters who occupy the left peak position (the shaded area) may well be unwilling to settle for that 'compromise'. As the number of multi-peaked issues increase (or as the multi-peaked issues become more important), it becomes increasingly difficult for the country to reach a democratic solution.[2] Thus, any innovation that tends to produce single-peaked distributions may make a significant contribution to the stability of a democratic system and may therefore increase the welfare of those who value stability. If that function can be performed by an educational system, an economist would argue that there

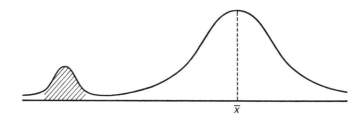

$\bar{x}$

Figure 10.1

[1] In Chapter 2 we did not use the words 'single-peaked' but they are the political scientists' (and economists') words for a distribution of voters along a scale when that distribution has only one hump. If the voters bunch together at several non-adjoining points the distribution is said to be multi-peaked.
[2] A bi-peaked distribution of the type illustrated in Figure 10.1 may well underlie the present ferment and near-revolutionary agitation for separatism by the residents of French Canada.

are substantial consumption externalities that could be captured by the innovation of these educational arrangements.

In the United States the education system has produced a largely single-valued (and therefore single-peaked) electorate from an otherwise extremely heterogeneous population. By inculcating the young (at state expense) with a particular set of values, it is possible to go a long way toward guaranteeing single-peakedness far into the future. The pressure to capture these consumption externalities has played an important role in determining the structure of education in the United States. One of the best statements of this position was made by Thaddeus Steven in 1835. Speaking against a measure designed to repeal the public education system in Pennsylvania he said: 'Hereditary distinctions of rank are sufficiently obvious, but that distinction which is founded on poverty is infinitely more so. Such an act should be entitled, "An act for branding and marking the poor, so that they be known from the rich and proud"'.

Such was the rhetoric of the 1830s and '40s. The political struggle for public education was intense, but the advocates of single-peakedness won, and the evidence suggests that the internalization was profitable. Even today to a very large extent both rich and poor remain part of a single-valued society. The support given parochial education by the Catholic Church can be viewed as an attempt by one group to preserve an element of multi-peakedness in at least one dimension of the socio-economic spectrum – a multi-peakedness that was threatened by the unifying force of state financed secular education.[1]

Over the more recent past it appears that the 'peak-molding' effects of education have been diminishing, and as they do, the size of the potential external profit declines concomitantly. The model predicts that when the capturable revenues fall below the net costs of supporting the arrangement, there will be a shift away from that arrangement. As black ghetto schools begin to teach value systems that are alien to the white middle class community, the external revenues from public education as perceived by that community decline. Similarly, when the nation's colleges and universities produce graduates whose value systems differ markedly from those of the typical voter, the voters will realize that the external economies in education have become external diseconomies (there are substantial political costs inherent in multi-peaked distributions), and one can expect a substantial cutback in the level of the public subsidy to higher education. In California,

---

[1] Although the argument was not cast in economic terms, it is clear that many of the critics of the Catholic Church were angered by the Church's attempts to interfere with the process of voter homogenization. See for example, Josiah Strong, *Our Country* (Cambridge, Mass., 1963 ed.).

The theory applied

for example, the voters have already begun to demand tuition from students in the state universities and colleges, but they have not made similar demands from junior college students. It is interesting to note that the junior colleges still turn out graduates with values that are consistent with those held by the majority of the voters.

(c) *Differences between private and social rates of discount*

The model implies that the choice between arrangemental alternatives may turn on the rate of discount. If the social rate is below the private rate, total income might be maximized if the innovation is at the governmental level.[1] Moreover, these gains would be additive to any that might be captured by governmental arrangements when there are social revenues (or costs) that cannot be internalized by individual or voluntary alternatives. In the early stages of development, investment in some forms of education (particularly those with long delayed returns) may appear to be unprofitable from the point of view of the individual forced to discount those earnings at private rates, but if the social rate of discount is used the investment might appear attractive. At the same time, such educational investment might constitute a necessary precondition for further economic development.

It appears likely that engineering education provides such an example from American history. Without a viable transport network the gains from interregional specialization could never be realized, but no system could be either built or maintained without the services of trained engineers. Without a transport network the earnings from an engineering education were at best long deferred, and when discounted at the very high private rates that prevailed, the present value of such investment was very low indeed. At social rates (and when the revenues were adjusted to reflect both the gains accruing to the individual and those that were available to the rest of society) the investment appeared highly profitable. Since only the government had access to low interest loans, governmental organization of engineering training became the arrangement of choice.

The first formal instruction in engineering in the United States was provided by the military academy at West Point. Although that institution had opened and begun to train engineers in 1802, the program was much

---

[1] We assume that the divergence is the result of the poor state of development of the private capital markets and the relatively better state of the market for government funds, a situation that was probably characteristic of the United States in the early decades of the nineteenth century (see Chapters 6 and 7 for a detailed examination of this phenomena). Clearly, if voluntary groups could have gotten access to the markets at favorable rates (so that it was only individuals who had to suffer the costs of market failure), the gains could only be realized by voluntary organizations.

strengthened in 1816. In that year, the President of the United States appointed Claudius Crozet Professor of Engineering and charged him with the task of establishing a first quality engineering curriculum in the mold of the Polytechnic School in Paris. When Crozet left in 1823, West Point had become one of the world's best engineering schools and was turning out a steady stream of trained graduates. Subsidization, however, did not end there. The graduates were commissioned in the United States army and, since there were still no jobs on the railroad network, they were employed on the nation's rivers and harbors as well as on a number of western survey- ing projects. As the first canals and railroads entered the planning stages, the newly trained engineers were loaned to the planners to provide technical help. When actual demands began to materialize in the private sector, a pool of trained personnel was available. Thus, by 1830 army engineers were employed in almost every major transport project, and ex-army engineers began to assume managerial and technical positions in many.

Once the potential demand for engineers had become a real demand, engineering education became profitable even at private rates of discount,[1] and it was no longer necessary for the government to continue its subsidy. As the gains from the innovation diminished, West Point began to alter its curriculum in the direction of military science and private engineering schools (a voluntary solution) opened their doors. In 1824 the Rensselaer School (later RPI) opened its doors, and by 1850 both Yale and Harvard had added engineering to their curricula. Although state support for engineering training reemerged with the passage of the Morrill Act, it appears that this reversal reflected political rather than economic motives.

(D) *Income redistribution*

In some areas, however, the process of socialization of the educational process can only be explained in terms of attempted income redistribution. In the case of vocational education, for example, the returns tend to be realized over a relatively short period of time and there are few externalities (either in consumption or investment).[2] One would, therefore, expect that most such education would be organized either as an individual or as a voluntary cooperative enterprise. Many trade schools are private and a great deal of vocational education is combined with regular work (i.e. on-the- job training). Still the last two decades of the nineteenth century saw a

[1] Of course, the private capital markets were improving rapidly in the period and the differences between private and social rates were declining.
[2] In terms of the Mincer–Becker discussion, vocational education can be viewed as education for a specific purpose (see *Journal of Political Economy*, Special Supplement, 1962).

241

The theory applied

rising cry for public vocational education, and public vocational schools were launched in most eastern and midwestern cities. To whom was such an innovation profitable and what was the source of those profits?

As we saw earlier in this chapter, by the 1880s those unions with some effective control over the supply of a skill had demonstrated that through unified action they could raise their wages and force a redistribution of income from business (and/or the consumers). As a result the employers were searching for an arrangemental alternative that would provide them with a mechanism to break the control the unions exercised over that supply. Public vocational education was one alternative arrangement that they thought could accomplish this redistribution. When in 1892 Colonel Richard T. Auchmuty organized the New York Trade School, he solicited funds from business groups with the argument that the school's graduates would work for less than union wages and that they would remain relatively free of union control. His arguments were telling enough that they elicited a $500,000 grant from J. P. Morgan and both vocal and active opposition from the unions. Samuel Gompers wrote:

'It is not only ridiculous but positively wrong for trade schools to continue their turning out both workmen who are ready and willing, at the end of their so called "graduation", to take the places of American workmen far below wages prevailing in the trade. With practically half of the toiling masses of our country unemployed, the continuance of the practice is tantamount to a crime.'[1]

The employers could, of course, have chosen a voluntary cooperative solution and financed vocational education through private contributions. The free rider problem, however, loomed large; and like many other primary action groups, they believed that it is always better if you can transfer the costs of an arrangement to a broader base while retaining the revenues for themselves. To this end they opted for public vocational education, and in the early 1890s they launched a compaign to widen public education to include specific vocational training. Among the first programs initiated by the newly formed National Association of Manufacturers was one designed to propagandize the benefits that accrue from public support for 'practical arts, industrial, manual training, or other technical schools'. Nor did their demands fall on deaf ears. While not all citizens might agree that 'trade schools properly protected from the domination and withering blight of organized labor are the one and only remedy from the present intolerable conditions', the majority of city voters were convinced that vocational

[1] Quoted in E. W. Benis, 'Relation of Labor Organizations to the American Boy and to Trade Instruction', *Annals of the American Academy of Political and Social Science*, 5 (1894–5), 227.

242

education should become a part of the offerings of the public school system. By 1908 the employers' viewpoint had won the day in most eastern and midwestern cities and that primary action group felt that they had initiated the innovation of an arrangement that would effect a redistribution of income towards itself while incurring very few costs in the process. Unfortunately, at least for the employers, the choice of any governmental alternative carries with it the possibility of substantial 'stuck costs', and these the employers had incorrectly estimated.

As any student of practical politics might have suggested, redistribution schemes based on direct electoral action are not apt to be stable if the groups who bear the cost of the redistribution command a majority of the votes. By the first decades of the twentieth century, while the trade unionists did not constitute a majority of the voters in the large cities they almost certainly had the sympathetic ear of that majority. All that was necessary was that the unions recognize the losses they would assume from the redistribution and then that they select and innovate a counter-arrangement. The potential revenues were substantial and the political mechanisms well known. As a result, the lag(s) was very short indeed.

By 1908 the A. F. of L. Council had come to recognize that industrial education was 'necessary and *inevitable*', and that the federation should move to assume a major voice in the determination of the aims and goals of vocational education. The council's advisory committee recommended that local boards representing 'both unions and management' be created to advise the local school authorities as to the appropriate level and content of their vocational offerings. The recommendations of the report were quickly effected in most large cities, and, with union representatives on the advisory boards, the forces aimed at overcoming the supply restrictions were effectively blunted. As our model would lead one to expect, the history of the past half century contains little evidence that vocational education has speeded the flow of workers into those skilled trades dominated by the craft unions.

(E) *Education: some special problems in interpretation and a need for theory revision*

Thus far we have examined the arrangemental response of the educational sector to a number of economic pressures, and, in these cases at least, it appears that the model helps us explain the evolution of the public school system in the United States. A further examination of that sector raises two quite disquieting problems, and it appears useful to examine them in some detail. The first involves the definition of the relevant decision-making unit and the second the optimal geographic size of an arrangemental innovation.

243

The theory applied

As we have seen in Chapter 1, the mere existence of an externality is not sufficient for arrangemental innovation. If the individual decision-making unit sees private justification for optimal action, the social revenues can be realized without any arrangemental reorganization. In the case of education, despite the existence of important externalities, it is possible (although not probable) that the private returns from investment in education may be sufficient to induce optimum levels of expenditure without 'socialization'. However, these private motives may be blunted if the goals of individual members of a family differ, and this fact raises important questions about the correct definition of a decision-making unit (not only for questions of educational arrangements, but in many other areas of economics as well).

In the case of education, while the private gains from education accruing to the family may well exceed the costs of that education, that relationship may not hold true for every member of the family. In fact, given the long deferral of the realized income, it is almost always the case that one generation is being asked to subsidize another, and many parents may be unwilling to sacrifice their consumption for the benefit of their children. This unwillingness ought to become more prevalent as society devalues the responsibilities of children for their parents' welfare and it clearly varies between ethnic and cultural groups. (Some – the Jews, for example – are certainly more 'child oriented' than others.) Where 'intra-family' divisions lead to suboptimal choices it may be necessary to innovate new arrangements if social income is to be maximized. In the educational history of the United States, such divisions may go a long way toward explaining the need for public expenditure on ghetto schools and the low rate of college enrollment among Catholic girls. In the more general case, it suggests the need for careful examination of the intra-unit distribution of costs and revenues when decisions are made by 'super-individual' individual units.

An examination of American educational history suggests that a large proportion of the consumption externalities associated with education could have been (and usually were) internalized within a relatively small geographic area. This fact may go a long way toward explaining the emergence of 'local school systems' and the support that local (as opposed to non-local) schools have received in the political arena.[1] If, however, the goal

---

[1] In the recent past as national decisions have become more important, it is possible that the optimal geographic area may have widened. However, in the absence of further arrangemental adjustment, it is not clear to the typical citizen that he will recoup much in the way of external benefits if distant schools teach value systems that are very different from his own. Thus without new arrangements it may be that national subsidization may appear uneconomic even though there are potential external benefits that could be captured with a new arrangement.

244

is not an increase in income but equality of opportunity (a redistributive rather than an income-increasing end), the optimal geographic area is very likely to be larger than 'the locality'. If education is to be the tool for effecting a rich to poor income redistribution (a likely choice in a society where votes are more evenly distributed than income), it is necessary that both the tax and the educational base encompass the rich as well as the poor. One should not, however, be surprised if attempts to redefine (i.e. broaden) the area within a given school district meet with substantial resistance from those who will lose in the transfer. There is, after all, no increase in total income that can be used as a bribe to make the change more palatable, since the potential profits from the consumption externality have already been internalized within the smaller area. The present resistance to bussing may be usefully viewed in this context, since it suggests that such resistance may be based on more than 'racist attitudes'.

(VI) Conclusions

The examination of the process of arrangemental innovation in the labor sector has provided us with some useful insights into redistributive arrangements, but perhaps more important, it has demonstrated quite markedly an important methodological weakness in the model. We have assumed that the institutional environment is exogenous, but in fact it is at times affected by the process of arrangemental innovation. The three landmark labor cases have been treated as exogenous events, and the model has been used to trace out the arrangemental responses to those changes. However, to some degree, those decisions reflect changes in political arrangements that themselves flowed from attempts by organized labor to redistribute income in its favor. Although our current level of understanding of psychology and the judicial process does not enable us to predict the timing of those decisions, it is clear that such decisions were, at least in part, a response to the increasing political and economic strength of organized labor. The model would be more useful in the long run if it were modified so that at least some parts of the institutional environment can be treated as endogenous.

Throughout the book we have been aware that arrangements designed to increase information flows can provide a mechanism for increasing total income. In the case of labor, however, we see that the failure to innovate adequate informational networks can lead to some laborers working at less than competitive wages, and that better information could lead to a redistribution of income from those who have exploited the lack of knowledge to the factors themselves. It is clear, however, that the free rider problem makes it very difficult for an individual or voluntary cooperative arrangement to

245

provide information unless, as in the case of the NEA, some tied benefits act to bind the group together. It is not surprising that arrangements to disseminate information are sometimes innovated by altruistic groups; however, our model does not explain why exploited workers have not turned to some governmental arrangement. Perhaps the same ignorance that makes exploitation possible makes it difficult for the affected groups to operate in the political arena. Certainly the fact that most exploited workers are in small minority groups with little ability to effect political coercion contributes substantially to the inability of those groups to perceive a positive present value to governmental arrangements.

Finally, the evolution of the education arrangements in the United States suggests very strongly that the public recognizes the political externalities inherent in a single valued system, and it also suggests that the same public is unwilling to support redistributive arrangements that fail to accrue those externalities.

PART THREE

CONCLUSIONS

CHAPTER II

THE CHANGING PUBLIC-PRIVATE MIX

(I) Introduction

Although the composition of the public–private mix is not directly predictable from our analysis, our study does permit us to make some useful comment on that subject – a subject that has long been of interest to economic historians. Our model attempts to predict the level of arrangemental response given some initiating disequilibriums, and the nature of that response makes a marginal contribution to the public–private ratio. However, the ratio is also a product of the initial condition (the legal and political structure as well as the citizens' tastes as they relate to public and private institutions) and the initial mix. If, however, we can combine the prediction of the model with an understanding of the initial conditions, we should at least be able to provide some description of the variations in the 'mix' over time.

In the past there has been a concern with temporal changes in the public–private mix; however, the earlier chapters also suggest that there were important regional and sectoral differences in that mix. That is, the public–private mix has not only changed over time but has displayed significant differences in the spatial and sectoral dimensions as well. While the bulk of this chapter will explore this change over time, it appears worthwhile to separate out the other two dimensions in a study of the role of government in the American economy.

(II) Sectoral differences in the public–private mix

A number of sectoral differences – differences that have produced varying amounts of government involvement in economic activity – have already been described. In this section of the chapter we can pull them together to contrast the pattern of government involvement in different parts of the economy. While these intersectoral differences, too, have varied over time and space, some are attributable to the innate characteristics of the sectors themselves.

249

Conclusions

The transport sector has always been deeply involved in government activity and, as noted in that chapter, the reasons are consistent with our model and worth re-emphasizing at this point. It has been self-evident to our citizenry (as indeed it has to those of other nations as well) that transport has a bigger impact on our economy than its private activities would appear (the social return is higher than the private return). More than that, many of these same citizens have felt that the entire social return should not redound to the private company itself, and therefore there has been persistent and continual conflict over the degree to which those transport companies should be allowed to discriminate in an attempt to capture the whole social product for themselves. As a result, while on the one hand, the citizens acting through government have provided a series of mechanisms designed to equate the private and social rates of return (land grants, for example), on the other hand, the citizenry have also attempted to get the government to redistribute the social proceeds. Witness the persistent and continuous efforts of farmers, merchants, and other transport using groups to capture some of the benefits from improved transport facilities.

A second part of the explanation for the deep involvement of government in transport arises from the fact that land has been a large input and therefore the construction of a national transport system has involved the property rights of other groups more than any other industry. The granting of a priority for transportation development over prior property claims involved eminent domain proceedings that by definition have stemmed from the coercive power of government. Without eminent domain proceedings, any individual property owner would have a potential veto over an entire transport route if his property was strategic for its development. And, therefore, the dependence of transport facilities upon the coercive power of eminent domain has inevitably led to a tie between the transport firm and the source of that power.

A third source of dependence of transport upon governmental arrangements has been in the high capital–output ratio of transport facilities. Because of the importance of fixed costs, in the short run average variable cost lies well below average total cost, and for transport the short run may be very long indeed. In addition, because of the nature of West–East v. East–West trade patterns, a substantial number of two-way hauls are unequal in volume and, as a result, the back-haul capacity was only partially utilized. Because of these two characteristics private cartel efforts and informal agreements aimed at price fixing have proved very unstable. It is not surprising that under these circumstances transport groups have turned to government to provide coercive backing for enforceable rate agreements in order to avoid the instability of the potential competition that would exist otherwise.

The history of manufacturing contrasts sharply with that of the transportation sector. Experience showed that the corporation (a voluntary organization) could realize most of the inherent economies of scale with no more governmental help than the passage of general incorporation laws (a legal change that preceded manufacturing developments in most states). There were few manufacturing developments that required eminent domain proceedings. While some held the view that there were external economies associated with manufacturing (in the early days of the Republic, Hamilton argued the case for subsidies and tariffs in his famous Report on Manufacturing), and such attitudes undoubtedly helped in the enactment of the early 'revenue' tariffs, the passage of real protectionist legislation reflected much more a small action group's systematic efforts to prevent external competition and redistribute income. The tariff, however, stands out as the exception and the overwhelming arrangemental pattern in manufacturing in the nineteenth century depended on the use of voluntary organization without recourse to government. In contrast to Germany, the employment of government to enforce industry cartelization was not an American option in a country where the legal heritage was the English common law and where there was a widespread anti-monopoly sentiment (a sentiment that later took legal form in the Sherman and Clayton Acts).

In modern times the most striking change in the relationship between government and manufacturing enterprise has been a consequence of the manufacturing induced agglomerate activities in the urban setting. The history of the social costs of urban agglomeration goes back to an earlier era and we see that the externalities associated with unrestricted manufacturing enterprise were becoming a concern to the populace in the early muckraking literature at the end of the nineteenth century. The view that there was a difference between private and social costs in the exploitation of natural resources led to the creation of national forests. But despite the extension of this view to the ills engendered by the manufacturing sector there was little legislative response. Recently attempts to reorganize property rights to make private and social costs coincide have become a major issue, and have led to growing efforts to take into account the social costs of manufacturing activities, particularly those associated with pollution, transport congestion, and other consequences of propinquity of economic activity.

Agriculture, like manufacturing in its early period, could achieve its ends through voluntary organization and had little need for recourse to government. That is, the underlying structure of property rights, taken with the lack of significant economies of scale or other potential sources of external profit, made agriculture essentially a proprietary, small-scale type of activity, relying on individual or voluntary organization. However, changes in the income expectations of farmers in the last third of the nineteenth

251

Conclusions

century altered this pattern. Farmers became convinced that their incomes were not growing rapidly enough and that they were unfairly discriminated against by businesses in other sectors in the economy (particularly transport and warehousing); and as a result they turned to the political process to redistribute income in their favor. Since that time, shifting patterns of farmer involvement in politics have closely reflected the changing income expectations of farmers. There was growing farm participation in political activities until 1896, a decline of such participation through World War I, and an increased participation in the depressed '20s and '30s. (In this respect the changing pattern of farmers' behavior has also been to some degree paralleled by that of labor as well.)

We also observed that the development of new knowledge and the underwriting of its diffusion were not profitable endeavors for voluntary organization when farm size was small, and therefore farmers pressed at both the state and federal level for public agricultural colleges, experiment stations, and the proliferating scientific activities of the Department of Agriculture.

The service sector, because of its heterogeneity, presents a more varied pattern. Some parts of it remained effectively outside of government involvement, while others became most closely connected with such activity. Those enterprises which seem to be most closely connected with the consumer's welfare and where there were direct costs to consumers from misinformation, have tended to become subject to governmental regulation at both the federal and state level.

It is not hard to see why banking should be regulated at the federal level since the externalities associated with the supply of money and its consequences in terms of the price level are clear. But the early involvement of state legislatures in the regulation of banking, insurance, and consumer loans must rest upon the more specific generalization described above. That is, these industries have intimately involved the well being of consumers, and 'watchdog' regulatory authority was invoked to protect the consumer who felt incapable of evaluating their performance and did not trust competitive pressures to produce ideal results. However, the story does not end there since once a regulatory arrangement was innovated it almost inevitably was transformed into a cartel device controlled by the industry to regulate and eliminate competition.

(III) Regional variations in the public–private mix

The varying degrees to which different sectors of the American economy would become involved in government organization to 'capture' potential profits would, of course, also show up in regional variations to the extent that regional specialization led to a spatial concentration of industry. In addition, as the Davis–Legler study shows, there were striking redistributive effects as a result of the structure of taxation and expenditure policy of all levels of government.[1] Nor was the redistribution static: regions that provided the taxes and regions that were the major beneficiaries of government expenditures changed throughout the nineteenth century. Since the major source of federal revenue was the tariff, it was collected in the major maritime states. However, the burden of the tariff rested on all consumers of the goods upon which tariffs were laid. Until the Homestead Act, land sales, a significant source of federal revenue, tended to drain income from the newly settled regions. The Old South, site of the nation's capital, was the major recipient of tax revenues; however, since about 40 percent of the budget went for military purposes (garrisoning soldiers to fight Indians), the western and particularly the mountain states were also large net beneficiaries. In the post-Civil War period, the New England states profited greatly as a result of transfer payments accruing from the Civil War (veterans' payments as well as much of the interest on the Civil War indebtedness accrued to New England).

In the twentieth century the regional pattern of revenues and expenditures changed, although it still produced substantial interregional redistributive effects. The major source of federal government revenue has been the income tax (both personal and corporate), and revenues have by and large reflected the spatial distribution of population, income, and urban industrial conglomeration. Expenditures, on the other hand, have in part continued to be concentrated in the Washington D.C. area, but they have been very heavily influenced by the geographic distribution of military expenditures – expenditures that have been a growing share of the total since 1940. Federal expenditures on public works have typically favored newer and less settled regions in the West as compared with older settled regions of the East and Midwest. In particular, the Army Corps of Engineers and the Bureau of Reclamation have engaged in large-scale power and irrigation projects in the West where stream flows and climate encouraged such developments.

One source of regional variation that has gradually declined in importance since the early national period flowed from the nation's public land policy. The land ordinances of 1785 and 1787 evidenced the basic decision to shift the land from public to private hands, and as settlement proceeded westward the western domain moved into private hands. However, this shift of land from public to private hands slowed down and was even reversed at the end

---

[1] L. Davis and J. Legler, 'The Government in the American Economy 1815–1902: A Quantitative Study', *Journal of Economic History* (December, 1966), 514–52.

of the nineteenth century with the decision to preserve the nation's resources by establishing a system of national forests and parks.

Still another source of regional variation stemmed from the change in the locus of political power, a process touched off by the Civil War but still continuing today. At the end of southern occupation and reconstruction in 1877, the South's influence upon political policies and particularly Federal Government largess was limited. The South's power in national councils was small and their shares of federal expenditures reflected the limited political muscle. Gradually, as the committee structure of Congress with its seniority privileges ensconced southerners into key committee positions, their role was dramatically changed.

(IV) Changes over time in the public–private mix

In 1800 the institutional environment that conditioned the public–private mix was in part a heritage from colonial times and in part a deliberate result of decisions made at the Constitutional Convention, the subsequent legislative enactments of the Federalists, and certain judicial decisions of the Marshall-dominated Supreme Court. The heritage from colonial times and English policy was mercantilist and had conditioned the populace to a public–private mix in which governmental activities were widely accepted. In part, this heritage itself had come from undeveloped markets and a highly developed governmental infra-structure that made the government a preferred and profitable vehicle for arranging the structure of economic activity. The long history of regulated and joint stock companies and the privileges they enjoyed as well as the wide variety of policies encompassed in the 'Navigation Acts' were in large part based on political policies of the English crown and the efforts of particular primary action groups to capture gains in such uncertain markets.

During the Constitutional era – roughly the period beginning with Confederation and continuing through the era of the Marshall-dominated Supreme Court (i.e. 1781–1835) – a set of decisions was made that shaped the fundamental institutional environment in a direction favoring voluntary organization by reducing the costs of such arrangement and at the same time raising the costs of governmental ones. These decisions were:

(1) those related to the disposition of land which was initially held by the government;

(2) those related to eliminating or reducing externalities or uncertainties associated with voluntary organization; and

(3) those related to the structure of political organizations that were designed to raise the costs of redistributive policies.

Let us look at each in turn.

We do not need to dwell at great lengths on the first since the pattern of distribution of public lands in the nineteenth century was discussed in the agricultural chapter. Suffice to emphasize here that one of the greatest assets of this new nation was the vast expanse of unexploited land and the decisions made in the constitutional era placed that land in the hands of the federal government. The land ordinances of the Confederation period stipulated that this land should pass from public to private hands, and the subsequent pieces of legislation (beginning with the Land Ordinance of 1787 and continuing to the Homestead Act in 1862) spelled out the specific conditions under which this transformation would occur.

The second set of decisions was, perhaps, the most important of all. The relative profitability of voluntary organizations can be enhanced to the degree that externalities are eliminated or reduced in a market economy. To do this it is essential that private property rights be specified and enforced in such a way that the gains accrue directly to the participating parties. The heart of private property arrangements is contracts, and the legal structure must provide that the contracts relating to market economy decisions can be specified and enforced to insure the interests of participating parties. The Constitution, the subsequent enactments of the Federalist-dominated Congress of the 1790s, and the interpretations of the Marshall Supreme Court, did just this.

The structure of property rights in the society and their embodiment in specific contracts reflects the degree to which contractual arrangements can be inclusive of all the benefits and costs involved in transactions. To take but one example, if property rights are not enforced then the expected private return from forming a voluntary organization to undertake some form of economic activity will be lower than if enforcement exists. The decisions of the Marshall-dominated Court can be viewed as a deliberate and systematic effort to reaffirm property rights and to widen the use of contracts, in order to reduce these externalities. In addition, the Constitution provided for military and naval forces to protect the United States from external threat and for militia and police to guarantee law and order at home; both enhanced the enforceability of such contracts. The powers granted to Congress in the Constitution (such as the ability to establish uniform bankruptcy laws, and to create patent laws) were one step in this specification of property rights. Still others were taken by the Supreme Court in a set of decisions of its first twenty years. These, as we have seen in Chapter 4, included *Fletcher* v. *Peck*, *New Jersey* v. *Wilson*, and *Dartmouth College* v. *Woodward*.

The third set of national decisions that shaped the basic institutional environment involved the innovation of a set of political institutions that

255

Conclusions

effectively increased the costs of enacting government policies. We have seen in Chapter 2 that a majority of the Constitutional Convention were conscious of the danger to the economy, as they viewed it, of factions whose objective was to redistribute income from rich to poor. In order to forestall such attempts, the structure of the body politic was carefully arranged to make the costs of such redistribution extremely high. There was a tripartite division of power among the legislative, executive, and judicial. The legislative branch was elected on different staggered terms (two years for the House, six years for the Senate), and senators were not elected directly but indirectly by the state legislative bodies. In addition, the Constitution specifically allowed the states to establish voting requirements. The states, in turn, had already ensconced in their constitutions certain property qualifications that made it very difficult for the poor to vote. Moreover, many powers were explicitly delegated to the states and, the authors thought, permanently removed from the purview of the federal government. The aim of this complicated structure was clearly enunciated by Madison in *Federalist Paper No. 10*. If the faction was, in fact, a minority, then the policies of the majority would take care of the problems and prevent wicked legislation from being enacted. If the faction was, in fact, the majority, the costs of getting through such a complicated political structure would probably make it an unprofitable venture and therefore forestall and prevent such activities.

The three changes in the basic environment described above were exogenous to our model. In addition another source of disequilibrium in the arrangemental structure was an increase in the relative size of the capital stock. This increase led to a secular decline in the rate of interest that had an important effect on arrangemental development. Given the cost of getting stuck with an unfavorable governmental solution and given the fact that these stuck costs tended to be deferred in time, decreases in the rate of interest increase the present value of these costs and therefore reduce the present value of governmental solutions.

Another source of change to our system that led to a shift from governmental to voluntary arrangements flowed from the revolutionary technological changes that occurred in nineteenth-century America. In manufacturing and transport, there were important new economies of scale in production that required arrangemental reorganization if they were to be realized. The prior development of the corporation taken with the progressively increasing stuck costs of governmental solutions biased the results in favor of voluntary organizations.

The cumulative effect of the influences described above was to shift the benefit/costs of arrangemental innovation in favor of voluntary solutions

256

over governmental ones. Yet, there were some important exceptions. There were frequently instances where, despite the careful specification and enforcement of property rights, significant externalities developed which could only be captured by direct government coercion.

Government played a major role in the transportation sector, although the basis of this participation changed. In the early part of the century, government participation both in turnpike and canal construction reflected, on the one hand, the primitive state of the private capital market and, on the other, the relatively well-developed structure of government. Taking the two together, it was cheaper to finance canals by government bonds than through the private capital market. Moreover, because of the high discount rate, the costs of being stuck with the consequences of governmental action did not appear large.

The state's default in their bond obligations severely shook the public's confidence in government arrangement. More fundamental, however, were the improvements in the private capital markets that made it possible to float securities and underwrite the large capital investment necessary in transportation at relatively much lower interest rates.

Despite these changes a persistent source of demand for governmental activity stemmed from the railroads' inability to discriminate perfectly. This inability yielded substantial externalities, and many of the policies of the federal government and state government were designed to capture them although the primary action group was sometimes the railroads and sometimes the railroad users – groups with diametrically opposed objectives.

Externalities were equally the moving force in the growth of public education. In 1840 less than half of total investment in education was public, by 1900 almost 80 percent of it was, and it was only in the pre-school grades and in colleges and universities that private education remained an important force. Albert Fishlow documents the evolving pattern of governmental activity in education and the surge of public education that took place after 1840.[1] Americans were early convinced that the returns to society from primary and secondary education exceeded the returns to the individual and that therefore public subsidy was the answer. Gradually, they became convinced that this divergence extended to the college level as well, and the Morrill Act that established a federal subsidy to the 'land grant colleges' was a further move in that direction.

We see few major efforts to redistribute income in the nineteenth century, but some did exist and they are predictable in terms of our model. The groups that found it profitable to undertake redistributive activity had to be

[1] A. Fishlow, 'Levels of Nineteenth Century Investment in Education', *Journal of Economic History* (December, 1966).

Conclusions

small so that the free rider problem was minimized, and they had to have some special 'in' with legislature. We have argued elsewhere that the costs of influencing legislation by an elite were lower in the nineteenth century, and when the history books talk about special 'ins' with the legislature, they are really talking about this low cost environment. These two qualifications for successful redistribution were met, for example, by the interests who lobbied for higher tariffs throughout most of the nineteenth century. The structure of political representation in Congress favored groups that were friendly to manufacturing. In addition, the pressure groups were small in numbers and as a result policing was relatively easy. Their success is attested to by the history of American tariffs from the 1840s to Smoot-Hawley.

The only other major effort at redistribution of income in the nineteenth century was that undertaken by the farmers in the Grange and Populist eras. We have already seen that local organizations could be profitably employed to solve local problems, and these provided the base for large scale organizations designed to effect favorable political policies at the state and federal level. The expansion of the farmer's political activity was triggered by changes in his income expectations, but, despite widespread effort, the structure of political organization that Madison had envisioned, effectively thwarted these attempts. The failure of the Grange and Populist movements provides a classic example of a faction, in Madison's terms, being unable to overcome the complicated political structure that had been designed almost solely to fend off such attacks on the establishment.

The history of the farmers' efforts to influence railroad rates had a different history but ultimately similar results. We saw in Chapters 5 and 7 how early state regulatory efforts led to a succession of Supreme Court decisions that turned the farmer to federal regulation and the creation of the Interstate Commerce Commission. The ICC in turn became a creature of the railroads and put on a legal basis the monopoly prices that the farmer had originally protested.

By the end of the nineteenth century, the basic institutional environment was changing. The franchise had steadily widened as property qualifications of states were reduced or completely abrogated. While it is true that for the Negro minority the change was more in theory than in practice, it foreshadowed increasing realization at a later time. The Supreme Court's interpretation of the Constitution had gradually widened the authority of the federal government over economic activity, and the most important source of this authority was the liberalizing interpretation of the commerce clause. With the ICC we have the first example of the delegation of legislative and regulatory power from elective legislative bodies to appointed commissioners, an example that was only a precursor of a continued increase in the delegation of such legislative power in the twentieth century both at the federal and state levels.

The most widely acknowledged sources of the increase in governmental activity in the twentieth century have been exogenous to our model – that is, war and the depression of the 1930s. Two world wars have left an immense heritage in terms of government expenditure. While World War I and its consequences for government participation were in good part reversed in the 1920s, the effects of World War II were not so readily eradicated. Whatever the justification, American military expenditure remained at a high level. The great depression left a heritage of two kinds, both of which had lasting effects on the public–private mix. First, it changed people's attitudes towards government participation. The public's belief that a system in which voluntary arrangements dominated economic activity produced optimal results was shaken by persistent and widespread unemployment and the economy's obvious inability to recover. The result was a reduction in the public's confidence in voluntary solutions and an increase in their estimate of returns of governmental solutions. Second, the New Deal produced a multitude of regulatory agencies designed to control and regulate the economy, and these by replacing legislative bodies with appointed regulatory commissions changed the structure of government. The Securities and Exchange Commission, the Federal Communications Commission, and the National Labor Relations Board are but three of many examples. The result was a substantial reduction in the cost of using government as a vehicle for capturing potential redistributive profits.

However, it would be misleading to look on war and the great depression as providing all – or even most – of the basic underlying sources for the changing public–private mix that we observe. Even the extension of the franchise to women and in recent years to Negroes is only a part of the story. A third important source has stemmed from the externalities associated with the growth of urban agglomerates and the increasing interdependence of individuals in society. Economies of scale inherent in modern technology have produced an urban society in which private and social costs diverge; problems associated with congestion, pollution, and health are not easily resolved by voluntary organizations, and effective solutions have often depended on the coercive power of government. At the same time, the specialization of functions that has accompanied growth has been a source of mutual interdependence. As a result, it has become increasingly apparent that the policies of one group have significant welfare effects on others.

Specifically, in terms of our model, in the twentieth century, the initial conditions have changed and so have the variables endogenous to our

Conclusions

model and the new equilibrium has tended to favor government institutional arrangements. The widening of the electorate has encompassed low income and minority groups with a stake in redistributing income and, predictably, the major political parties have pragmatically shifted their political umbrella to cover them as well. It is no accident that the first explicit overall effort to redistribute income nationally – the negative income tax – has become a real political alternative only in the decade of the '70s.

The widening divergence between private and social costs and benefits has not been amenable to solution by voluntary organization. Vested interests stemming from existing property rights can frequently be overcome only by the coercive power of government. Since problems of the environment typically involve the reorganization of property rights and accompanying redistribution of income, institutional arrangements have invoked government authority. Buchanan and Tullock make the case that government is not necessarily the only arrangement that can effectively capture such externalities; however, the dilemma of the 'single holdout' and the 'free rider' make voluntary solutions infrequent. Moreover, the heritage of the 1930s persists and governmental solutions have continued to be the preference of the electorate, as the policies of five post-war administrations (three Democratic and two Republican) have abundantly illustrated.

For public goods in general, and military expenditures in particular, the costs of excluding nonparticipants and preventing free riders have clearly militated against voluntary solutions. The relative rise in the demand for such services requires no further explanation. In addition, the potential benefits of government institutional arrangements have risen with the widening regulatory authority of government; the expanding rights of eminent domain; and increased taxing power (in each case the basic Supreme Court decisions were exogenous to our model).

On the other hand, the costs have fallen – not the stuck costs it is true – but those associated with the costs of effecting the new arrangement have decreased. The transfer to boards and agencies of decision-making authority by the legislative and executive branches of government at all levels (local, state and federal) stems partly from deliberate delegation and partly consideration of size and functional specialization. Whichever the reason, one need only influence a small commission and not the diverse legislative and executive authorities that Madison had envisioned as a safeguard against factional redistribution.

The ebb and flow of governmental economic activity in our history is only partly explainable within our model. Changes in the fundamental institutional environment have been considered exogenous even though we are quite conscious of the fact that a more complete model should in principle be able to encompass the interrelationship between the institutional arrangements endogenous to our system and long run changes in the fundamental institutional environment. Even so, the foregoing description is, we feel, a major improvement upon earlier examinations of this subject. It does provide a new (and we believe promising) approach to exploring the public–private mix.

CHAPTER 12

HISTORY AND THE ANALYSIS OF ARRANGEMENTAL CHANGE: A LOOK TO THE PAST WITH AN EYE TO THE FUTURE

(I) Introduction

In the first three chapters we sketched the outline of a theory of arrangemental innovation and mutation that made it possible for us to understand better certain aspects of the economic development of the United States, and that we hoped might have some predictive value. We recognize that the model is far from complete. The results of our attempts to apply the model indicate that we are still a very long way from being able to understand all of the arrangemental aspects of American development. We do believe, however, that we have provided the historian *cum* economist with a small window (albeit a dirty one) through which he may better examine some of those problems. Moreover, we still think that some theory of arrangemental change is a necessary prerequisite for any adequate theory of economic growth.

Since we would like to both clean that window and discover a more adequate predictive theory, it appears useful to consider our success – or lack thereof – in explaining the arrangemental aspects of American development. In particular, an examination of those areas where the model has failed to provide an adequate explanation of arrangemental change ought to provide: some clues as to the directions in which the model should be extended; the portions of the model that ought to be revised; and/or some caveats to the unwary who might attempt to use the model in its present form.

Although logically the categories are neither mutually exclusive or all inclusive, it appears heuristically useful to classify the areas of failure into four broad groups: those arising from (1) fundamental methodological problems, (2) the lag structure, information flows, and the menu of arrangemental alternatives, (3) the selection of arrangemental level, and (4) the political process and attempts at the redistribution of income.

(II) Methodological problems

(1) We have employed a partial, not a general, equilibrium model, and it suffers from the same limitations as do all such analytical structures. As long as the sector in question can be examined in isolation, the model tends to work well. When, however, arrangemental decisions in one sector have significant influences on innovation in another, it doesn't work nearly as well (except in the few instances where the connecting link is provided by changes in the rate of interest). While we are able to suggest what effect arrangemental innovations in the capital markets had on the organization of the transportation sector in the 1930s and '40s, we have no way of examining, for example, the effect of the widespread innovation of labor unions after the Jones and Laughlin decision on the organization of the manufacturing sector.

(2) The model is not dynamic, and we know very little about the path from one comparative static equilibrium to another. The attempts at explaining the lags in successful arrangemental innovation are, of course, steps in the direction of a more dynamic model, but they are no more than steps (and faltering ones at that). The exogenous shocks to the system are just that, and all too often the economy has not had time to adjust to one before another sets the system off in a new direction. This problem was illustrated very clearly by attempts on the part of manufacturers to find an adequate cartelizing arrangement in a judicial–political environment, characterized by a continually changing definition of legal collusion. Arrangemental innovations may themselves engender profits external to the arrangemental structure that can only be captured by still further innovation. In the case of the capital markets, for example, the innovation of a system of commercial banks provided a mechanism for capturing certain profits inherent in the processes of capital accumulation and mobilization but also induced additional costs to some groups. These costs – the costs inherent in any unstable economy – could only be internalized by further arrangemental innovations (the Federal Reserve Board, to name one). There is nothing in the model that permits us to examine the intra-equilibria paths nor to predict with any precision the emergence of 'second round' profits.

(3) We have taken the institutional environment as given, and we have assumed that any changes in that environment are the result of random exogenous events. The assumption reflects our inability to formalize the mechanism that connects arrangemental innovation to changes in the

environment, but it does not reflect any belief that the two are in fact independent. It should be clear to the most casual observer that the environment is to a large extent dependent upon the current set of institutional arrangements and that arrangemental innovation frequently alters that environment. In the United States, for example, the Constitution can be amended either by the state legislative bodies or by the Supreme Court. Both groups are responsive to the wishes of the electorate, but it is difficult to formalize the connection. State legislatures must be elected, and constitutional amendment is not the sole election issue. In the case of the Supreme Court, Mr Dooley's comment ('Th' supreme coort follows th' illiction returns') is not far wrong, but the process of following is nowhere made explicit. The steps required to change the Constitution or the common law are not straightforward, and the lags may be (and frequently are) so unpredictable that any model which makes the environment a dependent variable is likely to be empirically vacuous. How, for example, is it possible to predict that the courts would rule on the conspiracy doctrine in 1847 rather than 1837 or 1857, or that it would be 1911 before the Supreme Court would hold that the interstate commerce clause of the Constitution can be made to apply to the manufacture of goods in one state for sale in another? Still, it is obvious that these changes do reflect a response to the need for an arrangemental technique capable of internalizing some external profit, and could usefully be treated endogenously if a better understanding of the judicial process ever allowed us to reformulate the model.

(4) Like all of economic theory, the assumption of profit maximization is fundamental; however, the areas in the arrangemental sector where the assumption is inappropriate may be larger and more important than in the more traditional parts of the discipline. Certainly more than economic self-interest often lies behind political or social behavior (moral values sometimes play a role, to cite only one example). In many of the areas of interest from the viewpoint of arrangemental innovation, an individual's economic benefits or costs are small; in these circumstances it is likely that moral or social values may dominate and predictions based on the assumption of monetary profit maximization are apt to be wrong. There is, for example, nothing in our model that would predict the abolition of slavery in 1863. If profit maximization had been the only criteria, there would have been no need to alter the existing arrangement. As a result, the Emancipation Proclamation produced a need for innovation among a list of arrangemental alternatives that were likely, from a strictly economic viewpoint, all inferior to the existing arrangemental structure. Despite these limitations, no other behavioral assumption appears to be more useful, although a reformulation might include some mixed set of goals. Recent work in the theory of

bureaucracies and oligopolistic firms suggests that at least some other criteria could be included. However, this latter work has not yet produced a truly operational theory, and thus there is something to be said for simplicity – as long as the user is warned of the potential pitfalls.

(III) Problems arising from the lag structure, information flows, and the menu of available alternatives

(1) The development of information systems is very important to any theory of arrangemental innovation, and our failure to understand this process penalizes our predictions at least at two points. At the same time, our attempts to apply the model to American development have suggested something about that process that should be incorporated in any extension of the model.

We have assumed that the length of the organization and the menu selection lags depends in part upon the knowledge of the primary action group about the size and certainty of potential profits and about the alternatives that are on the menu. If such knowledge were a free good, there would be no problem. Most frequently, however, resources must be expended to secure the requisite information. Since potential profits can not be computed until the information is purchased, there is a substantial area of indeterminacy in our predictions of the time it will take for the primary action group to recognize the profit potential and to select the most profitable arrangement. The more easily such information can be obtained, the less the uncertainty and the less (*ceteris paribus*) the area of indeterminacy.

We do know that the more open is the society and the better the state of communications and transportation, the less is the cost of information. We expect, therefore, that our lag predictions would be better for developed than for underdeveloped economies, and our experience with the American economy seems to bear out this contention. Even in a developed economy, however, the entire logical structure of the model would be greatly improved if we could specifically incorporate a theory capable of explaining the development and operation of an information system.

There are also a number of institutional arrangements whose sole function is the exploitation of a lack of information. The 'racketeer locals' of the labor chapter provide one example, but there are many others that are more respectable. Since we know very little about the barriers to information flows, it is difficult to predict the innovation of these redistributive arrangements. Similarly, altruism has led certain individuals to devote time and resources to innovating information-disseminating arrangements whose only function is to counter this exploitation. The Catholic Trade

Conclusions

Union Council is an example, but history and the current press provide many other examples (Nader's Raiders and the Sierra Club, to cite two). Since little income accrues to the primary action group in these altruistic arrangements, the model is useless in predicting their emergence.

Our examination of American history provided at least two clues to the process of development of information systems, and these should improve our understanding of that facet of arrangemental innovation. First, not all information has the same economic life, and the length of life appears to be connected to the distributive arrangement of choice. If the information can be used for only a very brief period, then its possession may have some substantial economic value. If it does, we expect some individual arrangement to emerge that will permit its owner to exploit its economic potential (he is, after all, willing to pay for the information).[1] If, however, the information can be used only over a very long period and if there are no extra profits to be earned from being the first to use it, the costs of maintaining secrecy greatly reduce the economic potential of any information. Information is not patentable, it can seldom be copywrited, and the more open the society, the more difficult it is to preserve a secret. In these instances (cases of what we might term long half-life information), the distributive arrangements will be either voluntary cooperative associations of all potential users, or because of the free rider problem, governmental arrangements. Thus, it appears reasonable to expect private firms to distribute stock market quotations and horse racing results (their half-life is very short), producers' cooperatives to undertake the distribution of technical information in the California citrus industry, and the government to provide the same function for the wheat farmers. In the first case the half-life of the information is very short; in the second, other benefits from association membership prevent free riding; but in the third, the government's coercive power alone makes the arrangement viable.[2]

Second, like other arrangements, those designed to improve information flows will be innovated more quickly (and at lower organizational costs) if they can be tied to some already existing or independently profitable arrangement. The Grange, for example, was able to become a clearing house for farm information because its organizational and operating costs were largely borne by its social functions.

(2) It pays an individual to acquire information only when the discounted stream of income that he expects to receive from that information exceeds

---

[1] The arrangement may be a voluntary cooperative one, if there are scale economies coupled with some capital constraints.

[2] In the third there is also the possibility that the full costs are not born by the wheat farmers, so there is potentially an element of income distribution as well.

266

its cost. Problems of arrangemental prediction arise when the costs of acquisition are so high that it does not appear worthwhile for an individual to acquire it, and he makes decisions that would be against his own self-interest if the information were free. In the absence of information, the individual may substitute ideology for the needed information and this has produced some strange results. The relationship between minimum wage legislation and black unemployment is not readily discernible, and as a result, blacks have tended to support increases in the minimum wage.[1] Their reasoning apparently runs along some line such as: 'the Democratic Party supports such legislation, that party represents my general ideology, I don't know what the effects of minimum wage legislation on me will be, and it is not worth the cost for me to acquire that information; therefore, I will support the party's position on this specific piece of legislation'. Such behavior, although not inconsistent with the model, is practically impossible to predict since it is very difficult to estimate the costs and revenues accruing to an individual from a particular piece of information.

(3) We have tended to define the menu of available alternatives to include only those that are legally permissible, but this is obviously an artificial restriction. Any time the primary action group decides that the calculation of the total costs of an arrangement (including the costs of the legal penalty) leaves an illegal alternative as the most profitable, they will choose that alternative as long as it does not violate some deep moral principle. Since techniques for estimating the depth of moral principle have never been among the sharpest of the economist's tools, there is an area of indeterminacy in the model's predictions. There is no way of telling at any moment of time which among the illegal alternatives appear on the menu and which are excluded by moral principles. Thus, economic action was the arrangement of choice for trade unions even before 1842, when prosperity reduced the probabilities of prosecution, and the electrical industry scandal of the past decade attests to the fact that collusive agreements are still among some businessmen's alternatives despite the potential penalties of the Sherman Act.

(IV) Problems in the prediction of arrangemental level

(1) In most of the discussion we have assumed that all arrangements can be classified in one of three level categories (individual, voluntary cooperative, or governmental), but in the world, arrangements are not limited to these

---

[1] In most industries affected by minimum wage legislation an increase in that minimum probably leads to reduced employment and quite likely to a decline in the total wage bill for the affected workers.

three pure forms. Instead, a myriad of combinations of voluntary cooperative and governmental often exist, and it is even possible to have impure individual–governmental arrangements. The possible existence of these mixed type arrangements does not mean that the model is useless. It works well when the alternatives are limited to the pure forms; and even when they are not, it suggests approximately where between the pure forms the new arrangement is most likely to emerge. Still, we would hope that a more refined model might be able to predict more precisely what combinational arrangement will be the innovation of choice.

(2) It should be clear that income increasing arrangemental innovations can have redistributive effects if all the requisite side payments are not made. When this redistributive potential exists, the model's predictions are frequently wrong. While a voluntary cooperative solution may appear to be the arrangement of choice, the political power of some primary action group may permit it to capture a larger share of the total income if it can effect the innovation of a governmental alternative.[1]

(3) We have assumed that withdrawal from a governmental arrangement is not possible, and, as a result, such arrangements carry the potential costs of getting stuck with a solution which an individual member of the primary action group may not like. Moreover, we have assumed that there are no costs withdrawing from a voluntary arrangement, and therefore, that the potential 'stuck costs' are zero. Neither assumption is strictly correct, and the model does not work well when the assumptions are widely at variance with conditions in the sector under examination.

In the case of governmental arrangements, it is almost always possible to withdraw 'with your feet' (i.e. migrate). Throughout much of American history inter-state migration was a fairly inexpensive alternative, and in these instances the stuck costs of governmental innovation must have been low. The shift from state to federal arrangements has increased migration costs, although the possibility of migration still exists as the flight of many draft-age men to Canada attests.

Of more historical importance, few voluntary arrangements are characterized by zero withdrawal costs, and in these cases there is always a potential stuck cost if that arrangement is selected. When membership in the primary action group carries with it benefits not associated with the capture of the profits in question, withdrawal involves surrendering these extra benefits.

---

[1] It may even be possible for them to capture not only all of the new, but a share of the existing income as well. In terms of the model, such an arrangement will be the choice whenever the present value of their increased share of the existing income plus whatever share of the new income the arrangement captures for them exceeds the present value of the stuck costs of the governmental arrangement.

Most voluntary groups concerned with the cohesiveness of the primary action group attempt to build such side benefits into their organization. Unions have long provided members with sickness and death benefits, and the Medical Association provides not only malpractice insurance but, more important, an easy road to 'hospital privileges'.

Despite these caveats, the model works fairly well. Most discontents do not choose to migrate, and in most voluntary groups the 'stuck costs' are not so high as to preclude withdrawal should the group act very much against the self-interest of an individual member. The reader should, however, be warned that when migration is made easy, the costs of governmental arrangements fall; and when withdrawal is expensive, the costs of voluntary association may be high. Few members withdraw from the Mafia because they are displeased with the group's decisions.

(4) Our sectoral studies suggest that voluntary groups work better when their strategy involves education or some lobbying activity than when they try to effect a collusive arrangement. Payments in support of education and political activity are explicit and a member's failure to contribute is readily apparent. In addition, the payment is likely to be small relative to the member's total income. The payments in support of a cartel decision are not explicit (they involve agreements to abide by particular production and marketing decisions), not easily noted, and may represent a very high proportion of a member's total income. In the first instance, the gains from cheating are likely to be small and detection rapid; in the latter, the gains are potentially much larger and the chance of detection much less.

(V) Political problems

(1) In politics, votes rather than dollars are counted, and since the rules prohibit vote buying, there is a strong presumption that a governmental arrangement will not maximize total income. Since many income increasing arrangements have some redistributional component, in the absence of a mechanism to effect appropriate side payment, one would expect that the arrangement of choice is one that maximizes voter, not total, income. Moreover, the fact that a passionate minority has more political strength than its numbers alone would justify, suggests that arrangements designed to redistribute income away from such a minority (even if they increase total income) tend to be long-delayed. On the other hand, since the revenues per voter from such an arrangement, when it is finally innovated, tend to be small, the voters are apt to choose arrangements that punish the minority for their past behavior rather than arrangements that will maximize income. Thus, both zoning and anti-pollution laws tend to be long-delayed in

Conclusions

passage, and once passed, to be all or nothing solutions (no regulation or total prohibition) rather than some intermediate alternative that might produce a higher total income. In these cases the model in its presently specified form does not predict well, and there is considerable need for an extension that would take into account this type of political behavior.

(2) The model also does not predict well when: the arrangemental choice involves at least one governmental alternative; the redistributive aspects are important; the opposing coalitions are evenly balanced; and the gains to one group are both large and approximately equal to the losses of the other. Unequal political strengths lead to decisions favoring the majority, and unbalanced gains and losses to some form of side payments or bribes. In the absence of substantial majorities or sufficient additional income to underwrite side payments, the arrangemental result is largely indeterminate. Extensions of game theory may at some later date provide the basis for meaningful predictions, but at the moment one should approach such predictions with extreme caution.

(3) Finally, the model suffers from a lack of understanding of bureaucratic behavior and the response of governmental bureaucracies to the political process, but again history provides some suggestions for possible modifications. The experience of the transport sector suggests that the more an arrangemental innovation can be insulated from the electoral process, the better that arrangement conforms to our predictions based upon maximization of money income. While this observation does not necessarily imply that it is more difficult to bribe bureaucrats than elected representatives, there is considerable evidence to suggest that, once established, governmental secondary action groups charged with a regulatory function (the ICC, for example) tend to act more in the interests of the regulated industry than of the citizenry at large. That is, their actions tend to conform more closely to the pattern that we would expect had the distribution of income rather than the distribution of votes been the determining factor.

(VI) Conclusion

This list of areas of weakness is clearly not complete, but even as it stands it suggests that this model will not be the final step in any attempt to reach an adequate theory of arrangemental innovation. Yet, we have apologized enough for the model's shortcomings. We should end on a note of strength. A wedding of economic theory with an explanation for institutional change is essential for further understanding of the process of economic growth – past, present, and future. This is a beginning. Even when the model is not predictive in the sense of providing a single, unique outcome, it nevertheless uncovers and makes explicit the forces tending to induce institutional change. It ties together both market and non-market decision making, thus moving in the direction of developing a unified theory of social change. The historical chapters in our view add a whole new dimension to the history of the American economy by permitting us to integrate economic analysis with institutional history in the exploration of the development of product and factor markets. Finally, after three years of developing and applying this model, we are more than ever convinced that this approach does offer a promise of resolving many of the problems discussed in this concluding chapter and ultimately providing an adequately specified, usefully predictive model of institutional change.

Index

education – *continued*
between private and social rates of discount, 240–1; employee, 18; engineering, 240–1; federal investment in scientific research, 234–6; governmental activity in, 240–1, 257; and income redistribution, 234, 241–3; industry-financed, 212; investment an externality in, 234–6, 257; parochial, 239; 'peak-molding' effects of, 238–40; political externalities in single valued system, 246; private *v.* public, 236; public, evolution of, 234–45, 246; and stuck costs, 243; vocational, 241–3
elections, 31–3; economic environment and rules governing, 6, 7; and lag, 60
Elkins Act, 161
Ellison, T., 193n
environment, *see* institutional environment
Erie Canal, 78, 141, 142, 147, 148; financing of, 110, 112, 113, 139–40; railroad competition with, 157; and savings bank, 119
Erie Railroad, 143, 144
Euclid Village v. *Ambler Reality Co.*, 188n
Evans, G. H., 137n
Evans, Oliver, 168–9
externalities: captured by government solutions, 257–60; changes in costs and revenues, 14–19; costs of erosion and water control, 182, 183–4; costs of pollution, 182, 183–4; costs of zoning laws, 187–8; in distribution of public lands, 89–91; in education, 234–40, 257; examples of, 15–18; government and legislation in finance, 127–32; internalization of, by voluntary and governmental arrangements, 11 and n; pollution as example of, 17–18, 163, 186, 187; political, in single valued educational system, 246; in production, 16; reduction of, in voluntary organization during Constitutional era, 254, 255; social costs of manufacture, 167, 182–9, 251, 259; as source of gains, 12, 14–19, 39, 41–2, 61; in transport, 136, 142n, 147–52, 257

Federal Radio Commission v. *Nelson Brothers Bond and Mortgage Co.*, 74n
Federal Reserve Act, 131
Federal Reserve Bank, 132
Federal Reserve Board, 165, 263
Federal Reserve System, 131–2
Federal Water Pollution Control Act, 186
Fink, Albert, 144
Fishlow, Albert, 236, 257 and n
Fletcher v. *Peck*, 72n, 255
Flexner, A., 204–5
Fogel, R., 3n, 148 and n, 149n

Ford, Henry, 48
Forestall System, 130
franchise, 33–5, 79; extension to women and Negroes, 45, 259; and labor, 225; and land units, 87; and Negro education, 237; and property qualifications, 45, 256, 258; and rules of political game, 65–8
Frary, D., 67n
free rider problem, 18, 31, 182, 260; and agricultural information, 101, 209; in education, 237; in information systems, 266; and information to workers, 233, 245–6; in insurance cartels, 134; in vocational education, 242
Friedman, M., 191n
Fuchs, V. R., 191 and n, 192, 205n

game theory, 35–7
Garrett, J., 205n
Gary, Elbert, 40n, 174–5, 177
Gates, Paul W., 88 and n
Georgia Railroad and Banking Co. v. *Smith*, 76n
Gibbons v. *Ogden*, 73
Gompers, Samuel, 242
Goodrich, Carter, 77n, 139n
Gould, Jay, 155
governmental arrangements, 7, 10–11, 25, 37–8, 39, 45–6, 56, 258–60, 266, 267–70; benefits of, 12, 27–30, 260; and cartelization, 177; and commerce, 73–4; conditions for choice of, 27–30; costs of, 12, 44, 55, 100–3, 260; during depressions, 259; in education, 234, 235, 236, 240; eminent domain, 166, 250, 260; employment exchanges, 11; and finance, 28, 113–14, 129–32; formulation for returns from, 52, 54; and Grange, 95–6; and income redistribution, 26, 27, 29, 44, 142n; incorporative laws, 138n; and information systems, 100–3, 266; and lag, 46, 60, 61, 63, 236; and manufacture, 182, 188–90; and market failure, 112–14; and medicine, 44, 207; military defense, 29; and pollution control, 9, 10, 18, 29, 185–8; and price legislation, 176; shifts in community's probability weights toward, 77–9; and side markets, 112; and social costs of manufacture, 182–8; and social rates of discount, 240; as solution for agglomeration effects, 42; and transport, 45–6, 49, 113, 113–14n, 138n, 140–1, 142n, 146–7, 149, 150, 155, 160–6, 250, 257; during war, 79, 259; *see also* agriculture, land, and other sectors, public–private mix
Grand Alliance, 96
Grand Trunk Western, 157
Granges, 43, 94–6; as clearing house for farm

Index

Pennsylvania Society for the Promotion of Manufacturers and the Mechanical Arts, 179–80
petroleum, 13, 110–11, 170, 186
Pickering v. *Moore*, 71n
political game, 26–7; theory, 35–7; rules of, 33, 38, 39, 61, 65–9, 219
political parties: and antitrust enforcement, 178; Democratic party, 32, 96, 260, 267; and farmers, 96; and franchise, 34–5, 66; and income redistribution, 31, 32–3; and labor, 225–7; Populists, 96–7, 154, 258; Republican party, 101, 260; Socialist Labor party, 226; Workingmen's Party, 225
pollution, 42; anti-pollution laws as political problem of arrangemental model, 269–70; and coercive power of government, 9–10, 18, 29, 185–8; as externality, 17–18, 163, 185; and political action, 9, 10, 186; social costs of, in manufacturing, 182, 184–8, 251
pools: in manufacturing, 172, 173, 175; in transport, 157, 162
property rights: in American colonies, 83; changes occurring in, 7, 10, 27, 79; court decisions relating to, 72–3, 255; legal basis for, as dimension of environment, 65; and pollution control, 10, 17; rules governing, as part of economic environment, 6; society's support for, 44–5; and transport, 165, 166, 250; vested interests in, and governmental arrangement, 28–9, 260; and zoning laws, 70, 187–8
Provident Institution for Savings in the Town of Boston, 119
public–private mix: changes in, 254–61; during Constitutional era, 254; English influence on, 254; institutional environment in 1800, 254; in railroads, 45–6, 141; regional variations, 252–4; sectoral differences, 249–52

Raiffa, H., 35n
railroads, 125, 135, 157; and airline competition, 163; and capital mobilization, 45, 111; and cartelization, 35, 47, 51, 157–62, 164, 172; colonization schemes, 88; and competitive pricing, 172; externalities captured by government, 257; and government subsidies, 49, 149–52; indivisibility of, 153–4; and Interstate Commerce Commission, 35, 47, 51, 160–1, 162, 164, 165, 258; investment decision theory, 144–7; land grants, 87, 89, 150; long- and short-haul problem, 154 and n, 157; Massachusetts' subsidy of, 157; and political subsidies, 156–7; price discrimination by, 157; private–government partnership in, 45, 141; rate regulation, 95, 159–62, 258; and regulation by court decisions, 75;

reorganizational profits and location of, 155; right-of-way, 166n; and scale economies, 45, 143–4; and stockholders' voting trust, 173; and technological competition, 163–4
Rand, E., 205n
rates of discount: divergence between private and social, in educational investment, 234, 240–1; in formulation of arrangemental innovation, 52–5; private and social, in conservation, 183n; private and social, in transport, 136, 145–7
Rayack, Elton, 205n, 207n, 208n
Reed–Bulwinkle Act, 162
Rensselaer Polytechnic Institute, 241
rent, 111n, 152n, 213n; locational, 154 and n, 155, 165
retail price maintenance, 176–7
retailers, 198, 201–2, 203
returns to scale, *see* economies of scale
Reynolds v. *Sims*, 7, 69n
Riker, W., 27n, 32, 57
risk: assessment for insurance companies, 19–20, 44; aversion as source of external gains, 11, 12, 19–20, 23, 25, 41, 61; reduction of, in agriculture, 101; reduction of, in cotton trade, 192, 194, 196; reduction through insurance, 11
Rochdale principle, 94, 97
Rockefeller, John D., 40n, 110–11, 117, 118, 122, 173, 185–6n
Roosevelt, Franklin D., 32, 43, 74, 99

Salter, W. E. G., 57 and n
Santa Clara County v. *Southern Pacific Railroad Co.*, 77n
Sapiro, Aaron, 97–8, 100
Savings Bank of Baltimore, 119, 120
savings and loan associations, 116, 120, 133
savings banks, 119–20, 122
scale, *see* economies of scale
Schafer, H., 204n
Schechter Poultry Corporation v. *U.S.*, 177 and n
Schmookler, J., 57 and n, 58
Schultz, Theodore, 103
Schwab, Charles, 173
Sears Roebuck, 202
Secretary of Agriculture v. *Central Roig Refining Co.*, 76n
securities market, 125–7, 169, 195; cost reduction in, 11, 43; futures markets in, 24–5; government issues, 126; side markets in, 24
self-service store, 198, 202–3
service industries: auction system, 198–9, 209; chain stores, 201; characteristics of, 192–3; defined, 191; department store, 201–2;

280